The
EUROPEAN
DRIVER'S
HANDBOOK

AA

Designed by Tracey Butler Design

Motoring regulations supplied by
AA International Motoring Services

Turkish Republic of Northern Cyprus motoring
regulations verified by George McDonald

Published by AA Publishing, a trading name
of AA Media Ltd, whose registered office is Fanum
House, Basing View, Basingstoke, Hampshire RG21
4EA. Registered number 06112600.

ISBNs: 978-0-7495-6584-8 and
978-0-7495-6632-6 (SS)

Mapping © Crown copyright and database rights 2011
Ordnance Survey. Licence number 100021153

Land &
Property
Services.
This is based upon Crown
Copyright and is reproduced with
the permission of Land
& Property Services under
delegated authority from the Controller of Her Majesty's
Stationery Office, © Crown copyright and database
rights 2011. Licence Permit No 110069.

Ordnance
Survey
Ireland
Ireland's National Mapping Agency
Republic of Ireland mapping based
on Ordnance Survey Ireland. Permit
No. MP000611. © Ordnance Survey
Ireland/Government of Ireland.

Words and phrases taken from AA Phrase Book series
first published in 1992 as Wat & Hoe.
© Uitgeverij Kosmos bv – Utrecht/Antwerpen. Van Dale
Lexicografie bv – Utrecht/Antwerpen

Visit **theAA.com/motoring_advice/overseas** for the
latest information on driving in Europe.

A CIP catalogue record for this book is available from the
British Library.

Printed and bound by Oriental Press

Visit AA Publishing at **theAA.com/shop**

A04856

The Automobile Association would like to thank the
following photographers, companies and libraries for
their assistance in the preparation of this book.

Abbreviations for the picture credits are as follows: (t)
top; (b) bottom; (l) left; (r) right; (c) centre; (AA) AA World
Travel Library.

1 AA/P Kenward; 6 AA; 8/9 AA/A Baker; 11 AA; 12 South
West News Service; 13 AA; 14l AA; 14tr AA; 14cr AA; 15
AA; 16 AA/J Smith; 18 AA PR; 19 Digitalvision; 20 AA;
21 AA/M Birkitt; 25 AA/P Baker; 32 E.J. Baumeister Jr./
Alamy; 39 Graham Lawrence; 42 AA/T Souter; 45 AA/J
Smith; 48 AA/A Kouprianoff; 56 AA/J W Jorgensen;
59 Pictures Colour Library; 62 AA/B Smith; 76
AA/P Wilson; 79 AA/D Tarn; 80 AA/T Souter; 85 AA/C
Sawyer; 93 AA/L Blake; 97 AA/K Paterson; 103 Pictures
Colour Library; 106 Pictures Colour Library; 109 Pictures
Colour Library; 112 isifa Image Service s.r.o./Alamy; 117
DIOMEDIA/Alamy; 120 AA/A Kouprianoff; 124 AA/K
Naylor; 127 AA/J Smith; 130 AA/A Mockford & N Bonetti;
131 AA/A Kouprianoff; 134 Pictures Colour Library; 137
AA/K Paterson; 140 Pictures Colour Library; 143 AA/J
Smith; 146 Pictures Colour Library; 149 AA/P Enticknap;
150 AA/M Chaplow; 155 Pictures Colour Library; 161
AA/P Kenward; 164 AA/J Smith; 166/167 AA/J Tims; 169
AA/R Moore; 170 AA/R Moore; 173 AA/B Smith; 175
AA/A Baker; 176 AA/A Baker; 179 AA/C Jones; 181 AA/N
Ray; 185 AA/C Coe; 186 AA/D Forss; 191 AA/C Sawyer;
195 AA/P Enticknap; 197 AA/S Watkins; 198/199 AA/A
Kouprianoff; 217 AA/P Kenward; 218 AA/P Baker; 220
Digitalvision; 224 AA/C Sawyer; 225 AA/R Strange

Every effort has been made to trace the copyright
holders, and we apologise in advance for any accidental
errors. We would be happy to apply any corrections in
the following edition of this publication.

Contents

REYKJAVÍK
ICELAND

Norwegian Sea

0   200   400   600   800 km
0   100   200   300   400   500 miles

Östersund
Sundsvall

NORWAY

SWEDEN

OSLO

STOCKHOLM

ATLANTIC OCEAN

Inverness

Aberdeen

NORTHERN IRELAND Glasgow
Londonderry

Edinburgh

North Sea

Aalborg

Gothenburg

Galway

Belfast

Newcastle upon Tyne

DENMARK

Karlskrona

Killarney
REPUBLIC OF IRELAND   DUBLIN

York

Esbjerg

Malmö   COPENHAGEN

Liverpool   Manchester

Odense

Cork

BRITAIN

Birmingham

Hamburg

Bristol

Oxford

NETHERLANDS
AMSTERDAM

BERLIN

LONDON

Plymouth   Southampton   Bruges   The Hague   BRUSSELS   GERMANY
English Channel   Calais   Ghent   BELGIUM

Le Havre   Cologne

Brest

Frankfurt-am-Main   PRAGUE

Nantes   PARIS   LUXEMBOURG   CZECH REPUBLIC

Strasbourg   Stuttgart

Bay of Biscay   FRANCE   Munich   VIENNA

BERN   Zürich   Salzburg

La Coruña-
A Coruña   Bordeaux   Clermont-Ferrand   Geneva   SWITZERLAND   Innsbruck   AUSTRIA

Santiago de
Compostela   Santander   Lyon   Milan   Trieste   SLOVENIA   ZAGREB

Porto   Biarritz   Genoa   Venice   CROATIA

Toulouse   Bologna   BOSNIA
HERZEGOVIN

PORTUGAL   Zaragoza   ANDORRA   Marseille   Nice   Florence   SARAJEVO

LISBON   MADRID   Barcelona   *Corsica*   ITALY   Pescara   *Adriatic Sea*

SPAIN   Ajaccio   ROME   Foggia

Seville   Valencia   Olbia   Naples   Bríndisi

Cádiz   *Balearic Islands*   *Sardinia*   *Tyrrhenian Sea*

Málaga   Murcia   Cagliari   Messina

Gibraltar   Palermo   Réggio di Calábria

Mediterranean Sea   *Sicily*

MOROCCO   ALGERIA   TUNISIA   MALTA

Coverage map

Introduction

This essential handbook, now covering 42 European countries, has been compiled to ensure you are well prepared for motoring in Europe, whether you are an experienced motorist or adventuring abroad with your car for the first time.

We have included information on requirements by country (see pages 16–165) – from Andorra to Ukraine – with local rules for drivers, including seat-belt and drink-driving laws, speed limits and headlight requirements. There are also details of the documents you should take, equipment to carry in your car and what toll charges you will encounter. Useful quick-reference charts detail compulsory requirements, winter motoring information and distances. Principal mountain passes are also included. Easy-to-read maps, showing both toll and toll-free motorways, will help with route planning and budgeting.

A selection of scenic tours, each with an accompanying route map, will guide you through the best places of interest the region has to offer (see pages 166–197) and the words and phrases section is tailored to assist if you encounter difficulties on the road, from asking directions to reading traffic signs (see pages 198–217). With all this information at your fingertips, *The European Driver's Handbook* is your passport to a safe and enjoyable trip.

The car tours featured in this handbook were reproduced from the AA's Best Drives series of top-selling guides to all the most interesting driving destinations. The words and phrases are from the AA Phrase Books, which contain everything you would expect from a comprehensive language series. For information on the full range of the AA's guides, maps and atlases visit **theAA.com/shop**.

Before you go

Documents and insurance

Documents you should take with you

- A valid full driving licence (not provisional), with paper counterpart if you have a photocard licence.
- An International Driving Permit where necessary.
- The original vehicle registration document.
- Your motor insurance certificate.
- Your passport.
- You may need a visa for certain countries, too. It is your responsibility to ensure that you have all documentation needed to comply with the requirements of immigration, customs, health and other regulations.
- If you're travelling in a vehicle other than a motor car or motorcycle or taking a boat, make sure you have any additional documentation that may be required.
- If the vehicle you're driving is company owned, hired or borrowed, try to obtain the original V5 registration document together with a letter of authorisation from the owner. If you can't get the V5 then obtain a Vehicle on Hire Certificate, also known as the VE103b, available from BVRLA/All fleet services on **01452 887686**. This is the only legal alternative to the vehicle registration document. The Vehicle on Hire Certificate must be carried in addition to a letter of authorisation from the registered keeper.

Breakdown cover

Make sure that you have adequate cover. AA European Breakdown Cover provides cover for many European countries, **tel: 0800 072 3279** or visit **theAA.com** and follow the link **European Breakdown Cover** for information.

Car insurance

Contact your insurer for advice at least a month before taking a vehicle overseas. Ensure that you're adequately covered and have the necessary documents to prove it. A Green Card (proof of insurance cover while using your vehicle abroad) is compulsory in Bosnia and Herzegovina.

Credit cards

Occasionally we hear that UK-issued credit cards are not accepted at stores or petrol stations in other countries. Check with your card company to confirm that it can be used in the countries you are visiting.

Driving licence

You must always carry your full UK driving licence, and other qualified drivers in your party should take their licences in case of an emergency. All valid UK licences should be accepted in most of the countries listed in this book.

European Health Insurance Card

National Health treatment is not available outside the UK but you may be able to get free or reduced-cost treatment within the EU with the European Health Insurance Card (EHIC). The EHIC entitles UK residents who are travelling in Europe to reduced-cost, sometimes free, state-provided emergency healthcare when visiting a European Union (EU) country, Iceland, Liechtenstein, Norway or Switzerland. The card is available free of charge and is valid for up to five years. Each person needs their own card. You can

least three weeks (six weeks for a first adult passport) for your application to be processed. Holders of passports from outside the UK should check regarding any visa requirements with the appropriate embassy or consulate. Note down your passport number and the date of issue and keep this information in a safe place, separate from your passport. Carry your passport at all times as proof of identity and take one other form of photo ID with you.

Personal insurance

It is essential that you are fully covered by travel insurance. Make sure you have at least the minimum cover for medical expenses, theft and losses abroad.

Pets

If you intend to take your pet abroad contact the Pet Travel Scheme (PETS) helpline **tel: 0870 241 1710** or visit the PETS website **www.defra.gov.uk/wildlife-pets/pets/travel/pets/index.htm**

Travel advice

For up-to-date travel advice from the Foreign and Commonwealth Office **tel: 0845 850 2829** or visit **www.fco.gov.uk/en/travel-and-living-abroad/travel-advice-by-country/**

apply online at **www.nhs.uk/NHSEngland/Healthcareabroad**, or by phoning the EHIC Application Line on **0845 606 2030**. Postal application packs are available from post offices. The EHIC may not cover you for all medical costs incurred (the cost of bringing a person back to the UK in the event of illness or death is never covered) so you are strongly advised to arrange travel insurance also to ensure that you are covered for all possible eventualities.

Passports

Each person (including children and babies) must hold an up-to-date passport. Some countries require a passport to remain valid for a minimum period (usually at least six months) beyond the date of entry – check before you travel. Information and application forms are available from main post offices and from Passport Offices or you can apply for an application form online at **www.direct.gov.uk/en/TravelAndTransport/Passports**. Allow at

Your documents

You may be asked to produce your documents at any time. To avoid a police fine and/or confiscation of your vehicle, be sure that they are in order and readily available for inspection.

Preparing your car

Child restraints

Never fit a rear-facing car seat in any seat with an active air bag. Use only an approved restraint suitable for the child's weight and height. Visit **theAA.com/motoring_advice/child_safety/carseats.html** for further information.

Fire extinguisher/first-aid kit

In some countries it is compulsory to equip your vehicle with these items (see individual country sections).

Headlights

If you're driving to the Continent you must adjust the headlamp beam pattern to suit driving on the right so that the dipped beam doesn't dazzle oncoming drivers. Headlamp beam converter kits are widely available, but a dealer may need to make the adjustment, especially if your car has high-intensity discharge (HID), halogen-type or xenon headlamps – check the car's handbook. Remember to remove the converters as soon as you return to the UK.

Keys

Many modern cars have a 'transponder' key to prevent theft. If you lose the key, recovery to an authorised dealer is usually the only answer. Even a dealer may take several days to obtain a replacement, which will be expensive, so always carry a spare set of keys.

Loading your car

Visit **theAA.com/motoring_advice/loading-your-car-safely.html** for rules on how to pack your car. Overloading your car can incur fines and possibly invalidate your insurance.

Nationality plate/GB sticker

Vehicles must display a nationality plate/GB sticker of the approved pattern, design and size. UK registration plates displaying the GB Euro symbol (Euro plates) make display of a conventional sticker unnecessary when driving within the EU. In some countries outside the EU a conventional sticker is required even if you have Euro plates, so it is always safer to display one on your vehicle.

Rear-view mirrors

It is essential to have clear all-round vision. If your vehicle is not equipped with a door or wing-mirror on the left-hand side we recommend that you get one fitted to aid driving on the right.

Reflective jacket/waistcoat

It is now compulsory in many European countries for visiting motorists to carry/wear reflective jackets (see individual country sections). We recommend that you carry at least two jackets/waistcoats in the passenger compartment – one for the driver and one for a passenger, who may assist in changing a wheel. If you intend to hire a car, be aware that not all rental firms provide jackets with their cars. Check with the car hire company before you travel.

Seat belts

If seat belts are fitted to your vehicle it is compulsory to wear them.

Servicing

Service your car well in advance of your journey to reduce the chance of expensive breakdowns when abroad.

Speed-trap detection devices

The use or possession of devices to detect police radar is illegal in most European countries. Penalties can include a fine, driving ban and even imprisonment. Some countries now also prohibit the use of GPS-based navigation systems that have maps indicating the location of fixed speed cameras, meaning that you must deactivate the 'fixed speed camera PoI (Points of Interest)' function. See individual country sections.

Toolkit

Check the handbook for the location of the basic toolkit for the car, which should contain at least a jack and wheel-removal tools. If locking wheel nuts are fitted make sure that the toolkit includes the key or removal tool.

Tyres

Like in the UK, most countries require a minimum tread depth of 1.6mm over the central three-quarters of the tread and around the whole circumference. We recommend a minimum of 2mm but consider changing tyres if the tread is down to 3mm before you go. Tyres wear out quickly after they get down to 3mm.

Warning triangle

The use of a warning triangle is compulsory in many European countries in the event of an accident or breakdown (not always required for two-wheeled vehicles). In certain circumstances two triangles are required.

Wheel chains

Wheel chains are important for any winter motoring and compulsory in some countries even when using winter tyres (see the individual country sections). Snow chains are available from the AA's Dover and Folkestone shops (Dover **tel: 01304 208122**; Folkestone **tel: 0800 072 4372**).The Folkestone shop is beyond the customs point. Telephone ahead to check availability. You will be asked for the vehicle make and model and the tyre size, read from the sidewall of the tyre.

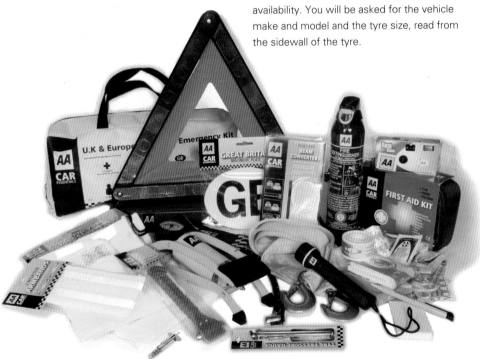

A selection of travel and emergency kits are available from accessory stores, theAA.com/shop and the AA Travelshops at Folkestone (Eurotunnel) and Dover.

Driving in

General motoring information   **18**
Driving requirements chart   **22**
Winter motoring requirements chart   **24**

Countries

General motoring information

Accidents

If you are involved in an accident, you must stop, switch on your hazard warning lights and place a warning triangle on the road at a suitable distance. If the accident necessitates calling the police, leave the vehicle in position and phone them, also obtaining medical assistance if needed. Notify your insurance company within 24 hours, making sure all the essential particulars are noted. If you can, take photographs of the scene of the accident. (See the individual country sections for emergency telephone numbers.) In Serbia and, in certain circumstances, in Switzerland, you are required to carry and complete a European Accident Statement form (available from some insurers).

Blue Badge users

The Blue Badge is recognised in all European countries. When displayed on the dashboard

of a car, it allows you to make use of the same parking concessions provided for the country's own citizens with a disability.

The concessions do differ from country to country so it's important to know where, when and for how long you can park in each country. Visit **theAA.com/motoring_advice/overseas/ blue-badge-users.html** and click on the 'Publications' link to download a leaflet giving details of parking concessions in 27 countries. **Remember, if you are in any doubt about your rights, don't park**.

Breakdown

Stop your car in a safe place where possible, out of the way of traffic. If you have a reflective jacket, put it on. Switch on your hazard warning lights and side lights and place a warning triangle to the rear of the vehicle at a suitable distance. Find the nearest telephone to call for assistance. On motorways, emergency telephones are generally located every 2km (1.24 miles) and automatically connect you to the authorities.

Car crime

Never leave handbags and other attractive items in obvious view even when you are in the car, and never leave anything in an unattended car. For advice on car crime or personal safety in specific countries, contact the Foreign Office Travel Advice Unit on **0845 850 2829** or visit **www.fco.gov.uk**

Crash or safety helmets

The wearing of crash or safety helmets by motorcyclists and their passengers is compulsory in all countries.

Delays and diversions

Roadworks and major events can mean that roads are sometimes closed completely. If this is the case, follow locally signed detours. There may be delays at peak travel periods, delays on some main routes and at frontier crossing points. Mountain passes and alpine roads may be closed during the winter months (see pages 224–235 for more information on Mountain passes).

General motoring information

Drinking and driving

There is only one safe rule – if you drink, don't drive. Laws are strict and the penalties are severe.

Emergency contact

Telephone **112**, the European emergency number you can use in the all the member states of the European Union, in case of accident, assault or in any other distress situation. See individual country entries for contact numbers in non-EU countries.

Fines

Some countries impose on-the-spot fines for minor traffic offences. Fines are generally paid in the currency of the country concerned. You must obtain a receipt as proof of payment.

Leaded petrol

Leaded petrol is no longer generally available in northern European countries and Lead Replacement Petrol (LRP) is getting more difficult to find. If LRP is not on sale, an anti-wear additive (for treating unleaded petrol) can be bought from the filling station shop.

Low Emission Zones

More than 70 cities and towns in eight countries around Europe already have in place, or are preparing to launch, Low Emission Zones (LEZs) – areas where the most polluting vehicles are regulated in some way. Currently most of these zones affect only vans and lorries but some, including those in Germany and Italy, affect passenger cars too. To find out where these LEZs are, what kinds of vehicles are affected, what emission standards are required and whether registration is required or not visit **www.lowemissionzones.eu** (in English). Low Emission Zones are also known as Environment Zones, *Umweltzonen*

(Germany), *Milieuzones* (Netherlands), *Lavutslippssone* (Norway), *Miljozone* (Denmark), *Miljözon* (Sweden).

Mobile phones

Before you take your phone abroad ask your network provider whether your phone is enabled for international roaming, what it charges for international roaming services in the countries you will be visiting and whether your handset will work in these countries. It may be worth buying a new SIM card when you arrive at your destination (the SIM card will work only on that country's network) and you can top it up as you

would a 'pay as you go' phone in the UK. Visit
**www.direct.gov.uk/en/TravelAndTransport/
TravellingAbroad/BeforeYouTravel/** for
further information. The use of hand-held
mobile phones while driving is prohibited
in many countries.

Rule of the road
In all countries covered in this guide, apart from
Cyprus (north and south), Malta, Great Britain
and Ireland, the rule of the road is to drive
on the right and overtake on the left. For UK
drivers it's easy to forget to drive on the right,
particularly after doing something familiar, such
as leaving a petrol station or car park.

Signposting
Signposting between major towns and along
main roads is generally efficient, but on some
secondary roads and in open country, advance
direction signs may be less frequent. Signs are
often of the pointer type and placed on walls or
railings on the far side of the turn; they tend to
point across the road they indicate, which can
be confusing at first. Difficulties may arise with
spellings when crossing frontiers, and place
names may not be so easily recognised when
written in a different language. Extra difficulties
may arise in countries with two or more official
languages or dialects, although some towns
may have both spellings, e.g. San Sebastian
– Donostia in Spain, Antwerpen – Anvers in
Belgium, Basel – Bâle in Switzerland.

Size restrictions
Check with your national camping or
caravanning club that your vehicle and/or trailer
complies with the weight and size legislation in
the countries that you intend to visit.

Spectacles
Take a spare pair of spectacles if you wear them
– especially if you are the sole driver.

Speed limits
Speed limits for individual countries are listed in
the appropriate country sections. Lower limits
will apply to motorcycles in some countries
and also generally when towing a trailer unless
otherwise indicated. Visiting drivers who have
held a full licence for under two years may also
have to adhere to lower speed limits.

How far in miles? Conversion table: kilometres to miles

kms	1	2	3	4	5	10	15	20	25	30	35	40	45	50
miles	0.62	1.24	1.86	2.49	3.11	6.21	9.32	12.43	15.53	18.64	21.75	24.85	27.96	31.07

Driving requirements chart

DRIVING REQUIREMENTS	Austria	Belgium	Croatia	Denmark	France	Germany
Minimum age/UK licence holders (1)	18	18	18	17	18	18
International Driving Permit required for UK licence holders (IDP)	No (2)	No	No	No	No	No
Original registration document	C	C	C	C	C	C
Motor vehicle insurance (4)	C	C	C	C	C	C
Motorway tax	C & Tolls	No	Tolls	Tolls	Tolls	No
GB sticker (5)	C	C	C	C	C	C
Warning triangle	C (6)	C (6)	C (6&8)	C	C (6)	R (7)
Reflective jacket/waistcoat	C (6)	C (11)	C	No	C (11)	No
First-aid kit	C	R (17)	C (6)	R	No	R (17)
Fire extinguisher (6)	No	R (17)	No	R	No	No
Headlamp adjustment (12)	C	C	C	C	C	C
On-the-spot fines	Yes	Yes	Yes (13)	Yes	Yes	Yes
Radar dectectors (18)	F	F	F	F	F	F
Daytime headlights/passing lights: cars	No (16)	No (16)	C (16)	C	R (16)	R (16)
Daytime headlights/passing lights: m/cycles	R	C	C	C	C	C

C = Compulsory R = Recommended by AA/respective country F = Forbidden.
The above chart covers some of the most popular countries featured in this book. It must be read in conjunction with the 'Driving in' information for the relevant country. The numbers in brackets refer to the notes below. Check **theAA.com/motoring_advice/overseas/compulsory_equipment.html** for the latest information. Items or associated equipment highlighted in **bold** in the chart above can be purchased online from the AA at **theAA.com/shop**.

NOTES

(1) Minimum age at which a visitor may drive a car.

(2) UK driving licences that do not incorporate a photograph are recognised, but drivers must be able to produce photographic proof of identity (e.g. passport).

(3) All valid UK licences should be accepted. However, this cannot be guaranteed on older all-green-style UK licences. Drivers may wish to update them voluntarily before travelling abroad, if time permits. Alternatively, older licences may be accompanied by an IDP.

(4) Before taking a vehicle abroad, contact your motor insurer or broker to notify them of your intentions, and ask their advice. It is important to know what level of cover you will have and what documents you need to prove it.

(5) GB stickers are compulsory within the EU unless your UK registration plates display the GB Euro symbol (Euro plates), which became a legal option from 21

March 2001. The Euro plate must comply with the new British Standard (BS AU 145d). The Euro plate is legally recognised only in the EU; it is still a requirement to display a GB sticker when travelling outside the EU.

(6) Not required for two-wheeled vehicles.

(7) Although it is not compulsory for visiting motorists to carry a warning triangle, its use is compulsory in an accident/breakdown situation.

(8) **Spain:** One warning triangle is compulsory for non-Spanish-registered vehicles; two for Spanish-registered vehicles. **Note:** Drivers of non-Spanish-registered vehicles should consider carrying two triangles as, regardless of regulations, local officials may impose an on-the-spot fine if only one is available. **Croatia:** Two triangles are compulsory for vehicles towing a trailer. **Switzerland:** Warning triangle must be kept within easy reach (not in the boot).

(9) The use of hazard warning lights or a warning triangle is compulsory in an accident/breakdown

Ireland	Italy	Netherlands	Norway	Portugal	Spain	Sweden	Switzerland
17	18	18	18	17 (14)	18	18	18
No	No (3)	No	No	No (3)	No (3)	No (2)	No
C	C	C	C	C	C	C	C
C	C	C	C	C	C	C	C
Tolls	Tolls	No	Tolls	Tolls	Tolls	Tolls	C & Tolls
C	C	C	C	C	C	C	C
C (10)	C (6)	R (9&6)	C (6)	R (9)	C (8&6)	R	C (6&8)
No	C (11&6)	No	R (11)	R (11)	C (11)	No	No
No	No	No	R	No	No	R	No
No	No	No	R	No	No	R	No
No	C	C	C	C	C	C	C
Yes (13)	Yes (13)	Yes	Yes	Yes	Yes	Yes (13)	Yes
F	F	F	F	F	F	F	F
No (16)	C (15)	R	C	No (16)	No	C	R
C	C	R	C	C	C	C	R

situation. However, a warning triangle should always be carried as hazard warning lights have no effect at bends or rises in the road, or may become damaged or inoperative.

(10) Compulsory for vehicles with an unladen weight exceeding 1524kg.

(11) It is compulsory for driver and/or passenger(s) to wear a reflective jacket/waistcoat when exiting a vehicle immobilised on the carriageway, in **Italy** at night or in poor visibility, in **Spain** on all motorways and busy roads. In **Croatia** wearing a jacket is compulsory whenever you have to get out of the vehicle at the roadside in an emergency. In **Portugal** and **Norway** the actual law applies to residents; however, regardless of the regulations local officials may impose an on-the-spot fine. In **Belgium** the wearing of a reflective jacket applies only to the driver; it must be worn should you be stranded on a Belgian motorway or on a major road or should you stop at a place where parking is not allowed. In **France** drivers must have one warning triangle and one reflective jacket in their vehicle (the requirement does not apply to two- or three-wheeled vehicles). In **Austria** the regulation applies only to the driver.

(12) The legal requirement is to 'not dazzle oncoming drivers' rather than specifically to adjust/convert the headlamp beam pattern. Without adjustment the dipped beam will dazzle oncoming drivers and this could result in a fine. Headlamp beam converter kits are widely available but may not be suitable for all types of headlights. The AA shop sells beam converters suitable for all vehicles and individual fitting diagrams are included for the latest 'clear glass', 'projector and xenon' headlamps inside the packaging. In some countries it is compulsory to use dipped headlights at all times when driving during the day. Note: This adjustment is not required for two-wheeled vehicles as the beam pattern is more symmetrical, but check that any extra loading has not affected the beam height. On some cars it is inadvisable or impossible for anyone other than a qualified technician to change a headlamp bulb unit e.g. high-intensity discharge (HID) headlamps and carrying spares is not an option. However, it is recommended that spare bulbs are carried for any lights that may be easily and/or safely replaced by the owner/driver. Spare bulbs are compulsory for **Spain** and **Croatia**; for **Spain** you must also carry the tools to change them.

(13) Sweden: Police are not actually authorised to collect fines, which must be paid in accordance with notice instructions. **Italy:** Police will collect a quarter of the maximum fine amount from drivers of foreign registered vehicles. **Ireland:** Police are not actually

Winter motoring requirements chart

(Driving Requirements Chart, Notes – continued)

authorised to collect fines; they will issue a notice, which must be paid within 21 days. **Croatia:** The fine does not have to be paid on the spot; however it does need to be paid within eight days.

(14) Portugal: Visiting drivers of 17 years of age may encounter problems even though they hold a valid driving licence in the UK.

(15) Outside built-up areas, during snow or rain causing poor visibility.

(16) Compulsory during daylight hours if visibility is poor. Also for **Croatia** during daylight hours from the last Sunday in October to the last Sunday in March.

(17) Recommended as their carriage is compulsory for vehicles registered in that country.

(18) Many countries now stipulate that GPS-based navigation systems that have maps indicating the location of fixed speed cameras must have the 'fixed speed camera PoI (Point of interest)' function deactivated.

Winter tyre/snow chain requirement chart

	Andorra	Austria	Finland	France	Germany
Winter tyres	R	C (1)	M (3)	–	R (4)
Snow chains (5)	C	C (7)	P	C	C

P = Permitted

R = Recommended

M = Mandatory

C = Compulsory. Chains should be carried and used as dictated by local signs or road conditions. Reduced speed limits may apply.

The information in the table above applies to vehicles not exceeding 3500kg.

This chart shows only specific winter requirements and should be read in conjuction with the general compulsory equipment chart and the general Driving in information for the country of interest.

Tyre tread/snow chains

Check all tyres for condition, pressure and tread depth. Where winter tyres are fitted, a minimum tread depth of 3mm is required in most countries (the **Czech Republic** now requires 4mm). For other tyres, while the legal minimum is 1.6mm the AA recommends at least 3mm of tread for winter motoring, and certainly no less than 2mm.

Snow chains may be purchased from the **AA Travelshop** at Dover and Eurotunnel (Folkestone) – the one-stop shop for all your motoring accessories.

NOTES

(1) All vehicles driving on snow-covered roads must have winter tyres (or all-season tyres marked M&S/mud and snow) during the winter season (from 1 November to 15 April) and if roads have a covering of snow, slush or ice outside these dates. Tyres must have a minimum tread depth of 4mm. Theoretically, snow chains on summer tyres can be used as an alternative to winter tyres where the entire road is heavily covered with snow and no damage to the road is caused by the snow chains. In practice though, because road conditions and the

Great Britain	Italy	Norway	Sweden	Switzerland
–	R (4)	R	C (6)	R (2)
P	C (8)	C	R	C

weather cannot be predicted, use of winter tyres is effectively compulsory.

(2) Snow tyres are not compulsory but vehicles not equipped to travel through snow and that impede traffic are liable to a fine.

(3) From 1 December to the end of February unless otherwise indicated by road signs. Tyres must be marked M&S on the sidewall. Spiked tyres may be used from 1 November to the first Monday after Easter.

(4) As the weather cannot be predicted and because snow chains may not be used in slushy/icy conditions it is recommended that visitors fit winter tyres to their vehicle. Winter tyres (or 'all year' tyres) must bear the mark M&S or the snowflake symbol on the sidewall.

(5) Snow chains must be fitted on at least two drive wheels. In any country, snow chains may be used only where there's sufficient snow covering to avoid any possibility of damage to the road surface. A fine may be imposed if damage is caused.

(6) Winter tyres, marked M&S (with or without spikes), with a tread depth of at least 3mm, are compulsory from 1 December until 31 March for Swedish-registered vehicles and trailers and also for foreign-registered vehicles.

(7) Must be carried – and used when advised by local signs.

General advice
In any country the driver is responsible for equipping and controlling their vehicle correctly. Drivers may be liable to a fine if they impede the normal flow of traffic or cause an accident as a consequence of not adapting their vehicle (tyres/snow chains) to suit the prevailing weather and road conditions. Road conditions in winter in many resorts will be much more severe than anything encountered in the United Kingdom. The AA recommends driving in extreme winter conditions only if the driver is confident and the vehicle suitably equipped.

Driving in Andorra *(South West Europe)*

The regulations below should be read in conjunction with the General motoring information on pages 18–21.

Drinking and driving
The permitted level of alcohol in the bloodstream is 0.05 per cent.

Driving licence
The minimum age at which a UK licence holder may drive temporarily a imported car and/or motorcycle is 18.

Fines
On-the-spot fines can be imposed.

Fuel
Leaded (98 octane), unleaded petrol (95 and 98 octane) and diesel *(gasoil)* is available, but not LPG. It is forbidden to carry petrol in a can. Credit cards are accepted at most filling stations; check with your card issuer for usage in Andorra before travel.

Lights
Dipped headlights should be used in poor daytime visibility.

Motorcycles
The use of dipped headlights during the day is compulsory. The wearing of a crash helmet is compulsory.

Motor insurance
Third-party insurance is compulsory.

Passengers/children in cars
A child under 10 cannot travel as a front-seat passenger.

Seat belts
It is compulsory for front-seat occupants to wear seat belts, if fitted.

Speed limits
The standard legal limits, which may be varied by signs, for **private vehicles with or without trailers** are: in built-up areas 50km/h (31mph), outside built-up areas between 60 and 90km/h (37 and 55mph).

Additional information
- It is compulsory to carry spare bulbs, a warning triangle and a reflective yellow waistcoat.
- Winter tyres are recommended.
- Snow chains must be used when road conditions or signs indicate.

Travel facts: Andorra

Embassy of Andorra
63 Westover Road
London SW18 2RF
Tel: 020 8874 4806.
www.andorra.ad
Information for UK residents planning a trip to Andorra.
By appointment only.

Banking hours
Banks are generally open Monday to Friday 9pm to
1pm and 3pm to 5pm and Saturday 9am to 12pm. In the
summer months all banks close on Saturday.

Credit/debit cards
Banks have money exchange facilities and automatic
cash machines. International credit cards such as
Visa, MasterCard and American Express are widely
accepted.

Currency
The euro (€) is the currency of Andorra. It is not a
member of the EU, does not issue its own euros and
therefore uses euros from other European countries.

Electricity
The power supply is 220/230 volts AC. Round two-hole
sockets take two-round-pin plugs. British visitors will
need an adaptor.

Health care
Comprehensive travel insurance is essential for all
visitors.

Pharmacies
The pharmacies in Andorra, identified by a green
cross, stock cosmetics, perfumes, and recognised
international pharmaceutical products. They offer
specialist advice from expert staff.

Post offices
There are two conventional postal systems in Andorra:
Spanish post (post offices open Monday to Friday
8.30am to 2.30pm, Saturday 9am to 1pm) and French
post (post offices open Monday to Friday 8.30am to
2.30pm, Saturday 9am to 12pm). All parishes have post
offices for stamps and related postal items.

Safe water
Bottled mineral water is cheap and widely available.

Telephones
All telephone numbers in Andorra comprise six digits.
There are no area codes. The country code for Andorra
is 376. To call home from Andorra dial the international
code (00) followed by the country code. To call the UK
from Andorra dial 00 44.

Time
Andorra is on Central European Time, one hour ahead
of Greenwich Mean Time (GMT + 1). From late March,
when the clocks are put forward one hour, until late
October, Summer Time (GMT + 2) operates.

Emergency telephone numbers
Police **110**
Ambulance/Fire Brigade **118**
Mountain Rescue **112**
Medical Emergency Service **116**

Driving in Austria *(Central Europe)*

The regulations below should be read in conjunction with the General motoring information on pages 18–21.

Drinking and driving
The maximum permitted level of alcohol in the blood is 0.049. If between 0.05 per cent and 0.079 per cent there is a fine, 0.08 per cent or more a severe fine and/or a driving ban for Austria. A limit of 0.01 applies to new drivers who have held a licence for under two years.

Driving licence
The minimum age at which a UK licence holder may drive a temporarily imported car is 18, motorcycle (up to 50cc) with a maximum design speed of 45km/h (27mph) 16 and motorcycle (over 50cc) 18. **Note:** UK driving licences that do not incorporate a photograph are valid only when accompanied by photographic proof of identity, e.g. passport.

Fines
On-the-spot fines can be imposed. The officer collecting the fine should issue an official receipt. For higher fines the driver will be asked to pay a deposit and the remainder of the fine within two weeks. Parked vehicles obstructing traffic may be towed away.

Fuel
Unleaded petrol (95 and 98 octane) and diesel are available; there is limited LPG. Leaded petrol is not sold, although you can buy a lead-substitute additive. Carrying petrol in a can is permitted. Credit cards are accepted by the larger filling stations; check with your card issuer for usage in Austria before you travel.

Lights
Passing lights (dipped headlights) must be used when visibility is poor due to bad weather conditions. It is prohibited to drive only with side lights (position lights).

Motorcycles
The wearing of crash helmets is compulsory for the driver and passenger. It is prohibited to drive only with side lights (position lights). The use of dipped headlights during the day is compulsory.

Motor Insurance
Third-party insurance is compulsory, including cover for trailers.

Passengers/children in cars
Children under 14 and less than 1.5m (4ft 11in) in height cannot travel as a front- or rear-seat passenger unless using suitable restraint system for their height/weight. Vehicles without such protection (e.g. two-seater sports cars or vans/lorries) may not carry children under 14 years. Children under 14 but over 1.5m (4ft 11in) in height must use the adult seat belt. Children 14 or over and over 1.35m (4ft 5in) in height are allowed to use a *Dreipunktgurt* (three-point seat belt) without a special child seat, if the belt does not cover the child's throat/neck.

Seat belts
It is compulsory for front- and rear-seat occupants to wear seat belts, if fitted. If you do not comply there is a fine of €35.

Speed limits

The standard legal limits, which may be varied by signs, for **private vehicles without trailers** are: in built-up areas up to 50km/h (31mph), outside built-up areas 100km/h (62mph) and motorways up to 130km/h (80mph). Lower limits apply to a **car towing a trailer (not over 750kg)**: in built-up areas areas 50km/h (31mph), outside built-up areas and motorways 100km/h (62mph). For a **car towing a trailer over 750kg (not exceeding 3500kg)** it is 100km/h (62mph) on motorways and 80km/h (49mph) on other roads. The speed limit for the total weight of a **car towing a trailer over 3500kg** is 70km/h (43mph) on motorways and 60km/h (37mph) on other roads.

Vehicles not capable of sustaining a minimum speed of 60km/h (37mph) are not permitted on motorways. Mopeds must not exceed 45km/h (28mph). The maximum recommended speed limit for vehicles with snow chains is 40km/h (24mph). Vehicles equipped with spiked tyres must not exceed 100km/h (62mph) on motorways and 80km/h (49mph) on other roads.

Additional information

- It is compulsory to carry a warning triangle conforming to EC regulation 27 (for vehicles with more than two wheels) and a first-aid kit which must be in a strong dirt-proof box..
- Every car driver has to carry a reflective jacket/waistcoat (compliant with European regulation EN471) to be used in the case of a breakdown or accident and when setting up a warning triangle on the road. This regulation does not apply to mopeds/motorcycles, although it is recommended.
- All motorists have the legal obligation to adapt their vehicle to winter weather conditions.
- Between 1 November and 15 April vehicles must be fitted with winter tyres (which must

be marked M&S (mud and snow) on the sidewalls and have a minimum tread depth of 4mm) or all-season tyres, which must be marked M&S, and if roads have a covering of snow, slush or ice outside these dates. Theoretically, snow chains on summer tyres can be used as an alternative to winter tyres where the road is heavily covered with snow and no damage to the road surface is caused by the snow chains. In practice, because conditions and the weather are unpredictable, use of winter tyres is effectively compulsory. **Note:** It is the driver's legal responsibility to carry the required winter equipment; therefore, it is essential to check that it is included in any hire car.

- All vehicles using Austrian motorways and expressways must display motorway tax sticker *(vignette)*. The stickers, valid for one year, two months or 10 days, may be purchased at some petrol stations close to the border and in Austria at the frontier, at petrol stations, post offices or in ÖAMTC offices. A *Korridor Vignette* is required for vehicles travelling from Hohenehms to Horbranz on the German border if you don't have a standard *vignette*. The minimum fine for driving without a *vignette* is €120.
- Tolls are also payable when passing through certain motorway tunnels, see page 30.
- The use of the horn is generally prohibited in Vienna and in the vicinity of hospitals.
- Drivers are not permitted to overtake a school bus that has stopped to let children on and off (indicated by a yellow flashing light).
- Spiked tyres may be used from 1 October until 31 May; special local regulations may extend this period.
- It is prohibited to use radar detectors.
- Parking vouchers can be obtained from tobacconists, banks and petrol stations.

Travel facts and toll charges: Austria

Austrian National Tourist Office
The tourist office in London is for press and marketing purposes only; however, you can make enquiries by phone direct to Austria.
Tel: 0845 101 1818 (local UK call charges apply)
www.aboutaustria.org

Banking hours
Banks are generally open Monday to Friday 8am to 3pm and up to 5.30pm on Thursday.

Credit/debit cards
Visa, MasterCard, Amex and Diners Club are accepted by the larger hotels, restaurants and some garages, but smaller establishments prefer cash.

Currency
The euro (€) is the currency of Austria. Euro coins are issued in denominations of 1, 2, 5, 10, 20 and 50 cents and €1 and €2. Banknotes are issued in denominations of €5, €10, €20, €50, €100, €200 and €500.

Electricity
Electric current is 220 volts AC and appliances need two-round-pin continental plugs.

Health care
Free or reduced-cost medical treatment is available in Austria to European visitors on production of a valid European Health Insurance Card (EHIC). See page 10. Comprehensive travel insurance is still advised and is essential for all other visitors.

Pharmacies
Pharmacies (apotheken) are the only places that sell over-the-counter medicines. Take all prescription medicines with you.

Post offices
Post office (postamt) opening times are generally Monday to Friday 8am to12 and 2 to 6pm. In major cities hours extend through lunchtime and into Saturday morning and at least one office will be open 24 hours. Stamps are sold at post offices and tobacco kiosks (tabak-trafik). Post boxes are yellow.

Safe water
Tap water throughout Austria is safe to drink. Bottled mineral water from local springs is available – look out for well-known brands Vöslauer and Römerquelle.

Telephones
Phone booths are generally dark green with yellow roofs. All boxes, even the new glass ones, display the symbol of a post horn. Most boxes will accept phone cards that are sold by post offices and tobacconists only. The country code for Austria is 43. To call home from Austria dial the international code (00) followed by the country code. To call the UK from Austria dial 00 44.

Time
Austria is on Central European Time, one hour ahead of GMT (GMT + 1). Daylight Saving Time comes into effect from the end of March to the end of October (GMT + 2).

Emergency telephone numbers
Police **133** or **112** Fire **122** or **112** Ambulance **144** or **112**

Toll charges in euros
For details of where to buy the motorway tax sticker (vignette) see page 29.

General		Car	Car towing caravan/ trailer
10-day *vignette*		7.90	7.90
2-month *vignette*		22.90	22.90
Annual *vignette*		76.20	76.20
Road			
A10	Tauern Autobahn	9.50	9.50
A13	Innsbruck – Brenner pass	8.00	8.00
	Grossglockner Alpine Road	28.00	not permitted
Bridges and tunnels			
Bosruck Tunnel on **A9**		4.50	4.50
Gleinalm Tunnel on **A9**		7.50	7.50
Karawanken Tunnel on **A11**		6.50	6.50

Driving in Belarus *(Eastern Europe)*

The regulations below should be read in conjunction
with the General motoring information on pages 18–21.

Drinking and driving
It is strictly forbidden to drink and drive;
nil percentage of alcohol is allowed in the
driver's blood.

Driving licence
The minimum age at which a visitor may drive
a temporarily imported car and/or motorcycle
is 18. National driving licences that bear the
photo of the holder are recognised for three
months, but an International Driving Permit (IDP)
is recommended. An IDP is compulsory for
licences not incorporating a photograph.

Fines
The police can fine motorists and demand
payment on the spot for minor traffic offences.

Fuel
Unleaded petrol (80, 92 and 95 octane) is
available; 98 octane is seldom available; diesel
(solyarka) and LPG are available. Leaded petrol
is not available. Up to 20 litres of fuel can be
imported free of duty if held in a metal container
(must be declared on entry). Credit cards are
accepted at large filling stations; check with your
card issuer for usage in Belarus before travel.

Lights
Vehicles must use lights in poor visibility and
when towing or being towed. Avoid driving
at night.

Motorcycles
The wearing of crash helmets is compulsory.
It is compulsory to use dipped headlights at
all times.

Motor insurance
Third-party insurance is compulsory, but fully
comprehensive insurance is recommended.
A Green Card is accepted. Short-term insurance
is available at the border.

Passengers/children in cars
A child under 12 cannot travel as a front-seat
passenger. Children under the age of 12 must
be seated in a suitable child-restraint system.

Seat belts
It is compulsory for front-seat occupants
to wear seat belts, if fitted.

Speed limits
The signs indicating speed limits must be strictly
adhered to. Standard legal limits, which may be
varied by signs, for **private vehicles without
trailers** are: in residential zones 20km/h
(12mph), in built-up areas 60km/h (37mph),
outside built-up areas 90km/h (55mph) and up
to 110km/h (68mph) on different sections of the
Brest–Moscow motorway. All motorists who
have held a driving licence for less than two
years must not exceed 70km/h (43mph).

Belarus

Additional information

- It is compulsory to carry a first-aid kit and a fire extinguisher. A warning triangle is also cumpulsory but not required for two-wheeled vehicles.
- A road tax is payable at the frontier.
- State Traffic Inspectorate officials will stop vehicles to check documents, especially if they are displaying foreign plates. Motorists entering Belarus are advised to ignore 'private facilitators' who offer to help travellers pass through checkpoints and border crossings.
- It is recommended that visitors carry an assortment of spares for their vehicles such as a fan belt, replacement bulbs and spark plugs.
- It is against the law to drive a dirty car.
- Radar detectors are strictly prohibited.
- It is advisable to pre-plan itineraries and book accommodation before departure.
- All foreign visitors are required to purchase health insurance on arrival.
- Poor road signs between small towns.
- Winter tyres are not a compulsory requirement, although they are highly recommended. All-year tyres and snow chains may be used instead of winter tyres.

Travel facts: Belarus

Belarus Embassy
6 Kensington Court
London
W8 5DL
Tel: 020 7937 3288
http://belarus.embassyhomepage.com
www.belintourist.com/eng

Banking hours
In Belarus banks are generally open Monday to Friday 9 or 10am to 1 or 5pm.

Credit/debit cards
Credit cards are not widely accepted but can be used to withdraw cash at major hotels and banks. Some large stores and restaurants will take them. The number of ATMs is steadily increasing in major cities. Amex is not accepted.

Currency
The unit of currency in Belarus is the Belarusian rouble (BYR). Notes are in denominations of BYR100,000, 50,000, 20,000, 10,000, 5,000, 1,000, 500, 100, 50, 20 and 10. Sterling is not widely accepted for exchange into Belarusian roubles. The US dollar or euros are the preferred foreign currencies. Foreign currency should be exchanged only at Government-licensed booths. These can be found in or near major stores, hotels, banks and shopping centres. Non-compliance can result in fines and/or arrest. Make sure you have enough money for the duration of your stay.

Electricity
The power supply is 220 volts AC, 50Hz. Plugs have two round pins.

Health care
The UK has a reciprocal health-care agreement with Belarus. If you're visiting Belarus and need urgent or immediate medical treatment it will be provided at a reduced cost or, in some cases, free. The range of medical services available may be more restricted than under the NHS, therefore it is essential for all visitors to have comprehensive travel insurance.

Visit **www.nhs.uk/NHSEngland/Healthcareabroad** for a country-by-country guide.

Pharmacies
You should bring essential personal medications as the availability of local supplies cannot be guaranteed.

Post offices
The Central Post Office in Minsk, near the railway station, is open Monday to Friday 8.30am to 5.30pm, Saturday and Sunday 10am to 5pm. Airmail to Western Europe takes a minimum of 10 days.

Safe water
Don't drink village well water. In cities, you should first boil, then filter tap water before drinking it. It is advisable to buy bottled water, which is widely available in shops.

Telephone
Public telephones take cards. Grey booths are for national calls and blue ones for international calls. Calls from Belarus to some countries must be booked through the international operator. The country code for Belarus is 375. To call home from Belarus dial the international code (00) followed by the country code. To call the UK from Belarus dial 00 44.

Time
Belarus is two hours ahead of Greenwich Mean Time (GMT + 2). From late March to late October it is three hours ahead of Greenwich Mean Time (GMT + 3).

Emergency telephone numbers
Police **102**
Fire **101**
Ambulance **103**

Driving in Belgium *(Western Europe)*

The regulations below should be read in conjunction with the General motoring information on pages 18–21.

Drinking and driving

The maximum permitted level of alcohol in the bloodstream is 0.049 per cent. If the level of alcohol in the bloodstream is between 0.05 and 0.08 per cent you will be banned from driving for three hours and issued an on-the-spot fine of €137.50. If you refuse to pay the fine the public prosecutor will prosecute and impose a fine up to €2,750; if it is 0.08 per cent or more there is an on-the-spot fine of up to €550 and a ban from driving for at least six hours; if prosecuted (more than 0.15 per cent alcohol) the fine is up to €11,000 and your licence suspended for up to five years. However, if you have held your licence for less than two years an on-the-spot fine will not be imposed, and you will automatically be prosecuted.

Driving licence

The minimum age at which a UK driving licence holder may drive a temporarily imported car and/or motorcycle is 18.

Fines

The officer collecting an on-the-spot fine must issue an official receipt showing the amount of the fine. Motorists can refuse to pay an on-the-spot fine; a foreign motorist refusing to do so may be invited to make a *consignation* (deposit). If he does not, his vehicle will be impounded by the police and permanently confiscated if the deposit is not paid within 96 hours. Fines can be paid in cash (euros) or by debit/credit card.

Fuel

Unleaded petrol (95 and 98 octane), diesel and LPG are available. Leaded petrol is not sold, although an anti-wear additive is available. Petrol in a can is permitted, but forbidden aboard ferries and Eurotunnel. Credit cards are accepted at filling stations; check with your card issuer for usage in Belgium before you travel.

Lights

Dipped headlights should be used in poor daytime visibility.

Motorcycles

The use of dipped headlights during the day is compulsory. The wearing of crash helmets is compulsory for both driver and passenger.

Motor insurance

Third-party insurance is compulsory. The police can impound an uninsured vehicle.

Motorways

Motorways are toll-free. See map page 36.

Passengers/children in cars

Children under 18 and less than 1.35m (4ft 5in) must use a suitable child-restraint system whether seated in the front or rear seat of a vehicle. When two child-restraint systems are used on the rear seats and there isn't adequate room for a third child-restraint system, then the third child may travel on the back seat protected by the adult seat belt. A child under three can not be transported in a vehicle without a child seat/restraint. It is prohibited to use a rear-facing child seat on a front seat with a front air bag unless it is deactivated.

Seat belts

It is compulsory for front- and rear-seat occupants to wear seat belts, if fitted.

Speed limits

The standard legal limits, which may be varied by signs, for **private vehicles with or without trailers (up to a maximum combined weight of 3.5 tonnes)** are: in built-up areas up to 50km/h (31mph), outside built-up areas 90km/h (55mph) and on motorways and dual carriageways separated by a central reservation 120km/h (74mph). The minimum speed on motorways is 70km/h (43mph). A limit of 30km/h (19mph) may be indicated at the entrance to a built-up area. Vehicles with spiked tyres must not exceed 60km/h (37mph) on normal roads and 90km/h (55mph) on motorways/dual carriageways.

Additional information

- Drivers stranded on a Belgian motorway or on a major road (usually four-lane roads, called *route pour automobiles* – sign E17), or stopping at places where parking is not allowed, must wear a reflective safety jacket as soon as they leave their vehicle. The fine for non-compliance is €50, but the amount can be much higher (€55–€1,375) if the driver refuses to pay or when he must go to court (e.g. in the event of an accident). The jacket is compulsory for vehicles registered in Belgium. While the driver of a foreign-registered vehicle will not be fined for not carrying a reflective jacket if there is a police check, he/she could be fined for not wearing a jacket in case the vehicle breaks down.
- A warning triangle is compulsory for vehicles with more than two wheels.
- A first-aid kit and fire extinguisher are recommended as their carriage is compulsory for Belgian-registered vehicles.
- The majority of roundabouts have signs showing that traffic on the roundabout has priority. If no sign is present, traffic joining from the right has priority.
- A road sign has been introduced banning the use of cruise control on congested motorways and can also appear during motorway roadworks.
- A white disc bordered in red, bearing the word *'Peage'* in black, indicates that drivers must stop. The Dutch word *'Tol'* sometimes replaces *'Peage'*.
- Any stationary vehicle must have its engine switched off, unless absolutely necessary.
- A car navigation system with maps indicating the location of fixed speed cameras is permitted but equipment that actively searches for speed cameras or interferes with police equipment is prohibited.
- The police can impound a vehicle with an unsafe load.
- Spiked tyres are permitted from 1 November until 31 March on vehicles weighing up to a maximum of 3.5 tonnes. Snow chains are permitted only on snow- or ice-covered roads. Winter tyres are permitted from 1 October to 30 April; a lower speed limit applies and the maximum design speed for the tyres must be displayed on a sticker on the dashboard.
- Vehicles with spiked tyres must display at the rear a white disc with a red reflectorised border showing the figure '60', when the spiked tyres are applied.

BELGIUM, NETHERLANDS & LUXEMBOURG

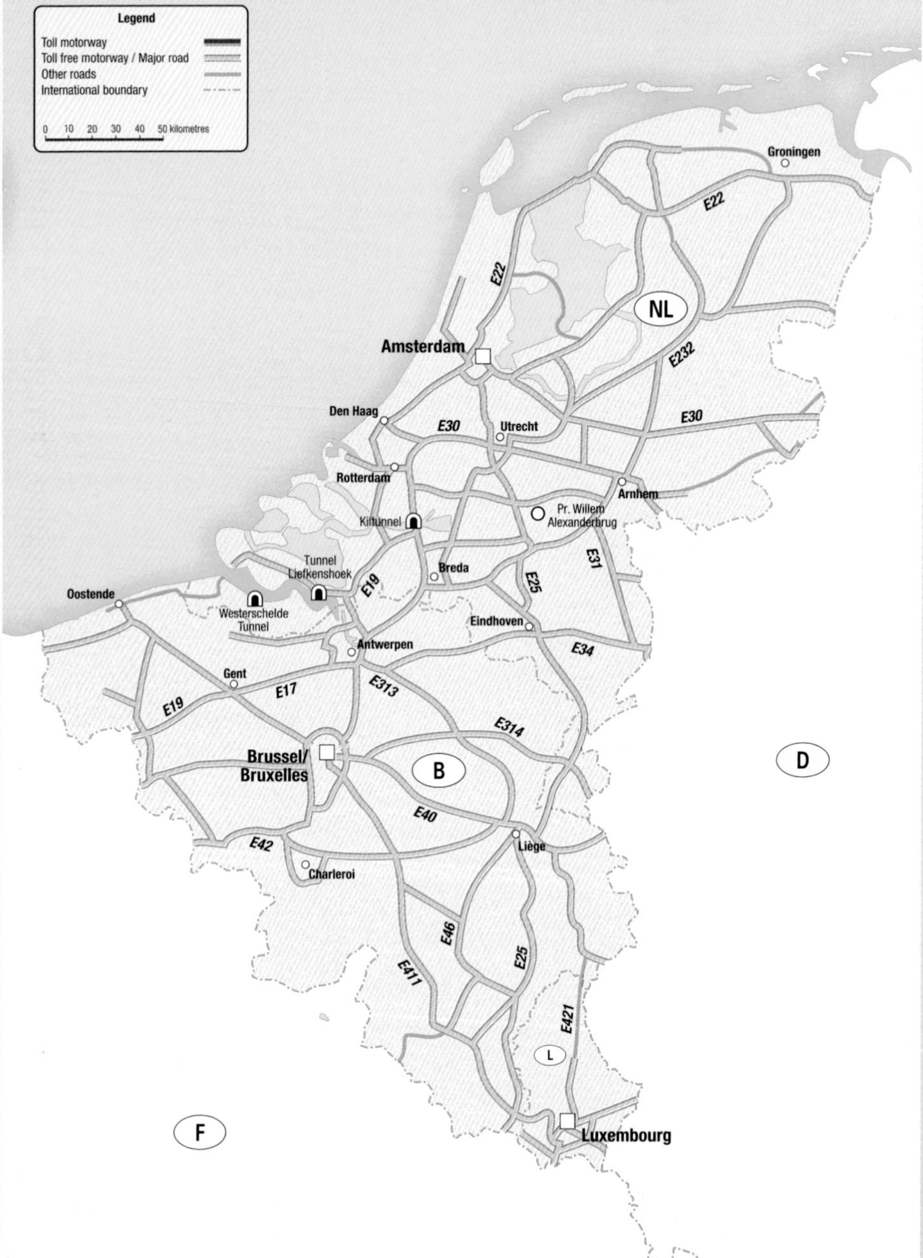

Legend

Toll motorway	
Toll free motorway / Major road	
Other roads	
International boundary	

0 10 20 30 40 50 kilometres

Groningen

E22

E22

NL

E232

Amsterdam

Den Haag

E30

Utrecht

E30

Rotterdam

Arnhem

Kiltunnel

Pr. Willem Alexanderbrug

Tunnel Liefkenshoek

Breda

E31

E19

E25

Oostende

Westerschelde Tunnel

Eindhoven

E34

Antwerpen

Gent

E19

E17

E313

E314

Brussel/ Bruxelles

B

D

E40

E42

Liège

Charleroi

E46

E25

E411

E421

L

F

Luxembourg

Travel facts and toll charges: Belgium

Tourism Flanders – Brussels
Flanders House
1a Cavendish Square
London W1G 0LD
Tel: 020 7307 7738
www.visitflanders.co.uk

Belgian Tourist Office Brussels & Wallonia
217 Marsh Wall
London E14 9FJ
Tel: 020 7537 1132
Tel: 0800 9545 245 (brochure line)
www.belgiumtheplaceto.be

Banking hours
Banks are generally open Monday to Friday 9am to 4pm. Some banks close for lunch.

Credit/debit cards
Most major credit cards are accepted by larger hotels, restaurants and some garages but smaller establishments prefer cash. ATMs for cash advances can be found outside banks in all the major towns.

Currency
The unit of currency in Belgium is the euro (€). Euro coins are issued in denominations of 1, 2, 5, 10, 20 and 50 cents and €1 and €2. Banknotes are issued in denominations of €5, €10, €20, €50, €100, €200 and €500.

Electricity
The power supply is 220 volts AC. Plugs are round with two pins. British appliances will need an adaptor.

Health care
Free or reduced-cost medical treatment is available in Belgium to European visitors on production of a valid European Health Insurance Card (EHIC). See page 10. Comprehensive travel insurance is still advised and is essential for all other visitors.

Pharmacies
Belgian pharmacies have many medicines available. Nevertheless, it is handy to take a supply of the medicines that you need regularly. It is also advisable to take a leaflet or list of active components, so that the pharmacy can find an alternative under a different product name, if necessary. Pharmacies are open weekdays 9am to 6pm. At night and at weekends at least one local pharmacy will be open.

Post offices
Stamps can be bought at the post office, machines, news-stands and souvenir shops. Most post offices are open Monday to Friday 9am to 5pm (some may close for lunch), Saturday 9am to noon. Post boxes are red and marked 'Poste'.

Safe water
It is safe to drink tap water, but sometimes bottled water may taste better. Café-restaurants usually offer still or sparkling mineral water.

Telephones
For most public telephones you need a phone card, available from post offices, kiosks and some supermarkets. Public phones displaying stickers showing flags of different countries can be used to make international calls with operator assistance. The country code for Belgium is 32. To call home from Belgium dial the international code (00) followed by the country code. To call the UK from Belgium dial 00 44.

Time
Belgium is on Central European Time, one hour ahead of GMT (GMT + 1). Daylight Saving Time comes into effect from the end of March to the end of October (GMT + 2).

Emergency telephone numbers
Police **101** or **112** Fire and Ambulance **100** or **112**

Toll charges in euros		
Bridges and tunnels	**Car**	**Car towing caravan/ trailer**
Liefkenshoek Tunnel on **R2**	5.50	18.00

Driving in Bosnia and Herzegovina *(South East Europe)*

The regulations below should be read in conjunction with the General motoring information on pages 18–21.

Drinking and driving
If the level of alcohol in the bloodstream is 0.031 per cent or more, severe penalties include a fine, imprisonment and/or suspension of the driving licence.

Driving licence
The minimum age at which a UK licence holder may drive a temporarily imported car and/or motorcycle (exceeding 125cc) is 18. We recommend that you obtain an International Driving Permit (IDP) to accompany your UK driving licence.

Fines
On-the-spot fines can be imposed or, for more serious violations, sentence by a local court. An official receipt should be obtained.

Fuel
Leaded petrol (98 octane), unleaded petrol (95 and 98 octane) and diesel *(dizel)* are available. LPG is available at approximately 60 filling stations throughout the country. Carrying petrol in a can is permitted. Credit cards are widely accepted throughout Bosnia and Herzegovina; check with your card issuer for usage before you travel.

Lights
The use of dipped headlights during the day is compulsory throughout Bosnia and Herzegovina.

Motorcycles
The use of dipped headlights during the day is compulsory. The wearing of crash helmets is compulsory for both driver and passenger.

Motor insurance
A Green Card is compulsory.

Passengers/children in cars
A person visibly under the influence of alcohol is not permitted to travel in a vehicle as a front-seat passenger. Children under 12 cannot travel as front-seat passengers. Children under five must use a suitable child-restraint system.

Seat belts
It is compulsory for front- and rear-seat occupants to wear seat belts, if fitted.

Speed limits
The standard legal limits, which may be varied by signs, for **private vehicles without trailers** are: in built-up areas 60km/h (37mph), outside built-up areas 80km/h (49mph) but 100km/h (62mph) on dual carriageways and 130km/h (80mph) on motorways. The maximum speed

for a **vehicle with trailer or caravan** under 3.5 tonnes combined weight, is 80km/h (49mph).

Additional information

- It is compulsory for visitors to equip their vehicle with a set of replacement bulbs.
- A first-aid kit and a warning triangle are also compulsory; two triangles are required if towing a trailer.
- Winter tyres or M&S tyres are compulsory between 15 November and 15 April.
- The authorities at the frontier must certify any visible damage to a vehicle entering Bosnia and Herzegovina and a certificate obtained; this must be produced when leaving.

- It is recommended that snow chains are carried as their use is compulsory if the relevant road sign is displayed or the snow covering is over 5cm (2in) deep. Spiked tyres are forbidden.
- During winter conditions, drivers are obliged to remove all snow and ice from their vehicles. Failure to comply will result in a fine.
- A GPS-based navigation system that has maps indicating the location of fixed speed cameras must have the 'fixed speed camera PoI (Points of Interest)' function deactivated.
- The use of radar detectors is prohibited.

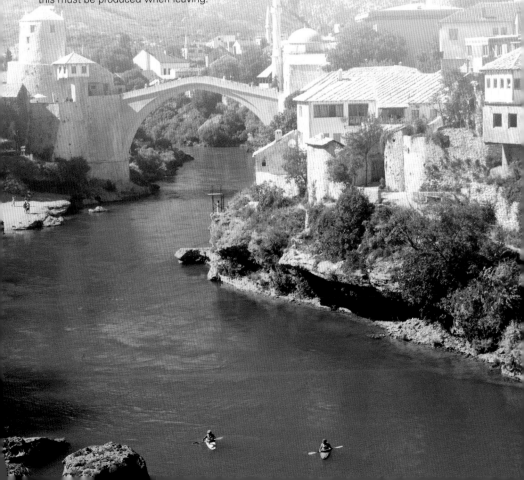

Travel facts: Bosnia and Herzegovina

Embassy of Bosnia & Herzegovina
5–7 Lexham Gardens
London W8 5JJ
Tel: 020 7373 0867
http://bosnia.embassy-uk.co.uk/
www.bhtourism.ba

Banking hours
Banks are generally open Monday to Friday 8am to 7pm.

Credit/debit cards
Most transactions are in cash. The acceptance of major credit and debit cards outside of Sarajevo is becoming more widespread (check with your card provider), but it is advisable to carry enough cash when travelling outside major cities. Cashing traveller's cheques is possible at some banks. ATMs are available in increasing numbers in the larger cities.

Currency
The official currency is the convertible mark (Konvertibilna Maraka or KM), abbreviated as BAM. It is linked to the euro (1.95KM = 1 euro). Notes are in denominations of BAM1, 5, 10, 20, 50, 100 and 200 and 1 and 50 pfenings. Coins are in denominations of BAM1 and 2, and 10, 20 and 50 pfenings. Some euro notes (but not coins) are widely accepted. Expect your change in KM.

Electricity
The power supply is 230 volts AC, 50Hz. Two-round-pin plugs are in use.

Health care
The UK has a reciprocal healthcare agreement with Bosnia and Herzegovina. If you're visiting Bosnia and Herzegovina and need urgent or immediate medical treatment it will be provided at a reduced cost or, in some cases, free. The range of medical services available may be more restricted than under the NHS, therefore it is essential for all visitors to have comprehensive travel insurance.
Visit **www.nhs.uk/NHSEngland/Healthcareabroad** for a country-by-country guide.

Language
The official languages are Bosnian, Serbian and Croatian. The Croats and Bosniaks use the Latin alphabet, whereas the Serbs use the Cyrillic. Most young people will know some English.

Pharmacies
To find a pharmacy, ask for *apoteka*. In major cities they will generally have regular prescription drugs readily available; there is usually at least one that is open 24 hours a day. Not all villages and smaller towns have a pharmacy. Contact your embassy if you need medical attention, as they will be able to recommend a doctor.

Post offices
You have to go to a post office to buy stamps and to send letters or postcards abroad.

Safe water
The water is generally considered safe to drink, although bottled water is recommended.

Telephones
Phone booths, at bus stations and post offices, accept 10KM and 20KM phone cards, which can be bought from post offices or small newspaper kiosks. Different phone companies provide services in different parts of the country and a phone card may not be valid once you leave the town you bought it in. It is cheaper to phone after 7pm. The country code for Bosnia and Herzegovina is 387. To call home from here dial the international code (00) followed by the country code. To call the UK from Bosnia and Herzegovina dial 00 44.

Time
Bosnia is on Central European Time, one hour ahead of GMT (GMT + 1). Daylight Saving Time comes into effect from the end of March to the end of October (GMT + 2).

Emergency telephone numbers
Police **122**
Fire **123**
Medical emergency **124**

Driving in Bulgaria *(South East Europe)*

The regulations below should be read in conjunction
with the General motoring information on pages 18–21.

Drinking and driving
If the level of alcohol in the bloodstream is 0.05
per cent or more the driver will be prosecuted.

Driving licence
The minimum age at which a UK driving licence
holder may drive a temporarily imported car and/
or motorcycle is 18. It is recommended that an
International Driving Permit (IDP) accompanies
an older licence that is not a European
Community model.

Fines
On-the-spot fines are issued. An official receipt
should be obtained. Wheel clamps are in use
for illegally parked cars. Vehicles causing an
obstruction will be towed away.

Fuel
Leaded petrol is no longer available in
Bulgaria. Unleaded petrol (95 and 98 octane),
diesel and LPG are available. Credit cards are
accepted at most filling stations but not all local
stations in small towns accept international
cards; check with your card issuer for usage in
Bulgaria before travel.

Lights
The use of dipped headlights during daylight
hours throughout the year is recommended;
however their use is compulsory from
1 November to 31 March.

Motorcycles
The wearing of crash helmets is compulsory for
both driver and passenger. Motorcyclists must
have their lights on at all times.

Motor insurance
Green Cards are recognised. Third-party
insurance is compulsory.

Passengers/children in cars
A child under 12 cannot travel as a front-seat
passenger. Children must be placed in special
restraints suitable for their size.

Seat belts
It is compulsory, for front- and rear-seat
occupants to wear seat belts, if fitted.

Speed limits
The standard legal limits, which may be
varied by signs, for **private vehicles without
trailers** are: in built-up areas 50km/h (31mph),
outside built-up areas 90km/h (55mph) and
motorways 130km/h (80mph). Lower limits
apply to **cars towing a caravan or trailer**:
outside built-up areas 70km/h (43mph),
motorways 100km/h (62mph).

Additional information
- A first-aid kit is compulsory.
- A fire extinguisher and a warning triangle
  are compulsory (neither are required for
  two-wheeled vehicles).
- It is compulsory to wear a reflective jacket

when leaving a car, day or night, in case of breakdown or emergency on a motorway. This regulation applies to all occupants and to motorcyclists.

- In built-up areas it is prohibited to use the horn between 10pm and 6am (9am on public holidays), and between midday and 4pm.
- Visiting motorists are required to drive through a liquid disinfectant on entry for which the charge is (approx.) €4, and to purchase a *vignette* (road tax). The *vignette* is available at the border, UAB offices, most petrol stations and offices of the CI and DZI bank, and are available for periods of one week, one month or a year. Heavy fines are imposed for non-compliance.

- Snow chains are permitted. Their use can become compulsory according to road conditions and will be indicated by the international road sign. Spiked tyres are forbidden.
- Drivers of luxury or 4 x 4 vehicles are advised to use guarded car parks.
- A GPS-based navigation system that has maps indicating the location of fixed speed cameras must have the 'fixed speed camera PoI (Points of Interest)' function deactivated. The use of radar detectors is prohibited.
- In one-way streets parking is on the left only.

Helpful road signs

Recommended
maximum speed

U-turn allowed

Travel facts: Bulgaria

Embassy of the Republic of Bulgaria
Commercial Section
186–188 Queen's Gate
London SW7 5HL
Tel: 020 7584 9400
Email: tourism@bulgarianembassy.org.uk
www.bulgariatravel.org
www.travel-bulgaria.com

Banking hours
Banks are generally open Monday to Friday 9am to
12 noon and 3pm to 5pm.

Credit/debit cards
Major international credit cards (Visa, MasterCard or
American Express) are accepted in larger hotels and
car hire offices, and in some restaurants and shops,
mainly in Sofia. Check with your provider for details.
Bulgaria is still a country that operates mainly on cash
rather than credit cards.

Currency
Bulgarian lev (Lv) = 100 stotinki. Notes are in
denominations of Lv50, 20, 10, 5, 2 and 1. Coins are in
denominations of 50, 20, 10, 5, 2 and 1 stotinki. The lev
is pegged to the euro. €1 = 1.955 BGN. Many banks will
cash euro cheques.

Electricity
The power supply is 220 volts AC, 50Hz. Appliances
need two-round-pin continental plugs.

Health care
Free or reduced-cost medical treatment is available in
Bulgaria to European visitors on production of a valid
European Health Insurance Card (EHIC). See page 10.
Comprehensive travel insurance is still advised and is
essential for all other visitors.

Pharmacies
Many pharmacies are not as widely stocked as at home.
Minor complaints can be solved at a pharmacy *(apteka)*,
but if you need a doctor *(lekar)* or dentist *(zâbolekar)*
visit the nearest health centre *(poliklinika)*,where staff

might speak English, German or French, and will almost
certainly understand Russian.

Post offices
Post offices in large towns are open 8.30 or 9am to
5.30pm. Postage stamps and postcards are sold in post
offices and at newspaper kiosks.

Safe water
Drinking water in major towns is generally safe to drink,
though you may prefer to buy bottled mineral water.

Telephones
Public phones on the streets operate with tokens
(0.20 lev) and phone cards, which are available from
post offices and newspaper kiosks. The country code
for Bulgaria is 359. To call home from here dial the
international code (00) followed by the country code.
To call the UK from Bulgaria dial 00 44.

Time
Bulgaria is on Eastern European Time. It is two hours
ahead of Greenwich Mean Time (GMT + 2) and from
late March to late October it is three hours ahead of
Greenwich Mean Time (GMT + 3).

Emergency telephone numbers
Police **166** or **112**   Fire **160** or **112**
First aid **150** or **112**   Road assistance **146**

Driving in Croatia *(South East Europe)*

The regulations below should be read in conjunction with the General motoring information on pages 18–21.

Drinking and driving

Drinking and driving is strictly forbidden for all drivers under the age of 24. Nil percentage of alcohol is allowed in a driver's blood. The legal limit for alcohol in the blood of drivers aged 24 years and over is 0.05 per cent. Exceptions to this rule apply to professional drivers. Tests for narcotics may be applied; if they prove positive, severe consequences include confiscation of the vehicle, a severe fine and removal of the driving licence. It is prohibited to drive after taking any medicine where the side effects may affect the ability to drive a motor vehicle.

Driving licence

The minimum age at which a UK licence holder may drive a temporarily imported car and/or motorcycle (exceeding 125cc) is 18.

Fines

The police officer will impose a fine on the spot; the fine must be paid within eight days at a post office or bank. The police may hold your passport until evidence of payment is produced. The driving licence of a foreign motorist can be suspended for up to eight days for driving under the influence of excess alcohol, driving without prescribed medical aids e.g. glasses, driving in a state of exhaustion or when ill. The driving licence must be collected within three days of the end of suspension.

Fuel

Unleaded petrol (95 and 98 octane) and diesel *(dizel)* are available; LPG is available at most motorway filling stations. It is forbidden to carry petrol in a can. Credit cards are accepted at filling stations; check with your card issuer for usage in Croatia before travel.

Lights

It is compulsory for all vehicles to use dipped headlights when visibility is reduced; a fine is imposed for non-compliance. Dipped headlights are compulsory in the daytime from the last Sunday in October to the last Sunday in March (out of the Daylight Saving Time period); there is a fine for non-compliance.

Motorcycles

The use of dipped headlights during the day is compulsory. The wearing of crash helmets is compulsory for both the driver and passenger. A child under 12 cannot travel as a passenger. A fine will be imposed if the passenger on a motorcycle is found to be under the influence of alcohol or narcotics.

Motor insurance

Third-party insurance is compulsory.

Passengers/children in cars

A child under 12 cannot travel as a front-seat passenger, with the exception of a child under two years seated in a suitable child seat. The seat must be fitted facing in the opposite direction of travel with the passenger air bags deactivated. Children aged two to five must be seated in a suitable child seat; other children must be seated using a suitable child restraint, using a booster seat where necessary.

Seat belts

It is compulsory for front- and rear-seat occupants to wear seat belts, if fitted.

Speed limits

The standard legal limits, which may be varied by signs, for **private vehicles without trailers** are: in built-up areas 50km/h (31mph), outside built-up areas 90km/h (55mph) but 110km/h (68mph) on expressways and 130km/h (80mph) on motorways, unless otherwise indicated by road signs. If **towing a trailer or caravan** the speed limit is reduced to 80km/h (49mph) on expressways and 90km/h (55mph) on motorways. All motorists under 24 years of age

must not exceed 80km/h (49mph) on normal roads outside built-up areas, 100km/h (62mph) on expressways and 120km/h (74mph) on motorways. The minimum speed on motorways is 60km/h (37mph).

Additional information

- It is compulsory for visitors to equip their vehicle with a set of replacement bulbs (this does not apply if the vehicle is fitted with xenon, neon, LED or similar lights); a first-aid kit (excluding motorcycles); a warning triangle (excluding motorcycles) – two triangles required if towing a trailer.

- During the winter months, especially in the Gorski Kotar and Lika regions, the use of snow chains is compulsory (see winter equipment below).

- All drivers of motor vehicles (except motorcycles with sidecars and mopeds under 50cc) must have a reflective safety jacket (EN471) in the vehicle and wear it whenever they have to get out of the vehicle at the roadside, in an emergency. Be aware, however, that car hire companies may not supply them to persons hiring vehicles.

- The use of spiked tyres is prohibited.

- It is generally prudent to have winter equipment ready between November and the end of April. This may consist of winter tyres marked M&S on the sidewalls or snow chains for the driving wheels. Vehicles not adapted to winter conditions may be prohibited from driving and can also encounter a fine. Snow tyres must have a minimum tread depth of 4mm.

- The authorities at the frontier must certify any visible damage to a vehicle entering Croatia and a certificate obtained; this must be produced when leaving the country.

- Radar detectors are forbidden.

Travel facts and toll charges: Croatia

Croatian National Tourist Office
2 The Lanchesters
162–164 Fulham Palace Road
London W6 9ER
Tel: 020 8563 7979
www.visit-croatia.co.uk; http://gb.croatia.hr

Banking hours
Banks are generally open Monday to Friday 7am to 4 or 7pm, Saturday until 1pm. In the larger cities some banks open on Sundays.

Credit/debit cards
Major credit cards are accepted in hotels, larger shops and restaurants. Large cities, towns and resorts have ATMs in banks, supermarkets, airports and elsewhere.

Currency
The currency in Croatia is the kuna (1 kuna = 100 lipa). There are 1, 2, 5, 10, 20, 50 lipa coins, 1, 2, 5 and 25 kuna coins and 5, 10, 20, 50, 100, 200, 500 and 1,000 kuna banknotes.

Electricity
Electric current is 220 volts AC, 50Hz. Appliances need two-round-pin continental plugs.

Health care
The UK has a reciprocal health-care agreement with Croatia. If you're visiting Croatia and need urgent or immediate medical treatment it will be provided at a reduced cost or, in some cases, free. The range of medical services available may be more restricted than under the NHS, therefore it is essential for all visitors to have comprehensive travel insurance. Visit **www.nhs.uk/NHSEngland/Healthcareabroad** for a country-by-country guide.

Pharmacies
Pharmacies sell over-the-counter medicines; most have English speaking staff.

Post offices
Post offices are open from 7am to 7pm, Saturday until 1pm. In larger cities some are open until 9pm in summer.

Postage stamps *(marke)* are sold in post offices and at newspaper and tobacco kiosks.

Safe water
The tap water in Croatia is chlorinated and safe to drink; however, it is advisable to drink bottled water.

Telephones
Public telephones are operated by phone cards, available from post offices, newspaper and tobacco kiosks and in hotel and tourist complexes. The country code for Croatia is 385. To call the UK from Croatia dial the international code (00) followed by the country code. To call the UK from Croatia dial 00 44.

Time
Croatia is on Central European Time, one hour ahead of GMT (GMT + 1). Daylight Saving Time comes into effect from the end of March to the end of October (GMT + 2 hours).

Emergency telephone numbers
Police **92** or **112**   Fire **93** or **112**   Ambulance **94** or **112**

Toll charges in kunas

Road		Car	Car towing caravan/ trailer
E59 (A2)	Zagreb – Macelj	42.00	69.00
E65 (A1)	Zagreb – Split – Dubrovnik	187.00	309.00
E65 (A6)	Zagreb – Rijeka	60.00	99.00
E70 (A3/ A5)	Zagreb – Lipovac (Slovenian border)	105.00	173.00
E71 (A4)	Zagreb – Gorican	36.00	60.00
A7	Rupa – Rijeka	5.00	8.00
A8	Kanfanar – Matuiji (Ucka Tunnel)	28.00	46.00
A9	Kastel – Pula (Mirna Bridge)	14.00	23.00

Bridges and tunnels

Krk Bridge		30.00	40.00

Driving in Republic of Cyprus

(Eastern Mediterranean)

The regulations below should be read in conjunction
with the General motoring information on pages 18–21.

Drinking and driving
The maximum legal level of alcohol in the blood
is 0.049 per cent. Persons suspected of driving
under the influence of alcohol may be subject to
a blood test.

Driving licence
All national driving licences are accepted.
The minimum age for driving a temporarily
imported car and/or motorcycle is 18.

Fines
The Cyprus traffic police are empowered to
impose on-the-spot fines for traffic offences.

Fuel
Unleaded petrol (95 and 98 octane) and diesel
are available. There is no LPG or leaded petrol,
but you can buy lead-substitute additive. It is
forbidden to carry petrol in a can. Credit cards
are accepted at most filling stations; check
with your card issuer for use in Cyprus before
you travel.

Lights
Vehicle lights must be used between half
an hour after sunset and half an hour before
sunrise. Spotlights are prohibited.

Motorcycles
The wearing of crash helmets is compulsory
for the rider and pillion passenger.

Motor insurance
Third-party insurance is compulsory.

Passengers/children in cars
Children under five cannot travel as a front-seat
passenger. Children over five and under 10
must use a suitable child-restraint system.

Seat belts
It is compulsory for front- and rear-seat
occupants to wear seat belts, if fitted.

Speed limits
The standard legal limits, which may be varied
by signs, for **private vehicles without trailers**
are: in built-up areas 50km/h (31mph) or 65km/h
(40mph) depending on the road, outside built-up
areas 80km/h (49mph) and 100km/h (62mph) on
motorways. The minimum speed on motorways
is 65km/h (40mph).

Additional information
- It is compulsory to carry two
  warning triangles.
- The rule of the road is drive on the left,
  overtake on the right.

Republic of Cyprus

- The use of the vehicle horn is prohibited between 10pm and 6am, and in the vicinity of hospitals.
- Spiked tyres and snow chains are permitted on mountain roads in winter.
- A GPS-based navigation system with maps indicating the location of fixed speed cameras must have the 'fixed speed camera PoI (Points of Interest)' function deactivated.
- The use of radar detectors is prohibited.
- Eating and drinking while driving is prohibited.

Travel facts: Republic of Cyprus

Cyprus Tourism Organisation
17 Hanover Street
London W1S 1YP
Tel: 020 7569 8800
www.visitcyprus.com

Banking hours
Banks are generally open Monday to Friday 8.30am to 1.30pm (some branches open in the afternoon).

Credit/debit cards
Hotels, large shops and restaurants normally accept major credit cards and traveller's cheques.

Currency
The currency of the Republic of Cyprus is the euro (€), introduced 1 January 2008, which is divided into 100 cents. Notes are issued in denominations of €5, €10, €20, €50, €100, €200 and €500; coins in 1, 2, 5, 10, 20 and 50 cents, and €1 and €2.

Electricity
The power supply is 240 volts AC, 50Hz and the type of socket is generally a European two-round-pin style, but there are some older buildings with UK-style three rectangular pins.

Health care
Free or reduced-cost medical treatment is available in Cyprus to European visitors on production of a valid European Health Insurance Card (EHIC). See page 10. Comprehensive travel insurance is still advised and is essential for all other visitors.

Language
The official language is Greek. English is widely spoken and French and German are spoken within the tourism industry.

Pharmacies
Minor ailments can be dealt with at pharmacies *(farmakio)*, which sell most branded medicines. Local newspapers list pharmacies that are open at night and on weekends/holidays, as well as the names of doctors who are on call on weekends/holidays.

Post offices
There are main post offices in large towns and sub-post offices in the suburbs. Post offices are open Monday to Friday 7:30am to 1:30pm (Thursday also 3 to 6pm). Post boxes are painted yellow.

Safe water
Tap water in hotels, restaurants and public places is generally safe to drink in Cyprus. Bottled mineral water is inexpensive and widely available.

Telephones
Phone cards for public phone boxes and mobile phones are sold in kiosks all over the island and are generally available in €5, €10, €20 and €50 units.The country code for Cyprus is 357. To call home from here dial the international code (00) followed by the country code. To call the UK from Cyprus dial 00 44.

Time
Cyprus is on Eastern European Time. It is two hours ahead of Greenwich Mean Time (GMT + 2) and from late March to late October it is three hours ahead of Greenwich Mean Time (GMR + 3).

Emergency telephone numbers
Police **199** or **112**
Fire **199** or **112**
Ambulance **199** or **112**

Driving in Turkish Republic of Northern Cyprus *(Eastern Mediterranean)*

The regulations below should be read in conjunction with the General motoring information on pages 18–21.

Drinking and driving
Drivers are permitted to have 50mg of alcohol in 100ml of their blood, provided they are capable of driving.

Driving licence
A UK licence is acceptable. The minimum age for driving a temporarily imported car and/or motorcycle is 17.

Fines
There are no on-the-spot fines.

Fuel
Leaded (98 octane), unleaded petrol (95 and 97 octane), diesel *(mazot)* and Euro-diesel are available but not LPG. It is permitted to carry petrol in a can, but not aboard ferries. Credit cards are accepted at most filling stations; check with your card issuer for use in Cyprus before you travel.

Lights
Vehicle lights must be used between half an hour after sunset and half an hour before sunrise.

Motorcycles
The wearing of crash helmets is compulsory.

Motor insurance
Third-party insurance is compulsory. A Green Card is not accepted. Short term insurance may be purchased at the port of arrival.

Passengers/children in cars
A child under five cannot travel as a front-seat passenger; children over five and under 10 must use a suitable child restraint system.

Seat belts
It is compulsory for front seat occupants to wear seat belts.

Speed limits
The standard legal limits, which may be varied by signs, for **private vehicles without trailers** are: in built-up areas 50km/h (31mph), outside built-up areas 70km/h (43mph), 80km/h (49mph) or 90km (56mph).

Additional information
- The rule of the road is drive on the left, overtake on the right.
- Two warning triangles are compulsory.
- Road signs are predominately in English.

Travel facts: Northern Cyprus

Northern Cyprus Tourism Centre
29 Bedford Square
London WC1B 3ED
Tel: 020 7631 1930
www.cypnet.co.uk/ncyprus

Banking hours
In North Cyprus banks are open Monday to Saturday 8.30am to 12 noon throughout the year. Afternoon times vary depending on the bank. Most major banks have ATMs which accept main credit and debit cards.

Credit/debit cards
Most major credit and debit cards are accepted by hotels, restaurants and shops.

Currency
The unit of currency in North Cyprus is Turkish lira (TL) divided into 100 kurus (Kr). Banknotes are issued in denominations of 1, 5, 10, 20, 50 and 100TL. Coins in 1, 5, 10, 25 and 50Kr and 1TL. Most businesses will accept the euro, pound sterling, US dollars and Cyprus pounds.

Electricity
The power supply is 240 volts AC, 50Hz. Sockets are generally European two-round-pin style, but there are some older buildings with UK-style three rectangular pins.

Health care
Comprehensive travel insurance is essential for all visitors.

Language
Turkish is the official language; English is widely spoken and understood.

Pharmacies
Pharmacies *(eczane)* sell many prescription drugs over the counter. Many pharmacists, provided they speak English, will advise you which medicine to take for your condition

Post offices
There are main post offices in large towns and sub-post offices in the suburbs. Post offices are open Monday to Friday 8am to 1pm and 2 to 5pm; Saturday 8.30am to 12.30pm. Post boxes are painted yellow. Mail posted in Northern Cyprus has to travel via Turkey.

Safe water
Tap water is generally safe to drink. If you are in any doubt, it is best to stick to bottled water that has either been opened in front of you or purchased by you.

Telephones
The international dialling code 90 392 should precede the seven-digit local telephone numbers when calling North Cyprus from abroad. Public telephone booths are available and telephone cards can be purchased from the Telecommunications Office. To call home from here dial the international code (00) followed by the country code. To call the UK from Cyprus dial 00 44.

Time
Cyprus is on Eastern European Time. It is two hours ahead of Greenwich Mean Time (GMT + 2) and from late March to late October it is three hours ahead of Greenwich Mean Time (GMT + 3).

Emergency telephone numbers
Police **155**
Fire **199**
Forest fire **177**
Ambulance **112**

Driving in Czech Republic *(Central Europe)*

The regulations below should be read in conjunction with the General motoring information on pages 18–21.

Drinking and driving

Drinking and driving is forbidden. Nil percentage of alcohol is allowed in the driver's blood. A fine of between 25,000 and 50,000CZK will be imposed and the driving licence withdrawn for up to two years. Random breath testing takes place frequently. Driving under the influence of alcohol or drugs is a criminal offence.

Driving licence

The minimum age at which a UK licence holder may drive a temporarily imported car is 18, a motorcycle up to 125cc 17 years, over 125cc (max 25kW) 18 years. Photocard licences are accepted; licences not incorporating a photo must be accompanied by an International Driving Permit (IDP).

Fines

On-the-spot fines of up to 5,000CZK can be imposed; the maximum fine for a traffic offence is 100,000CZK. An official receipt should be obtained. The police are empowered to retain the driving licence when a serious traffic offence has been committed. Illegally parked vehicles may be clamped or towed away.

Fuel

Unleaded petrol *(natural)*, (95 and 98 octane), diesel *(nafta)* and LPG *(autoplyn or plyn)* are available. It is permitted to carry up to 10 litres of petrol in a can. Credit cards are accepted at filling stations; check with your card issuer for usage in Czech Republic before you travel.

Lights

You must use dipped headlights during the day throughout the year. The fine for non-compliance is approximately 2,000CZK. Any vehicle warning lights, other than those supplied with the vehicle as original equipment, must be made inoperative.

Motorcycles

The use of dipped headlights during the day is compulsory throughout the year. The wearing of crash helmets is compulsory for the driver and passenger of motorcycles. It is forbidden for motorcyclists to smoke while riding their machine.

Motor insurance

Third-party insurance is compulsory.

Passengers/children in cars

All passengers must use seat belts. Children (persons with a weight under 36kg/79lb and under 1.5m/4ft 11in in height) are not permitted to travel in a vehicle unless using a suitable restraint system. A child in the front seat of a vehicle using a suitable child-restraint system and where the air bag is activated must travel facing forward.

Seat belts

It is compulsory for front- and rear-seat occupants to wear seat belts, if fitted.

Speed limits

The standard legal limits, which may be varied by signs, for **private vehicles without trailers** are: in built-up areas 50km/h (31mph), outside built-up areas 90km/h (55mph) and motorways (for vehicles not exceeding 3.5 tonnes and buses) 130km/h (80mph). On expressways that pass through built-up areas the limit is 80km/h (50mph). **Towing combinations** under 3.5 tonnes combined weight are limited by the maximum permissable speed of the slower part of the combination.

The maximum speed with snow chains is 50km/h (31mph). At railway crossings drivers must not exceed 30km/h (18mph) for 50 metres before the crossing. The arrival of a train is indicated by red flashing lights/red or yellow flag. Vehicles constructed with a maximum speed of 80km/h (49mph) or under are not permitted to travel on motorways.

Additional information

- A first-aid kit is compulsory.
- A warning triangle (not required for two-wheeled vehicles) is compulsory.
- During winter, vehicles must be fitted with either winter tyres (which must be marked M&S) or carry snow chains between 1 November and 31 March. Depending on weather conditions (if roads are covered with snow) this period may be extended. As snow chains can be used only when roads are completely covered, we recommend that winter tyres are fitted. The minimum depth on winter tyres is 4mm. A road sign showing a picture of a car and a snowflake is used to designate these road sections; the same road sign with a line across indicates the end of this restriction. One of these sections is also on the motorway D1 from Prague to Brno.
- The driver of a vehicle with two or more axles

must carry a reflective waistcoat (EU standard EN471), which has to be used in the event of a breakdown or emergency outside a built-up area on expressways and motorways. It has to be worn when exiting the vehicle in such circumstances and therefore must be kept within the car (not in the boot). The waistcoat is recommended for passengers and riders of mopeds and motorcycles.

- Motorway tax is payable for the use of motorways and express roads. A windscreen sticker must be displayed on all four-wheeled vehicles up to 3.5 tonnes as evidence of payment. The sticker can be purchased at the Czech frontier, UAMK branch offices, petrol stations or post offices for periods of one year, one month or 10 consecutive days. Fines are imposed for non-display.
- The authorities at the frontier must certify any visible damage to a vehicle entering the Czech Republic. If any damage occurs inside the country a police report must be obtained at the scene of the accident. Damaged vehicles may be taken out of the country only on production of this evidence.
- The use of an audible warning device is permitted only in built-up areas to avoid imminent danger; they are prohibited between 8pm and 6am, and in Prague.
- The use of spiked tyres is prohibited.
- A GPS-based navigation system with maps indicating the location of fixed speed cameras must have the 'fixed speed camera PoI (Points of Interest)' function deactivated. The use of radar detectors is prohibited.

Travel facts and toll charges: Czech Republic

Czech Tourist Authority
13 Harley Street
London W1G 9QG
Tel: 020 7631 0427
www.czechtourism.com
www.pis.cz/en

Banking hours
Banks are normally open Monday to Friday from 9am to 5pm. Some open Saturday morning.

Credit/debit cards
Payment by credit/debit card in the Czech Republic is not as widespread as it is in other European countries. There are plenty of ATMs throughout the country.

Currency
The local currency is the Czech koruna, or Czech Crown, (Kč) which is divided into 100 heller. Notes are issued in denominations of Kč50, 100, 200, 500, 1,000, 2,000, 5,000; coins in hellers 50 and Kč1, 2, 5, 10, 20, 50.

Electricity
The electrical supply is 220 volts AC, as in the rest of Europe. Czech plugs have two round pins.

Health care
Free or reduced-cost medical treatment is available in Czech Republic to European visitors on production of a valid European Health Insurance Card (EHIC). See page 10. Comprehensive travel insurance is still advised and is essential for all other visitors.

Pharmacies
Pharmacies (*lékánat* or *apothéka*) are the only places to sell over-the-counter medicines. They also dispense many drugs (*leky*) normally available only on prescription in other Western countries. Take a supply of your own prescription medicines with you as you may not be able to find exactly the same in Czech Republic.

Post offices
Post offices have distinctive orange *Posta* signs outside. They are normally open Monday to Friday 8am to 5pm and Saturday until noon. Stamps (*známky*) can be bought from news kiosks, tobacconists, some hotels and shops, as well as post offices.

Safe water
Tap water may not be particularly palatable, but it is safe to drink, though most people drink mineral water (*minerální voda* or *minerálka*).

Telephones
Most pay phones accept only telephone cards, which can be obtained from post offices, newsagents and any establishment displaying the blue and yellow *Ceský Telecom* logo. They come in denominations of 50 units upwards. The country code for Czech Republic is 420. To call home from here dial the international code (00) followed by the country code. To call the UK dial 00 44.

Time
The Czech Republic is on Central European Time (GMT + 1), but from late March, when clocks are put forward one hour, until late October, Czech Summer Time (GMT + 2) operates.

Emergency telephone numbers
General **112**
Police **158** or **112**
Fire **150** or **112**
Ambulance **155** or **112**

Toll charges in Czech koruna
For details of where to buy the motorway tax see page 53. You may be charged more if your vehicle is over 3,500kg.

General	Car (with or without trailer)
1 week	250.00
1 month	350.00
1 year	1,200.00

Driving in Denmark *(Northern Europe)*

The regulations below should be read in conjunction with the General motoring information on pages 18–21.

Drinking and driving

If the level of alcohol in the bloodstream is 0.05 per cent or more severe penalties can be imposed including licence suspension, fines or imprisonment, depending on the level of excess.

Driving licence

The minimum age at which a UK licence holder may drive a temporarily imported car and/or motorcycle is 17.

Fines

Visitors who infringe traffic regulations can expect to be fined on the spot. If you do not accept the fine, the police will take the matter to court to be settled by a judge. The police may retain the vehicle until such time. Vehicles parked against regulations will be taken away by the police at the owner's expense.

Fuel

Unleaded petrol (92 and 95 octane) and diesel are available. There is limited availability of LPG. Leaded petrol is no longer available; a leaded petrol substitute called *'Millenium'* is available. It is permitted to carry petrol in a can, but not aboard ferries or in the Eurotunnel. Credit cards are accepted at most filling stations; check with your card issuer for use in Denmark before travel.

Lights

The use of dipped headlights is compulsory during the day.

Motorcycles

The use of dipped headlights is compulsory during the day. The wearing of crash helmets with straps is compulsory for both driver and passenger.

Motor insurance

Third-party insurance is compulsory.

Passengers/children in cars

Children under three years must be seated in a child-restraint system adapted to their size. Children over three and less than 1.35m (4ft 5in) must be seated in a child-restraint system suitable for their height and weight. A child must not be placed in the front seat with their back to the road if the vehicle is fitted with an active air bag. As all rear-seat passengers must wear a seat belt it is not possible to transport three children if there are only two seat belts.

Seat belts

It is compulsory for front- and rear-seat occupants to wear seat belts.

Speed limits

The standard legal limits, which may be varied by signs, for **private vehicles without trailers** are: in built-up areas 50km/h (31mph), outside built-up areas 80km/h (49mph) or 90km/h (55mph), and motorways 110km/h (68mph) or 130km/h (80mph). Lower limits apply to **private cars towing a trailer or caravan**: outside built-up areas 70km/h (43mph) and on motorways 80km/h (49mph).

Additional information

- A red warning triangle is compulsory in case of an accident or breakdown. It is recommended that visitors equip their vehicle with a fire extinguisher and a first-aid kit.
- Generally there is a duty to give way to traffic approaching from the right.
- A bold line, a line of white triangles (shark's teeth) painted across the road or a white triangle with a red border indicate that you must stop and give way to traffic on the road you are entering.
- When roads are wet or slushy, speed must be reduced as far as possible to prevent other road users from being splashed.
- It is prohibited to use radar detectors.
- Spiked tyres may be used between 1 November and 15 April; they must be fitted to all four wheels.
- Right-hand drive vehicles must have wing-mirrors on both sides of the vehicle.
- Private cars must be equipped with an exterior side mirror and an interior rear-view mirror.

Road signs (a selection of standard and non-standard)

Traffic merges

Minimum speed limit

Recommended speed limit

Compulsory slow lane

1 hour parking zone

Place of interest

Maximum width

Travel facts and toll charges: Denmark

Danish Tourist Board
55 Sloane Street
London SW1X 9SR
Tel: 020 7259 5959
www.visitdenmark.com

Banking hours
Banks are normally open Monday to Friday from 10am to 4pm, and until 6pm on Thursday.

Credit/debit cards
Most shops accept major credit cards. The most common are Visa and MasterCard.

Currency
The monetary unit is the Danish kroner (DKK), which is divided into 100 øre. Banknotes are issued in denominations of DKK50, DKK100, DKK200, DKK500 and DKK1,000. Coins are found in DKK20, DKK10, DKK5, DKK2, DKK1 and 50 øre and 25 øre. Some shops, hotels and restaurants, particularly in larger cities, display prices in both Danish kroner and euros and many are likely to accept payment in euros. It is advisable to ask beforehand if you wish to pay in anything other than Danish kroner.

Electricty
The electricity supply in Denmark is 220 volts AC (50Hz). Appliances need two-round-pin continental plugs.

Health care
Free or reduced-cost medical treatment is available in Denmark to European visitors on production of a valid European Health Insurance Card (EHIC). See page 10. Comprehensive travel insurance is still advised.

Pharmacies
Only medicine prescribed by Danish or other Scandinavian doctors can be dispensed at a chemist (apotek). Many medicines that can be bought over the counter in the UK can be obtained only with prescriptions in Denmark. If you take prescribed medication, you should bring a supply large enough to last throughout the trip since some medicines may not be on the market in Denmark.

Post offices
Post offices are generally open Monday to Friday from 9 or 10am to 5 or 6pm. Some are closed on Saturdays. Opening hours for those that are open are usually from 9 or 10am to noon or 2pm. You can buy stamps from newsagents and post offices.

Safe water
The tap water in Denmark is safe to drink. Bottled mineral water is widely available.

Telephones
Most Danish public telephone boxes are operated by means of phonecards, but also by means of Danish currency and euros. Some of the public coin phones also accept credit cards. There are no area codes. The country code for Denmark is 45. To call home from Denmark dial the international code (00) followed by the country code. To call the UK dial 00 44.

Time
Denmark follows Central European Time (CET), which is one hour ahead of Greenwich Mean Time (GMT + 1). From the last Sunday in March to the last Sunday in October, clocks are put forward one hour (GMT + 2).

Emergency telephone numbers
Police **112**
Fire **112**
Ambulance **112**

Toll charges in Danish kroner

Bridges and tunnels	Car	Car towing caravan/ trailer
Oresund Bridge (one way)	275.00	550.00
Storebaelt Bridge (one way)	215.00	330.00

Driving in Estonia *(Eastern Europe)*

The regulations below should be read in conjunction with the General motoring information on pages 18–21.

Drinking and driving

Drinking and driving is strictly forbidden in Estonia. Nil percentage of alcohol is allowed in the driver's blood. A fine and/or imprisonment can be imposed for non-compliance.

Driving licence

The minimum age at which a UK licence holder may drive a temporarily imported car and/or motorcycle is 18.

Fines

Police can impose fines on the spot. They monitor speeds closely and will impose fines for even the smallest speeding offences. Illegally parked cars will be clamped.

Fuel

Unleaded petrol (95 and 98 octane), diesel and LPG are available. Leaded petrol is no longer available. Carrying petrol in a can is permitted, subject to payment of excise duty at the frontier. Credit cards are accepted at most filling stations; check with your card issuer for use in Estonia before travel.

Lights

The use of dipped headlights during the day is compulsory.

Motorcycles

Use of dipped headlights during the day is compulsory. The wearing of crash helmets is compulsory for both the driver and passenger.

Motor insurance

Third-party insurance is compulsory.

Passengers/children in cars

Children too small to wear seat belts must travel in a child seat adapted to their size.

Seat belts

It is compulsory for front-seat occupants to wear seat belts. Rear seat belts must be worn if fitted.

Speed limits

The standard legal limits, which may be varied by signs, for **private vehicles without trailers** are: in built-up areas 50km/h (31mph), outside built-up areas 90km/h (55mph) but up to 110km/h (68mph) on some roads during the summer months. Motorists who have held a driving licence for less than two years must not exceed 90km/h (55mph) outside built-up areas.

Additional information

- A first-aid kit, fire extinguisher, two wheel chocks (blocks of wood or plastic to put under a vehicle's wheels when parked, to prevent it from moving) and a warning triangle (not required for two-wheeled vehicles) are compulsory.
- Winter tyres (with a minimum tread depth of 3mm) are compulsory between 1 December and 1 March; however these dates may vary from October to April according to the weather conditions.

- It is recommended that visitors carry an assortment of spares for their vehicle, such as fan belt, replacement bulbs and spark plugs.
- In addition to the original vehicle registration document, it is recommended that an International Certificate for Motor Vehicles (ICMV) is also carried if visiting any Russian-speaking areas outside Estonia.

- The border police may ask visitors for proof of sufficient personal insurance cover on entry.
- It is prohibited to overtake a tram that has stopped to let passengers on or off.
- Motorists must pay a toll to enter the city of Tallinn.

Travel facts: Estonia

Estonian Embassy
16 Hyde Park Gate
London SW7 5DG
Tel: 020 7589 3428

Estonia does not have a tourist office in the UK, but the embassy can help tourists with information. You can collect tourist brochures from the embassy Monday to Friday 9am to 5pm.
www.estonia.gov.uk
www.visitestonia.com

Banking hours
Banks are generally open from Monday to Friday from 9am to 3 or 4pm. Most banks are closed on Saturday and Sunday. Currency exchange offices are open from Monday to Friday from 9am to 6pm; on Saturday from 9am to 3pm. Some are also open on Sunday.

Credit/debit cards
Credit cards such as Visa and MasterCard/Eurocard, are accepted in most of the major hotels, restaurants and shops. Most banks will give cash advances on credit cards supported by a valid passport. Check with the credit card company for further details before travelling.

Currency
The national currency is the kroon (EEK). The smaller unit is the cent, 1 kroon = 100 cents. The kroon is pegged to the euro at €1 = 15.65EEK. Foreign currencies can be easily exchanged in banks and exchange offices.

Electricity
The electricity supply in Estonia is 220 volts AC, 50Hz. Continental-style two-pin plugs are in use.

Health care
Free or reduced-cost medical treatment is available in Estonia to European visitors on production of a valid European Health Insurance Card (EHIC). See page 10. Comprehensive travel insurance is still advised and is essential for all other visitors.

Pharmacies
Over-the-counter medicines are available in pharmacies *(apteek)*, which can be found in every town. However, it may be more convenient to bring enough medicines to last throughout your trip.

Post offices
Post offices are generally open during normal shopping hours: Monday to Friday from 9am to 6pm, and Saturday 9.30am to 3pm. The Central Post Office in Tallinn, at Narva mnt, is open seven days a week.

Safe water
The tap water is safe to drink but you may prefer bottled mineral water.

Telephones
Pay phones accept phone cards, which can be purchased from hotel reception desks, tourist information offices, post offices, news-stands and some shops. The country code for Estonia is 372. To call home from Estonia dial the international code (00) followed by the country code. To call the UK dial 00 44.

Time
Estonia is on Eastern European Time. It is two hours ahead of Greenwich Mean Time (GMT + 2) and from late March to late October it is three hours ahead of Greenwich Mean Time (GMT + 3).

Emergency telephone numbers
Police **110** or **112**
Fire **112**
Ambulance **112**

Driving in Finland *(Northern Europe)*

The regulations below should be read in conjunction
with the General motoring information on pages 18–21.

Drinking and driving

The police can carry out random breath tests
and blood tests. If the level of alcohol in the
bloodstream is 0.05 per cent or more the driver
will be penalised, which could include a daily
fine or imprisonment and withdrawal of driving
licence. The police test for alcohol and narcotics.

Driving licence

The minimum age at which a UK licence holder
may drive a temporarily imported car is 18,
a motorcycle (not exceeding 125cc) 16,
exceeding 125cc 18. Motorists banned
from driving in an EU or EEA country are not
permitted to drive in Finland.

Fines

Police may impose, but not collect, on-the-spot
fines up to €115 for parking and other minor
infringements. The fine is payable at a bank
within two weeks. For more serious offences
there is a system of daily fines with a minimum
of €6 per day. The police can remove an illegally
parked vehicle; the release fee is up to €170.

Fuel

Unleaded petrol (95 and 98 octane) and diesel
is available. Leaded petrol and LPG are not
available. Carrying up to 10 litres of petrol in a
can is permitted. Credit cards are accepted at
most filling stations; check with your card issuer
for use in Finland before travel.

Lights

All motor vehicles must use their headlights
inside and outside built-up areas at all times
throughout the year.

Motorcycles

The use of dipped headlights during the day is
compulsory. Drivers and passengers of mopeds
or motorcycles must wear a crash helmet.

Motor insurance

Third-party insurance is compulsory.

Passengers/children in cars

A child less than 1.35m (4ft 5in) travelling in a
car, van or lorry must be seated in a child seat
or child restraint. A child under three years old
may not be transported in a vehicle without a
child restraint/seat, except in a taxi. Where a
child restraint/seat is not available, a child three
years and over must travel in the rear seat of the
vehicle using a seat belt or other safety device
attached to the seat. All child restraints/seats
have to conform with the ECE standard 44/03
or EU directive 77/541EEC. It is the
responsibility of the driver to ensure that
all children are safely restrained.

Seat belts

It is compulsory for front- and rear-seat
occupants to wear seat belts, if fitted.

Finland

Speed limits

The standard legal limits, which may be varied by signs, for **private vehicles without trailers** are: inside built-up areas 50km/h (31mph), outside built-up areas 80km/h (49mph) or 100km/h (62mph), according to the quality of road, with 80km/h (49mph) being the upper limit where there are no signs. On motorways the limit is 120km/h (74mph). There is no minimum speed on motorways. Temporary speed limits may be enforced on some or all roads by the local road districts. Reduced speed limits apply during the winter months, October to March (generally 20km/h or 12mph less than standard limits). Lower limits apply to **private cars towing a trailer or caravan:** outside built-up areas and on motorways 80km/h (49mph) and for a trailer without brakes 60km/h (37mph).

Additional information

- A warning triangle is compulsory.
- Winter tyres, marked M&S on the sidewall, are compulsory between 1 December and end of February. The recommended minimum tread depth is 3mm for winter tyres, but in difficult weather conditions it is 5mm.
- Pedestrians must use reflectors in the hours of darkness (any type of reflector is accepted). A car driver/passenger who steps out of a vehicle becomes a pedestrian and therefore must have a reflector, such as a jacket/waistcoat.
- Radar detectors are prohibited.
- Spiked tyres may be used from 1 November to the first Monday after Easter; if used they must be fitted on all wheels.
- Snow chains may be used temporarily when required by conditions. Drivers must be careful to avoid damaging the road surface.
- Beware of game (elk, reindeer, etc.) as they constitute a very real danger on some roads.
- It is prohibited to sound a horn in towns and villages except in cases of immediate danger.

Travel facts: Finland

Finnish Tourist Board
PO Box 33213
London W6 8JX
Tel: 020 7365 2512
www.visitfinland.com/uk

Banking hours
Finnish banks are open Monday to Friday 9.15am to 4.15pm. ATMs are fairly widespread and marked by the sign OTTO.

Credit/debit cards
Most major credit cards, including Visa, MasterCard and EuroCard, can be used for payment in many shops and restaurants.

Currency
The Euro (€) is the official currency of Finland. Banknotes are issued in €5, €10, €20, €50, €100, €200 and €500; coins in denominations of €1 and €2 and 1, 2, 5, 10, 20 and 50 cents.

Electricity
The electric current in Finland is 220V (230V) AC, 50Hz. A two-round-pin continental plug system is used.

Health care
Free or reduced-cost medical treatment is available in Finland to European visitors on production of a valid European Health Insurance Card (EHIC). See page 10. Comprehensive travel insurance is still advised and is essential for all other visitors.

Pharmacies
Medicines are available over the counter at pharmacies *(apteekki)*. Some have late opening hours.

Post offices
Post offices are open Monday to Friday 9am to 6pm. Post offices in grocery stores and petrol service stations may stay open until 8 or 9pm. Yellow post boxes on walls are for daily collections. Stamps are available at post offices, book and newspaper shops, R-kiosks, stations and hotels.

Safe water
Tap water is of the highest quality and can be consumed throughout the country. Bottled mineral water is available in shops and restaurants.

Telephones
Telephone calls can be made from booths, hotels and post offices. Many public telephones operate using a pre-paid card purchased from R-kiosks, Sonera shops and some post offices. The country code for Finland is 358. To call home from Finland dial the international code (00) followed by the country code. To call the UK dial 00 44.

Time
Finland is on Eastern European Time. It is two hours ahead of Greenwich Mean Time (GMT + 2) and from late March to late October it is three hours ahead of Greenwich Mean Time (GMT + 3).

Emergency telephone number
Emergency **112**

Driving in France and Monaco

(Western Europe)

The regulations below should be read in conjunction with the General motoring information on pages 18–21.

Drinking and driving

If the level of alcohol in the bloodstream is 0.05 per cent or more (0.02 per cent for bus/coach drivers), severe penalties include fine, imprisonment and/or confiscation of driving licence. Saliva tests will be used to detect drivers under the influence of drugs – severe penalties are as above.

Driving licence

The minimum age at which a UK licence holder may drive a temporarily imported car is 18, a motorcycle (up to 80cc) 16, a motorcycle (over 80cc) 18.

Fines

On-the-spot fines or 'deposits' are severe. An official receipt should be issued. Vehicles parking contrary to regulations may be towed away and impounded.

Fuel

Unleaded petrol (95 and 98 octane), diesel and LPG are available. Leaded petrol is no longer available – lead replacement petrol *(super carburant)* is available or a lead-substitute additive can be bought. Carrying petrol in a can is permitted, but not aboard ferries or in Eurotunnel. A new type of fuel, the SP95-E10 *(Sans Plomb* 95 octane, ethanol 10%: lead-free 95 octane containing 10 per cent of ethanol) is now sold throughout France. This fuel is not suitable for all cars and you should check with your vehicle manufacturer before using it. If in doubt use the standard SP95 or SP98 octane unleaded fuel, which continues to be available alongside the new fuel. Credit cards are accepted at most filling stations; check with your card issuer for usage in France and Monaco before travel. Many automatic petrol pumps are operated by credit/debit card. However, cards issued outside France are not always accepted by these pumps.

Lights

Dipped headlights must be used in poor daytime visibility. It is highly recommended by the French government that four-plus wheeled vehicles use dipped headlights day and night (this is already compulsory for motorcycles).

Motorcycles

The use of dipped headlights during the day is compulsory for motorcycles. The wearing of crash helmets is compulsory for both driver and passenger of any two-wheel motorised vehicle.

Motor insurance

Third-party insurance is compulsory.

Motorways

See motorway map, page 68. To join a motorway follow signs with the international motorway symbol or signs with the words *'par*

Autoroute' added. Signs with the words *'péage'* or *'par péage'* lead to toll roads. Motorcycles under 80cc are prohibited. Use green alternative routes to avoid traffic jams on major highways.

Most motorways charge tolls (see pages 69–70) except on certain sections in the immediate vicinity of towns such as Paris, Bordeaux, Lille, Lyon, Marseille and Metz.

On the majority of toll motorways in France a travel ticket is issued on entry and the toll is paid on leaving the motorway and also at occasional intermediate points. The travel ticket gives all relevant information about toll charges, including the toll category of the vehicle. At the exit point the ticket is handed in. On some motorways the toll collection is automatic; ensure you have the correct change ready to throw in the collecting basket. If change is required use the marked separate lane. **Note:** toll booths will not exchange traveller's cheques – ensure you have sufficient euros with you to meet the high toll charges (alternatively, credit cards are now accepted at most toll booths).

It is usually possible to obtain 24-hour service for a car and/or occupants every 40km (25 miles). Rest stops, most with toilet facilities, can be found every 15km (9 miles). Free emergency telephones are sited every 2km (1.24 miles) on most motorways.

Passengers/children in cars

Children under the age of 10 are not permitted to travel in the front seat of a vehicle, unless there are no rear seats or the rear seats are already occupied with children under 10, or there are no seat belts. In these circumstances a child must not be placed in the front seat with their back to the road if the vehicle is fitted with a passenger air bag, unless it is deactivated. They must travel in an approved child seat or restraint adapted to their size.

A baby up to 13kg must be carried in a rear-facing car seat. A child between 9 and 18kg must be seated in a child seat and a child from 15kg up to 10 years can use a booster seat with a seat belt or a harness. It is the driver's responsibility to ensure all passengers under 18 are appropriately restrained.

Seat belts

It is compulsory for front- and rear-seat occupants to wear seat belts, if fitted.

Speed limits

The standard legal limits, which may be varied by signs, for **private vehicles with and without trailers** are: in built-up areas 50km/h (31mph), outside built-up areas 90km/h (55mph), but 110km/h (68mph) on urban motorways and dual-carriageways separated by a central reservation and 130km/h (80mph) on motorways. Lower limits of 80km/h (49mph) outside built-up areas, 100km/h (62mph) on dual carriageways and 110km/h (68mph) on motorways apply in wet weather and to visiting motorists who have held a driving licence for less than two years. Additionally, speed limits are reduced on stretches of motorways in built-up areas. The minimum speed limit on motorways is 80km/h (49mph).

Note: Holders of EU driving licences exceeding the speed limit by more than 40km/h (25mph) will have their licences confiscated on the spot by the police.

Additional information

- It is compulsory to carry a warning triangle (excludes motorcycles).
- Snow chains must be fitted to vehicles using snow-covered roads in compliance with the relevant road sign.
- It is compulsory to carry one reflective jacket (EN471) in the vehicle. This does not apply to drivers of two-wheeled and three-wheeled vehicles.
- It is recommended that visitors equip their vehicle with a set of replacement bulbs.
- In built-up areas, give way to traffic coming from the right – *'priorité a droite'*. At signed

roundabouts bearing signs *'Vous n'avez pas la priorité'* or *'Cédez le passage'* traffic on the roundabout has priority; where no such sign exists traffic entering the roundabout has priority.

- Overtaking stationary trams is prohibited when passengers are boarding/alighting.
- Parking discs for 'blue zone' parking areas can be obtained from police stations, tourist offices and some shops.
- In built-up areas the use of the horn is prohibited except in cases of immediate danger.
- Any apparatus with a screen that could distract the driver (such as television, video, DVD equipment) should be positioned in a place where the driver is unable to see it. This excludes GPS systems. It is prohibited to touch or program the device unless parked in a safe place.
- It is prohibited to carry, transport or use radar detectors. Failure to comply with this regulation involves a fine of up to €1,500, and the vehicle and/or device may be confiscated.

Road signs (a selection of standard and non-standard)

Priority road

End of priority road

Traffic on the roundabout has priority

Give way

Continuation of restriction

Alternative holiday routes

Information centre for holiday route

Travel facts: France and Monaco

Atout France/The French Tourist Board
Lincoln House
300 High Holborn
LONDON WC1V 7JH
Tel: 090 68 244 123 (60p per minute at all times)
uk.franceguide.com

Banking hours
Banks are generally open Monday to Friday 9am to 4.30pm. Some open extended hours including Saturday morning, but may close on Monday instead. Banks close at noon on the day before a national holiday, as well as on the holiday itself.

Credit/debit cards
Credit cards are widely accepted in shops, restaurants and hotels. Visa (Carte Bleue), MasterCard (Eurocard) and Diners Club can be used in most ATM cash dispensers. Some smaller shops and hotels may not accept credit cards – always check first.

Currency
The currency in France is the euro (€). Euro coins are issued in denominations of 1, 2, 5, 10, 20 and 50 cents and €1 and €2. Banknotes are issued in denominations of €5, €10, €20, €50, €100, €200 and €500.

Electricity
The power supply in France is 220 volts. Sockets accept two-round-pin (or increasingly three-round-pin) plugs, so an adaptor is needed for most non-continental appliances. A transformer is needed for appliances operating on 110–120 volts AC.

Health care
Free or reduced-cost medical treatment is available in France and Monaco to European visitors on production of a valid European Health Insurance Card (EHIC). See page 10. Comprehensive travel insurance is still advised and is essential for all other visitors.

Pharmacies
Pharmacies – recognised by their green cross sign – have highly qualified staff able to offer medical advice, provide first aid and prescribe a wide range of drugs, although some are available by prescription (ordonnance) only.

Post offices
Post offices (bureaux de poste) are well signed, and generally open Monday to Friday 8am to 5pm, Saturday 8am to noon. In smaller places, opening hours may be shorter and offices may close for lunch. Main post offices sometimes stay open until later in the evenings. Post boxes are yellow.

Safe water
It is safe to drink tap water served in hotels and restaurants, but never drink from a tap marked eau non potable (not drinking water). Bottled water is cheap and widely available.

Telephones
All telephone numbers in France comprise 10 digits. There are no area codes; simply dial the number. In addition to coin-operated models, an increasing number of public phones take phone cards (télécartes). These can be bought from France Telecom shops, post offices, tobacconists and at railway stations. Some cards give cheaper overseas calls than standard télécartes, so ask before you buy if you need to phone abroad. The country code for France is 33. To call home from France dial the international code (00) followed by the country code. To call the UK from France dial 00 44.

Time
France is on Central European Time, one hour ahead of Greenwich Mean Time (GMT + 1). From late March, when clocks are put forward one hour, until late October, French Summer Time (GMT + 2) operates.

Emergency telephone numbers
Police **17** or **112**
Fire **18** or **112**
Ambulance **15** or **112**

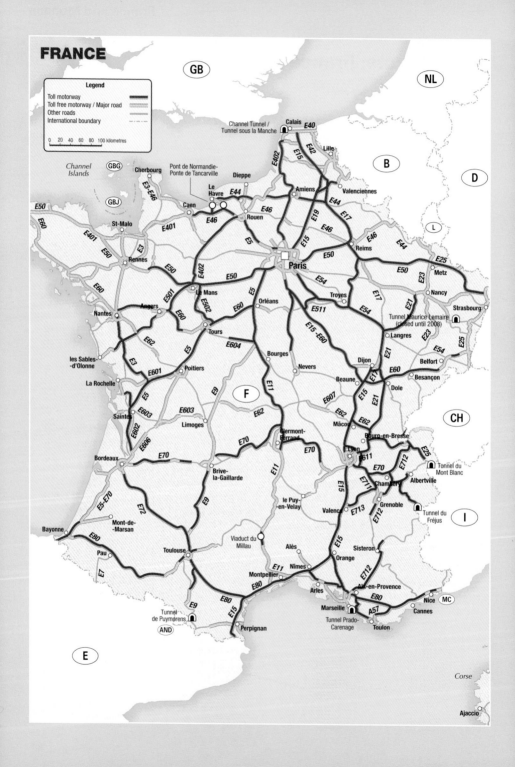

Toll charges in euros

Road	Car	Car towing caravan/ trailer	Road	Car	Car towing caravan/ trailer
E3/E5 (A83/A10) Nantes – Bordeaux	26.90	40.90	**E19 (A1/A2)** Valenciennes – Paris	13.00	19.10
E5 (A10/A837) Bordeaux – La Rochelle	12.60	19.10	**E19/E17**		
E5 Bordeaux – Hendaye			(A26/A2) Valenciennes – Reims	11.90	17.80
(Spanish border)	7.00	10.70	**E21 (A29)** Dijon – Dole	2.80	4.20
E5 (A10) Paris – Tours	20.80	33.90	Dole – Bourg-en-Bresse	8.20	12.80
Tours – Bordeaux	30.10	47.40	**E21 (A3)** Nancy – Langres	7.90	12.50
Tours – Poitiers	9.70	16.00	**E25 (A4)** Metz – Strasbourg	12.00	18.60
Poitiers – Saintes	11.30	17.90	**E25 (A40)** Genève – Tunnel du		
E5 (A13) Rouen – Paris	13.40	24.10	Mont Blanc	5.30	9.20
E5/E11(A10/A71)			**E44 (A29)** Le Havre – St Saens (**E402**)	7.20	10.80
Paris – Clermont-Ferrand	33.80	54.30	**E44 (A29/A16)** Neufchâtel-en-Bray –		
E9 (A66) Toulouse – Tunnel du			Amiens	6.30	9.80
Puymorens	4.50	6.80	**E44/E17 (A29/A26)** Amiens – Reims	12.10	18.30
Brive – Toulouse	13.90	21.60	**E46/E5 (A13)** Caen – Paris	21.60	26.40
E15 (A26/A1) Calais – Paris	18.90	27.30	**E50 (A4)** Paris – Reims	9.70	14.70
E15 (A1) Lille – Paris	14.60	21.50	**E50 (A4)** Paris – Metz	22.90	34.90
E15 (A7) Lyon – Montpellier	24.00	37.50	**E50 (A11/A81)** Paris – Rennes	26.70	40.80
E15 (A6) Paris – Beaune	19.60	30.40	**E50/E25 (A4)** Paris – Strasbourg	34.90	53.50
Paris – Mâcon	25.50	39.80	**E50/E501 (A11)** Paris – Angers	25.40	39.00
Paris – Lyon	30.90	48.20	**E54/E15**		
E15 (A9) Orange – Montpellier	1.10	1.70	(A5/A6) Paris – Lyon (via Troyes)	35.60	55.10
Montpellier – Le Perthus			**E60 (A11)** Angers – Nantes	8.20	12.40
(Spanish border)	12.60	20.00	**E60 (A11/A85)** Angers – Tours	8.80	12.40
E15/E17 (A26) Calais – Reims	20.20	30.20	**E60 (A36)** Beaune – Besançon	6.90	10.60
A4/A26 Reims – Troyes	10.20	15.20	Besançon – Belfort	7.00	10.70
E15/E17 (A4/A26/A5/A6) Reims – Lyon	37.30	57.00	Belfort – Mulhouse (German border)	2.80	4.10
E15/E80			**E62 (A40)** Mâcon – Genève	14.60	23.70
(A7/A8) Lyon – Aix-en-Provence	22.30	36.20	**E70 (A89)** Bordeaux –		
E17 (A31) Dijon – Beaune	2.60	3.80	Brive-la-Gaillarde	15.60	24.20
E17 (A31) Langres – Dijon	2.10	3.10	Brive-la-Gaillarde –		
E17/E21/E62			Clermont-Ferrand	9.30	14.40
(A26/A5/A39/A40) Reims – Tunnel			**E70 (A72)** Clermont-Ferrand – Lyon	8.40	12.90
du Mont Blanc	51.10	78.30	**E70 (A43)** Lyon – Chambéry	10.30	16.20

Toll charges in euros *continued*

Road	Car	Car towing caravan/trailer
E70 (A41/A43/		
A430) Chambéry – Albertville	4.90	7.60
E70/E711		
(A43/A48) Lyon – Grenoble	9.60	15.50
E72 (A62) Bordeaux – Toulouse	16.70	26.40
E80 (A8) Aix-en-Provence – Cannes	13.20	19.90
Cannes – Nice	2.80	4.30
Nice – Menton		
(Italian border)	2.10	3.20
E80 (A64) Bayonne – Toulouse	17.60	27.80
E80 (A54/A9) Montpellier – Arles	6.10	9.40
E80 (A8/A54) Montpellier –		
Aix-en-Provence	10.10	15.40
E80/E15		
(A9/A61) Toulouse – Montpellier	20.30	30.70
Toulouse – Le Perthus		
(Spanish border)	17.90	27.20
E402 (A28) Rouen – Le Mans	18.60	30.70
Le Mans – Tours	10.00	15.50
E402/401 (A16) Calais – Paris	18.70	27.80
E604 (A85) Tours – Bourges	11.90	18.20
E611/E62		
(A42/A40) Lyon – Genève	14.40	23.20
E712 (A51) Aix-en-Provence –		
La Saulce (Sisteron)	11.60	17.60
E712 (A41) Chambéry – Genève	8.20	12.40
Grenoble – Chambéry	5.50	7.90
E712 (A51) Grenoble – Sisteron	2.90	4.50
E712/E25		
(A41/A40) Chambéry – Chamonix	8.70	14.20
E713 (A49/A48) Valence – Grenoble	8.20	12.90
A14 Orgeval – Paris (La Défense)	7.70	15.40

Road	Car	Car towing caravan/trailer
A52/A50 Aix-en-Provence – Toulon	7.00	10.70
A57 Toulon – Le Cannet des Maures	2.20	3.20
A87 Angers – Les Sables d'Olonne	8.70	14.10
A13/E5 Le Havre – Paris	24.30	39.10
Bridges and tunnels		
Pont de Normandie (Le Havre)	5.00	5.80
Pont de Tancarville (Le Havre)	2.30	2.90
Tunnel du Puymorens		
(near Andorra/Spanish border)	6.00	12.20
Tunnel Prado Carenage (Marseille)		
(cars only)	2.60	
Tunnel du Fréjus (French/		
Italian border)	35.10	46.40
Tunnel du Mont Blanc (French/		
Italian border)	35.10	46.40
Le Viaduc de Millau (summer)	7.90	11.80
(rest of year)	6.10	9.20
Tunnel de Sainte Marie		
aux Mines	7.70	16.40

Driving in Germany *(Central Europe)*

The regulations below should be read in conjunction with the General motoring information on pages 18–21.

Drinking and driving

If the level of alcohol in the bloodstream is 0.050 per cent or more, penalties include fines and the licence holder can be banned from driving in Germany. The blood alcohol level is nil per cent for drivers under 21 and those who have held a licence for less than two years; if even a small amount of alcohol is detected in the blood the fine is €250.

Driving licence

The minimum age at which a UK licence holder may drive a temporarily imported car and/or motorcycle is 18.

Fines

On-the-spot fines or a deposit can be imposed. Should a foreign motorist refuse to pay, their vehicle can be confiscated. Motorists can be fined for offences such as exceeding speed limits, using abusive language, making derogatory signs and running out of petrol on a motorway. Wheel clamps are not used in Germany but vehicles causing obstruction can be towed away.

Fuel

Unleaded petrol (95 and 98 octane) and diesel are available. LPG is available from more than 5,000 stations. There is no leaded petrol, but you can buy a lead-substitute additive. It is permitted to carry petrol in a can in Germany, but it is forbidden aboard ferries and Eurotunnel.

Credit cards are accepted at most filling stations; check with your card issuer for usage in Germany before travel.

Lights

It is recommended to use dipped headlights or daytime running lights at all times. It is compulsory during daylight hours if fog, snow or rain restrict visibility. Driving with side lights (parking lights) alone is not allowed. Vehicles must have their lights on in tunnels.

Motorcycles

The use of dipped headlights during the day is compulsory. The wearing of a crash helmet is compulsory for both driver and passenger of a moped or motorcycle. Drivers of trikes and quads capable of exceeding 20km/h (12mph) must wear a helmet unless the vehicle is constructed with seat belts and they are worn.

Motor insurance

Third-party insurance is compulsory.

Passengers/children in cars

A child less than 1.5m (4ft 11in) and under 12 years old travelling in any type of vehicle must be seated in an approved child seat or child restraint. Where a child restraint/seat is not available because other children are secured by a child restraint/seat, a child three years and over must travel in the rear seat of the vehicle using a seat belt or other safety device attached to the seat. A child under three may not be transported in a vehicle without a suitable child restraint/seat. It is the responsibility of the driver to ensure that all children are safely restrained.

Seat belts

It is compulsory for front- and rear-seat occupants to wear seat belts, if fitted.

Speed limits

The standard legal limits, which may be varied by signs, for **private vehicles without trailers** are: in built-up areas 50km/h (31mph), outside built-up areas 100km/h (62mph) and on dual carriageways and motorways a recommended maximum of 130km/h (80mph). The minimum speed on motorways is 60km/h (37mph). Different speed limits apply in bad weather conditions. Lower limits apply for **private vehicles with a caravan or trailer** (up to 3.5 tonnes): outside built-up areas the maximum limit is 80km/h (49mph) and on motorways (100km/h) 62mph. UK and Irish caravanners wanting to travel at 100Km/h on motorways have to pass a TÜV (MOT) test in Germany to confirm outfit suitability. A 100km/h sticker will then be fixed to the back of the caravan/trailer. However, problems may be experienced when encountering officials in different regions. The maximum speed limit for vehicles with snow chains is 50km/h (31mph).

Additional information

- Visiting UK motorists are strongly advised to carry a warning triangle, as all drivers must signal their vehicle in case of breakdown; this is a compulsory requirement for residents.
- It is recommended that visitors carry a first-aid kit and set of replacement bulbs.
- Slow-moving vehicles must stop at suitable places and let others pass.

- It is prohibited to overtake or pass a school bus that is approaching a stopping point. Pass buses with caution. A fine will be imposed for non-compliance.
- Spiked tyres and the use of radar detectors are prohibited.
- A GPS-based navigation system that has maps indicating the location of fixed speed cameras must have the 'fixed speed camera PoI (Points of Interest)' function deactivated. Should you be unable to deactivate this function the GPS system must not be carried.
- All motorists are obliged to adapt their vehicles to winter weather conditions. This includes, but is not limited to, winter tyres and anti-freeze fluid for the washer system. Extreme weather may additionally require snow chains. The law does not specify which type of tyre is 'appropriate'. The general opinion is that any type of tyre except summer tyres is appropriate, including all-year tyres. Winter tyres must bear the mark M&S or display the snowflake on the sidewall. Motorists whose cars are equipped with summer tyres while there is snow and ice may not take the car on the road. Motorists in violation face fines of €20. If they actually obstruct traffic, the fine is €40.
- All vehicles entering certain German cities, indicated by signs *'Umweltzone'*, must display a coloured sticker *(plakette)* on the windscreen. These can be obtained from technical inspection centres or approved garages in Germany for a fee of €5 to €10, on production of the registration certificate. The fine for non-compliance is €40. The fee is a 'one-off' charge and is valid in any German city as long as it remains fixed in the vehicle i.e. not transferred to another vehicle. Visit **www.umweltbundesamt.de/umweltzonen** for maps and detailed information.

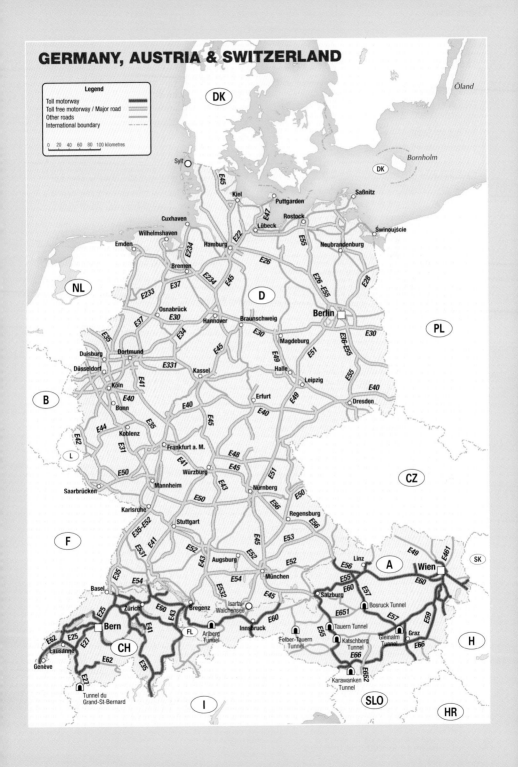

GERMANY, AUSTRIA & SWITZERLAND

Legend

Toll motorway
Toll free motorway / Major road
Other roads
International boundary

0 20 40 60 80 100 kilometres

Öland

Bornholm

DK

DK

Sylt

Kiel

Puttgarden

Saßnitz

E45

Cuxhaven

Rostock

Świnoujście

Wilhelmshaven

Lübeck

E47

E22

Emden

Hamburg

E22

Neubrandenburg

E234

E26

E28

Bremen

E45

E26 -E55

E233

E37

E234

D

Berlin

E26

Osnabrück

Braunschweig

E30

PL

E37

E30

Hannover

E30

E36 -E55

Duisburg

Dortmund

E34

Magdeburg

E30

Düsseldorf

E35

E331

Kassel

E45

E49

E51

Halle

E55

Köln

E41

Erfurt

Leipzig

E40

B

E40

Bonn

E40

Dresden

E44

E35

E49

Koblenz

E31

E45

E42

L

Frankfurt a. M.

E48

E50

Würzburg

E45

E51

Saarbrücken

E41

Mannheim

E43

Nürnberg

E50

E50

Regensburg

Karlsruhe

Stuttgart

E56

E56

CZ

E35-E52

E53

F

E41

E52

E45

E531

Augsburg

E52

Linz

E49

E461

E35

E54

München

E52

E56

A

Wien

SK

Basel

E54

E45

E55

E60

E57

E60

Zürich

E60

E43

Bregenz

Isartal-Walchensee

Salzburg

Bosruck Tunnel

E58

E25

Bern

E41

FL

Arlberg Tunnel

Innsbruck

E60

E651

Tauern Tunnel

E57

Graz

E62

E25

E27

CH

E35

Felber-Tauern Tunnel

Katschberg Tunnel

Gleinalm Tunnel

E66

H

Lausanne

E62

E66

Genève

E27

Karawanken Tunnel

E662

Tunnel du Grand-St-Bernard

I

SLO

HR

Travel facts: Germany

German National Tourist Office
PO Box 2695
London W1A 3TN
Tel: 020 7317 0908
www.germany-tourism.co.uk

Banking hours
Opening hours can vary greatly although banks tend to open at 8.30 or 9am and close at 4pm (6pm Thursday). They are closed at weekends although many have a foyer with ATMs that can be accessed 24 hours a day.

Credit/debit cards
Credit cards with a Maestro, Cirrus, Delta or Plus logo can be used to withdraw cash and pay for goods and services all over the country.

Currency
The currency in Germany is the euro (€). Euro coins are issued in denominations of 1, 2, 5, 10, 20 and 50 cents and €1 and €2. Banknotes are issued in denominations of €5, €10, €20, €50, €100, €200 and €500.

Electricity
The power supply in Germany is 220 volts AC. Sockets accept two-round-pin (or increasingly three-round-pin) plugs, so an adaptor is needed for most non-continental appliances. A transformer is needed for appliances operating on 110–120 volts.

Health care
Free or reduced-cost medical treatment is available in Germany to European visitors on production of a valid European Health Insurance Card (EHIC). See page 10. Comprehensive travel insurance is still advised and is essential for all other visitors.

Pharmacies
Pharmacies (apotheken) can be found in every town and most villages throughout Germany. German pharmacists are highly trained and can offer excellent advice and over-the-counter medicines.

Post offices
Post offices are generally open Monday to Friday 8am to 6pm, Saturday 8am until noon. Post boxes are bright yellow.

Safe water
It is safe to drink the tap water in Germany, although mineral water (Mineralwasser) is also widely available. It's sold mit Kohlensäure (carbonated) or still (still).

Telephones
Most pay phones in Germany accept only phone cards (telefonkarten), which can be bought at tourist or post offices, fuel stations, newspaper kiosks and elsewhere. International calls can be made from all pay phones except for those marked National. Phone calls can also be made from main post offices, where the connection will be made for you; you pay after the call has been completed. If you're using a phone card to call abroad, shop around for the best rates (these are usually printed on the back of the cards), as these vary from company to company. The country code for Germany is 49. To call home from Germany dial the international code (00) followed by the country code. To call the UK from Germany dial 00 44.

Time
Germany is on Central European Time, one hour ahead of Greenwich Mean Time (GMT + 1). From late March, when clocks are put forward one hour, until late October, Daylight Saving Time (GMT + 2) operates.

Emergency telephone numbers
Police **110**
Fire **112**
Ambulance **112**

Charges in euros

Bridges and tunnels	Car	Car towing caravan/ trailer
Warnow Tunnel (Rostock)	2.90	4.20
Herren Tunnel (Lübeck)	1.30	1.30

Driving in Gibraltar *(South West Europe)*

The regulations below should be read in conjunction
with the General motoring information on pages 18–21.

Drinking and driving
The maximum level of alcohol in the
bloodstream is 80mg of alcohol in 100ml of
blood, 35mcg of alcohol on 100ml of breath and
107ml of alcohol in 100ml of urine.

Driving licence
The minimum age at which a UK licence holder
may drive a temporarily imported car and or
motorcycle is 18.

Fines
There are no on-the-spot fines, except when a
vehicle is clamped or towed away.

Fuel
Leaded petrol and LPG is not available.
Unleaded petrol (97 octane) and diesel is
available. Carrying petrol in a can (in a purpose
made steel container) is permitted on payment
of duty. Credit cards are accepted at most filling
stations; check before you travel.

Lights
The use of full headlights is prohibited; use only
dipped headlights during the hours of darkness.

Motorcycles
The wearing of crash helmets is compulsory.

Motor insurance
A Green Card is compulsory (British motorists
may, if they wish, produce a British certificate of
motor insurance).

Passengers/children in cars
Children under three must use a child restraint
appropriate for their weight, in any vehicle.
There is only one exception in that they are
permitted to travel unrestrained in the rear
of a taxi if the right child restraint is not
available. A rear-facing baby seat may be used
only if the air bag has been deactivated. Children
aged three and over and under 1.35m (4ft 5ins)
in height must use an appropriate child restraint.
A child over 12 or 1.35m (4ft 5ins) may use an
adult seat belt.

Seat belts
It is compulsory for front- and rear-seat
occupants to wear seat belts, if fitted.

Speed limits
The standard legal limits for cars, motorcycles
and **towing combinations** under 3.5 tonnes is
50km/h (31mph) unless otherwise indicated by
traffic signs.

Additional information
- The use of a car horn is not permitted within
  the city limits.
- The Spanish–Gibraltar frontier at La Linea is
  open to pedestrian and vehicular traffic of all
  EU nationalities and to nationals who do not
  require a visa.

Travel facts: Gibraltar

The Gibraltar Government Office
150 Strand
London
WC2R 1JA
Tel: 020 7836 0777
www.gibraltar.gov.uk/holiday.php

Banking hours
Banks are generally open Monday to Thursday from 9am to 3.30pm, and until 4.30pm on Friday. Bureaux de change open from 9am to 6pm.

Credit/debit cards
UK debit cards and all major credit cards are readily accepted in Gibraltar.

Currency
Sterling is the currency in Gibraltar, and British notes and coins circulate alongside Gibraltar pounds and pence. Gibraltar notes and coins are not accepted in the UK, and Scottish and Northern Irish notes are not accepted by most businesses in Gibraltar. Euros are accepted and change normally given in sterling.

Electricity
The power supply in Gibraltar is 230 volts AC, 50Hz. Two-pin plugs are standard.

Health care
If you are a British national resident in the UK you can obtain emergency treatment in Gibraltar by presenting your UK passport as proof of residence. However, as some emergency treatment may require transfer to Spain or the UK, you should obtain a European Health Insurance Card (EHIC). See page 10. Comprehensive travel and medical insurance is advised and is essential for all other visitors.

Pharmacies
Gibraltar has well-stocked pharmacies *(farmacia)* providing for the local community and visitors alike. The range of products is greater than across the frontier in Spain. Pharmacies are identified by a green cross.

Post offices
The General Post Office, 104 Main Street, is open Monday to Friday 9am to 4.30pm (closes 2.15pm mid-June to mid-September) and Saturday 10am to 1pm.

Safe water
The municipal water supply in Gibraltar is considered safe to drink. Bottled water is widely available.

Telephones
The country code for Gibraltar is 350. To call home from Gibraltar dial the international code (00) followed by the country code. To call the UK from Gibraltar dial 00 44.

Time
Gibraltar is on Central European Time (GMT + 1). Clocks are put forward one hour (GMT + 2) between March and October.

Emergency telephone numbers
Ambulance **190** or **112**
Fire **190** or **112**
Police **199** or **112**

Driving in Great Britain *(Western Europe)*

The regulations below, which cover England, Scotland, Northern Ireland and Wales, should be read in conjunction with the General motoring information on pages 18–21.

Drinking and driving

The maximum permitted level of alcohol in the blood is 0.08 per cent. The police can ask a driver suspected of having committed an offence to undergo a breath test. A penalty of up to £5,000 and/or 6 months' imprisonment and 12 months' withdrawal of driving licence, if the first time, can be imposed. The police may also carry out tests to detect a driver who may be under the influence of narcotics.

Driving licence

Visitors may use their national driving licence only if they have reached the minimum age to drive a vehicle in the UK; a motorcycle with or without sidecar, up to 25kW and a power to weight ratio not exceeding 0.16kW/kg, 17 years; a motorcycle with or without a sidecar above 25kW, 21years; a temporarily imported car, 17 years. A provisional (learner's) driving licence issued abroad is not valid for use in the UK.

Fines

Drivers without a satisfactory UK address who commit traffic offences will have to pay a financial penalty deposit equal to the amount of the fixed penalty or £300 as a deposit in respect of a potential court fine. The deposit has to be paid on the spot. Those who can provide a satisfactory UK address will be issued with a fixed penalty that has to be paid within 28 working days. The police and examiners from the Vehicle Operator and Services Agency (VOSA) can collect on-the-spot payments.

Vehicles illegally parked are liable to a fine and may also be wheel-clamped or removed.

Fuel

Unleaded 95 octane petrol is sold as Premium Unleaded and unleaded 97 octane petrol as Super Unleaded. All UK petrol and diesel contains 10ppm or less sulphur. Leaded 4-star petrol and lead replacement petrol (LRP) are no longer available. Drivers of older cars designed to use leaded petrol are advised to use lead-replacement additives available widely in filling stations and accessory stores. Prices vary according to the region, fuel brand and type of outlet; supermarket prices may be lower. There are approximately 1,300 filling stations that sell Liquefied Petroleum Gas (LPG). If you are visiting the UK please be aware that UK filling stations use a bayonet-type LPG pump attachment that requires an adaptor for use with other European LPG vehicle connectors. UK filling stations do not generally have adaptors available so you should make sure that you have a suitable adaptor before travelling. The following two companies can supply 'European to UK' LPG adaptors: Autogas 2000 Ltd, **www. autogasshop.co.uk/autogaslpg-filling-adapters-1-c.asp**; Gasure LPG conversions and adapters, **www.gasure.co.uk/adaptors.htm**

Lights

Motorists must use side lights between sunset and sunrise and headlights at night (between half an hour after sunset and half an hour before sunrise) on all roads without street lighting and on roads where the street lights are more than 185m apart or are not lit. Motorists must use headlights or front and rear fog lights when visibility is seriously reduced, generally to less than 100m, use dipped headlights at night in built-up areas unless the road is well lit, and use headlights at night on lit motorways and roads with a speed limit in excess of 30mph (48km/h).

Motorcycles
It is compulsory for riders of motorcycles, scooters and mopeds to wear a safety helmet of an approved design. This also applies to passengers, except those in sidecars. The helmet must be manufactured to a standard similar to the British Standard. The use of headlights during the day is recommended.

Motor insurance
It is prohibited to drive an imported vehicle in the UK without adequate motor insurance. If the importer does not hold an insurance certificate valid for the UK, arrangements should be made prior to travel. Minimum third-party insurance, including trailers, is compulsory.

Motorway/bridge tolls
See motorway map on page 82. Tolls are payable when using certain motorway sections and some bridges and tunnels; see chart on page 83. Not all booths accept credit/debit cards. For information on the M6 toll visit **www.m6toll.co.uk**

Passengers/children in cars
Children under three years must use a child restraint appropriate for their weight in any vehicle (including vans and other goods vehicles). The only exception is that a child under three may travel unrestrained in the rear

of a taxi if the right child restraint is not available. Rear-facing baby seats must not be used in a seat with a frontal air bag unless the air bag has been deactivated manually or automatically. In vehicles where seat belts are fitted, children three years to 12 years and under 1.35m in height (4ft 5in) must use the appropriate child restraint. These children may travel in the rear and use an adult belt in a taxi, if the right child restraint is not available, or for a short distance in an unexpected necessity, or where two occupied child seats in the rear prevent the third being fitted. Drivers are responsible for making sure children under 14 years comply with these laws. Fines for non-compliance vary between £30 and £500

Seat belts

Seat belts must be worn in the front and rear of vehicles, if fitted.

Speed limits

The standard legal limits, which may be varied by signs, for **private vehicles without trailers** are: in built-up areas up to 30mph (48km/h) unless otherwise indicated, outside built-up areas 60mph (96km/h), motorways and dual carriageways up to 70mph (112km/h). Cars **towing trailers or caravans** are limited to 50mph (80kp/h) outside built-up areas, and 60mph (96km/h) on dual carriageways and motorways. Cars **towing a trailer or caravan**, motor caravans with an unladen weight exceeding 3.5 tonnes, and vehicles adapted to carry more than eight passengers as well as the driver must not use the outside lane of a motorway with three or more lanes.

Additional information

- The rule of the road is drive on the left, overtake on the right.
- While it is not compulsory, it is recommended that you carry a warning triangle, first-aid kit and fire extinguisher. Motorists must not use a warning triangle on a motorway.
- It is an offence to use a hand-held phone or similar device when driving.
- It is prohibited to use the horn when the vehicle is stationary, except at times of danger due to another vehicle in movement, or as an anti-theft device. The use of the horn is prohibited in built-up areas from 11.30pm to 7am.
- A toll (congestion charge) is payable when driving or parking in central London on weekdays (Monday to Friday excluding public holidays) between 7am and 6pm. The entrances to the zone are indicated by the letter 'C' in white on a red background. At present the standard charge for most vehicles is £8 if purchased on or before the date of travel. Visit **www.tfl.gov.uk/roadusers/ congestioncharging/** for further information. Tolls are also payable when using certain motorway sections, bridges and tunnels (see page 83).
- Visiting motorists driving left-hand drive vehicles should ensure that their headlights are adjusted for driving on the left, otherwise they risk being stopped by the police and subsequently fined up to £1,000.
- At some intersections called 'box junctions', criss-cross yellow lines are painted on the roadway. Traffic at these junctions must not enter 'the box' (i.e. the area of yellow lines) unless the exit road or lane is clear.

Travel facts: Great Britain

Britain and London Visitor Centre
1 Regent Street
London SW1Y 4XT
Tel: 0870 156 6366
www.visitbritain.com

Banking hours
Banks are generally open from Monday to Friday 9.30am to 4.30pm. Some banks open Saturday morning. Opening hours can differ considerably from branch to branch. Some banks in Scotland close for an hour at lunchtime. Many banks have 24-hour banking lobbies where you can access a range of services via machines.

Credit/debit cards
All credit/debit cards that bear the Visa, MasterCard or American Express logo are widely accepted in Britain. Retailers can charge more for goods and services bought by credit card, but they must display a notice if any price increase applies.

Currency
Britain's currency is the pound sterling (£), issued in banknotes of £5, £10, £20 and £50. There are 100 pennies or pence (p) to each pound and coins come in denominations of 1p, 2p, 5p, 10p, 20p, 50p, £1 and £2. Scottish £1 notes are still in circulation in Scotland. The Channel Islands and the Isle of Man have different coins and notes from the mainland but the monetary system is the same.

Electricity
The power supply in Britain is 230/240 volts AC. Sockets accept only three-square-pin plugs, so an adaptor is needed for continental appliances. A transformer is needed for appliances operating on 110–120 volts.

Health care
Free or reduced-cost medical treatment is available in Great Britain to European visitors on production of a valid European Health Insurance Card (EHIC). See page 10. Comprehensive travel insurance is still advised and is essential for all other visitors.

Pharmacies
Prescription and non-prescription drugs and medicines are available from chemists/pharmacies. Pharmacists can advise on medication for common ailments. Pharmacies operate a rota so there will always be one that is open 24 hours a day. Notices in pharmacy windows give details.

Post offices
Post offices are generally open Monday to Friday 9am to 5.30pm, Saturday 9am to noon.

Safe water
Tap water is safe to drink. Bottled mineral water is widely available but can be expensive.

Telephones
Traditional red phone booths are now rare; instead they come in a variety of designs and colours. Coin-operated phones take 10p, 20p, 50p and £1 coins (20p is the minimum charge), but phones taking British Telecom (BT) phone cards or credit cards are often more convenient. Phone cards are available from post offices and many shops. The country code for Britain is 44. To call home from Britain dial the international code (00) followed by the country code. To call Germany from Britain dial 00 49.

Time
Britain is on Greenwich Mean Time (GMT) in winter, but from late March to late October British Summer Time BST (GMT + 1) operates.

Emergency telephone numbers
Police **999** or **112**
Fire **999** or **112**
Ambulance **999** or **112**

GREAT BRITAIN

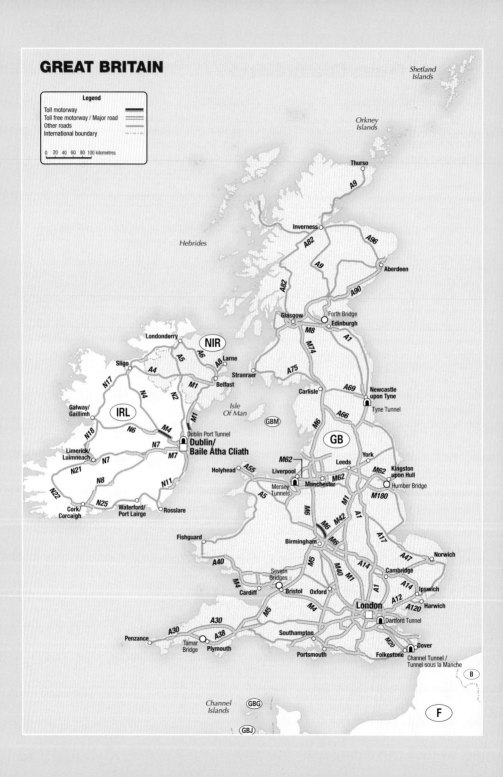

Shetland Islands

Orkney Islands

Legend

Toll motorway	
Toll free motorway / Major road	
Other roads	
International boundary	

0 20 40 60 80 100 kilometres

Hebrides

Thurso

A9

Inverness

A82   A96

A9   Aberdeen

A82   A90

Glasgow   Forth Bridge
Edinburgh
M8
M74   A1
A75

Londonderry

NIR

Sligo   A5   A6   A8 Larne
A4   M1   Belfast
N17   N4   N2
Galway/   N6   M4
Gaillimh   IRL   Dublin Port Tunnel
N18   Dublin/
Baile Átha Cliath
Limerick/   N7   M7
Luimneach   N7
N21   N8   N11
N22
Cork/   N25   Waterford/
Corcaigh   Port Lairge   Rosslare

Stranraer
Carlisle   A69   Newcastle
upon Tyne
A66   Tyne Tunnel

Isle
Of Man   GBM

M6   GB   York

Fishguard

Holyhead   A55   M62   Leeds   Kingston
Liverpool   M62   upon Hull
A5   Mersey   Manchester   Humber Bridge
Tunnels   M62   M180
M6   M1
M6   M42
A1   A17
Birmingham   M6
A40   M5   M40   A14   Norwich   A47
M4   Severn   M1   Cambridge
Bridges   A14
Cardiff   Bristol   Oxford   A1   Ipswich
M5   A12   A120   Harwich
M4   London
A30   A30   Dartford Tunnel
Penzance   A38   Southampton
Tamar   Plymouth   M20   Dover
Bridge   Portsmouth   Folkestone   Channel Tunnel /
Tunnel sous la Manche

B

Channel Islands   GBG

F

GBJ

Toll charges in £ sterling

General	Car	Car towing caravan/ trailer
Central London	8.00	8.00

Central London congestion charge zone. Charge applies between 7am and 6pm weekdays and allows unlimited trips into or out of the zone in one day. For more information see page 80.

Road

M6 Toll Road

	Car	Car towing caravan/ trailer
Weekday night charge (11pm to 6am) (Main Plaza)	3.50	7.00
Weekday night charge (11pm to 6am) (Local Junction)	2.50	7.00
Weekday day charge (6am–11pm) (Main Plaza)	5.00	9.00
Weekday day charge (6am–11pm) (Local Junction)	3.70	8.40
Weekend charge (6am–11pm) (Main Plaza)	4.50	8.00
Weekend charge (6am–11pm) (Local Junction)	3.50	8.00

Bridges and Tunnels

	Car	Car towing caravan/ trailer
Aldwark Toll Bridge between Little Ouseburn and Aldwark/ Linton on Ouse	0.40	1.00
Batheaston Bridge off **A4** near Bath	0.50	1.00
Cartford Bridge 5 miles (3km) east of Poulton-le-Fylde	0.40	0.80
Cleddau Bridge on **A477**	0.75	1.50

Bridges and tunnels	Car	Car towing caravan/ trailer
Clifton Suspension Bridge on **B3129**. Not suitable for caravans over 4 tonnes	0.50	0.50
Dartford River Crossing on **A282/ M25**	1.50	2.00
Dunham Bridge on **A57**	0.30	0.40
Humber Bridge on **A15**	2.70	4.90
Itchen Bridge on **A3025** (off-peak 0.50)	0.60	0.60
Mersey Tunnel (Kingsway) between Wallasey and Liverpool	1.40	2.80
Mersey Tunnel (Queensway) between Birkenhead and Liverpool	1.40	2.80
Middlesbrough Transporter on **A178**	1.20	2.00
Penrhyndeudraeth Bridge (Briwet Bridge; between **A496** and **A487**)	0.40	0.70
Second Severn Crossing on **M4** (westbound only)	5.50	5.50
Severn Bridge on **M48** (westbound only)	5.50	5.50
Swinford Bridge on **B4044**	0.05	0.10
Tamar Bridge on **A38** (eastbound only)	1.50	2.00
Tyne Tunnel on **A19**	1.20	1.20
Warburton Bridge on **B5159**	0.12	0.12
Whitchurch Bridge on **B471**	0.40	0.40
Whitney-on-Wye Bridge on **B4350**	0.50	0.50

Driving in Greece *(Southern Europe)*

The regulations below should be read in conjunction with the General motoring information on pages 18–21.

Drinking and driving

It is a criminal offence to drive if the level of alcohol in the bloodstream is 0.05 per cent or more. A lower unit of 0.02 per cent applies to drivers who have held a licence for less than two years, and to motorcyclists.

Driving licence

The minimum age at which a UK licence holder may drive a temporarily imported car and/or motorcycle (over 50cc) is 17.

Fines

Police can impose fines but not collect them on the spot. The fine must be paid at a Public Treasury office within 10 days. You can be fined for the unnecessary use of a car horn. Vehicles may be towed away if parked illegally, or if violating traffic regulations.

Fuel

Unleaded petrol (95 and 98 octane) and diesel *(petreleo)* is available. Leaded petrol is not available. Lead replacement petrol is sold as Super 2002 (98 octane). It is forbidden to carry petrol in a can in a vehicle. LPG may not be used in private cars, only in taxis. Credit cards are accepted at some filling stations. Check with your card issuer for use in Greece before travel.

Lights

Dipped headlights should be used in poor daytime visibility. The use of undipped headlights in towns is strictly prohibited.

Motorcycles

The use of dipped headlights during the day is compulsory. The wearing of crash helmets is also compulsory.

Motor insurance

Third-party insurance is compulsory.

Passengers/children in cars

It is prohibited for children over three years of age and under 1.5m (4ft 11in) to travel in the front seat of a vehicle. Children under five years must use the child restraint appropriate for their weight in all cars, vans and goods vehicles, except when travelling in the rear of taxis. They cannot be carried in the vehicle otherwise. Approved child restraints are those conforming with standard ECE R44/03 (or later). Children measuring 1.35m (4ft 5in) or over can use a seat belt. Placing a rear-facing child restraint in the front passenger seat is allowed only if the passenger air bag is deactivated.

Seat belts

It is compulsory for front-seat occupants to wear seat belts.

Speed limits

The standard legal limits, which may be varied by signs, for **private vehicles without trailers** are: in built-up areas 50km/h (31mph) for cars, 40km/h (24mph) for motorcycles; outside built-up areas 90km/h (55mph) or 110km/h (68mph) for cars, 70km/h (43mph) for motorcycles;

motorways 130km/h (80mph) for cars and 90km/h (55mph) for motorcycles. When **towing a trailer or caravan**, the limits outside built-up areas are 80km/h (49mph), and 90km/h (55mph) on motorways.

Additional information

- A fire extinguisher, first-aid kit and warning triangle are compulsory.

- The police are empowered to confiscate the number plates of illegally parked vehicles throughout Greece. Generally this applies only to Greek-registered vehicles, but the drivers of foreign-registered vehicles should beware of parking illegally.

Travel facts and toll charges: Greece

Greek National Tourism Organisation
4 Conduit Street
London W1S 2DJ
Tel: 020 7495 9300 (enquiries and information)
www.visitgreece.gr

Banking hours
Banks are generally open Monday to Friday 8am to 2pm
(Friday 1.30pm) and 8am to 6pm in major tourist areas.

Credit/debit cards
Cash is still the preferred method of payment in Greece.
Only the larger and more expensive hotels, restaurants
and shops will accept payment by credit card.

Currency
The currency in Greece is the euro (€). Euro coins are
issued in denominations of 1, 2, 5, 10, 20 and 50 cents
and €1 and €2. Banknotes are issued in denominations
of €5, €10, €20, €50, €100, €200 and €500.

Electricity
The power supply in Greece is 230 volts AC, 50Hz.
Sockets accept two-round-pin plugs.

Health care
Free or reduced-cost medical treatment is available in
Greece to European visitors on production of a valid
European Health Insurance Card (EHIC). See page 10.
Comprehensive travel insurance is still advised and is
essential for all other visitors.

Pharmacies
Pharmacies (farmakeío), indicated by a green cross,
give advice and prescriptions for common ailments.
Codeine is banned in Greece and you can be fined for
carrying it.

Post offices
Post offices, identified by a yellow OTE sign, are
generally open Monday to Friday 8am to 2pm (7pm in
major tourst areas). Stamps (ghramatósima) are also
sold at kiosks or shops selling cards. Post boxes are
yellow; use the slot marked Exoterico for overseas mail.

Safe water
Tap water is chlorinated and is regarded as safe to
drink. Bottled mineral water it is cheap to buy and is
widely available.

Telephones
Calls from phone booths can be made using a phone
card available from kiosks, OTE offices and some
shops. They are sold in units of 100, 500 and 1,000. You
can also make calls from street kiosks, which have
metered phones and charge at the end of the call,
although connections tend to be poor. The country code
for Greece is 30. To call home from Greece dial the
international code (00) followed by the country code.
To call Britain from Greece dial 00 44.

Time
Greece is on Eastern European Time. It is two hours
ahead of Greenwich Mean Time (GMT + 2) and from
late March to late October it is three hours ahead of
Greenwich Mean Time (GMT + 3).

Emergency telephone numbers
Police, Fire and Amulance **112**
Tourist Police **171**

Toll charges in euros

Road		Car	Car towing caravan/ trailer
1/E75	Lamia – Inofita	1.20	4.00
1/E75	Katerini – Larisa	1.40	4.00
1/E75	Larisa – Lamia	1.40	4.00
1/E75	Thessaloniki – Katerini	1.40	2.00
1/E75	Lamia – Afidnes	1.40	4.00
1/E75	Afidnes – Athina	1.40	2.00
7/E65	Korinthos – Tripoli	2.70	4.00
8A/E65–E55			
	Korinthos – Patra	1.80	5.00
8A/E94	Athina – Korinthos	1.40	4.00

Driving in Hungary *(Central Europe)*

The regulations below should be read in conjunction with the General motoring information on pages 18–21.

Drinking and driving

Nil per cent of alcohol is allowed in the driver's blood. Amounts of less than 0.08 per cent incur a fine, more than 0.08 per cent incur legal proceedings.

Driving licence

The minimum age at which a UK licence holder may drive a temporarily imported car and/or motorcycle is 17. All valid UK driving licences should be accepted in Hungary. This includes the older all-green paper-style UK licences (in Northern Ireland older paper-style with photographic counterpart) although the EC appreciates that these may be more difficult to understand and that drivers may wish to update them before travelling abroad. Alternatively, older licences may be accompanied by an International Driving Permit (IDP).

Fines

On-the-spot fines can be imposed. The police must hand over the payment order to transfer the amount of the fine to be paid within 30 days. The fine is payable only in the Hungarian forint (HUF) – credit cards are not accepted. Cash should not be given to a policeman at the roadside. Wheel clamps are in use.

Fuel

Unleaded petrol (95 octane), diesel *(dizel* or *gazolaj)* and LPG are available. Leaded petrol is not available. It is permitted to carry up to 40 litres of petrol in a can. Credit cards are accepted at some filling stations, check with your card issuer for usage in Hungary. Cash is the most usual form of payment.

Lights

The use of dipped headlights is compulsory at all times outside built-up areas. At night the use of full beam in built-up areas is prohibited.

Motorcycles

The use of dipped headlights is compulsory at all times. The wearing of crash helmets is compulsory for both driver and passenger.

Motor insurance

Third-party insurance is compulsory. Should a visitor cause an accident involving a Hungarian citizen they must report it to the Association of Hungarian Insurance Companies.

Passengers/children in cars

A child under three years of age may travel in a vehicle only if using a suitable child-restraint system appropriate for their weight; they are permitted to travel in the front of the vehicle using this restraint if it is rear facing and there is no air bag or it has been deactivated. Children under 1.5m (4ft 11in) and over three years must use a suitable child-restraint system and be seated in the rear of the vehicle.

Seat belts

It is compulsory for front- and rear-seat occupants to wear seat belts, where fitted.

Speed limits

The standard legal limits, which may be varied by signs, for **private vehicles without trailers** are: in built-up areas 50km/h (31mph), outside built-up areas 90km/h (55mph) or 110km/h (68mph) on semi-motorways and 130km/h (80mph) on motorways. When **towing a trailer or caravan** the limits are: 50km/h (31mph) in built-up areas, 70km/h (43mph) outside built-up areas and on semi-motorways, and 80km/h (49mph) on motorways. Vehicles with snow chains must not exceed 50km/h (31mph). In city centres, roads with a 30km/h (18mph) speed limit are increasingly common.

Additional information

- A first-aid kit and warning triangle are compulsory.
- All pedestrians walking on a road, or road shoulder outside a built-up area, must wear a reflective jacket at night and when visibility is poor. Any person exiting a vehicle outside a built-up area in a breakdown situation becomes a pedestrian and therefore must wear a reflective jacket.
- The use of snow chains or their presence in a car can be made compulsory on some roads when weather conditions require.
- A spare bulb kit is recommended as it is compulsory for Hungarian-registered vehicles.
- It is recommended that the driver of a conspicuously damaged vehicle entering Hungary obtains a police report confirming the damage at the time of entry, otherwise lengthy delays may be encountered at the frontier when leaving Hungary. This report should be obtained from the police of the country where the car was damaged.
- Motorway tax is payable for the use of M1 (Budapest–Hegyeshalom), M3 (Budapest –Gorbehaza–Nyiregyhaza), M5 (Budapest–Kiskunfelegyhaza–Szeged–Roszke/border with Serbia), M6 (M0–Erd–Dunaujvaros), M7 (Budapest–Lake Balaton–Letenye, border with Croatia), M30 (Emod–Miskolc), M35 (Gorbehaza–Debrecen). The electronic *vignette* and any toll charges must be paid in forints. Credit cards accepted: Visa, Eurocard/MasterCard, DKV and UTA. The *vignette* can be purchased in person, online, or by telephone (land line or mobile). When a motorist has purchased an *e-vignette*, a confirmation message will be sent or a coupon issued. This document must be kept for one year after the expiry of validity. The motorway authorities check all vehicles electronically, and verify the registration number, the category of toll paid and the validity of the *e-vignette*. For further information visit **www.motorway.hu**. *Vignettes* are available for four days (vehicles up to 3.5 tonnes only), one week, one month or 13 months. Fines are imposed for non-display. The Hungarian motoring association recommends that foreign motorists wishing to purchase a *vignette* at the border have cash in Hungarian forints. *Vignettes* should be purchased only from outlets where the prices are clearly displayed at the set rate. See toll charges, opposite.
- Motorist should be wary of contrived incidents, particularly on the Vienna–Budapest motorway, designed to stop motorists and expose them to robbery.
- There are restrictions on traffic entering Budapest when air pollution exceeds a fixed level on two consecutive days.
- Spiked tyres are prohibited.
- The use of the horn is prohibited in built-up areas, except in case of danger.

Travel facts and toll charges: Hungary

Hungarian Tourist Office
46 Eaton Place
London SW1X 8AL
Tel: 0800 360 00000
www.gotohungary.co.uk
www.hungary.com

Banking hours
Banks are generally open Monday to Friday 8am to 4pm, and some are open until noon on Saturday.

Credit/debit cards
The acceptance of credit cards is limited; they are becoming increasingly popular but they are not accepted everywhere. Most ATMs in Hungary accept Visa, MasterCard (including Cirrus and Maestro), American Express and Diners Club.

Currency
Hungary's currency is the forint (Ft or HUF). The denominations of forint banknotes are Ft200, 500, 1,000, 2,000, 5,000, 10,000 and 20,000. There are coins of 1, 2, 5, 10, 20, 50 and 100 forints.

Electricity
Hungary has 220–230V AC power supply. Electrical sockets take two-round-pin plugs.

Health care
Free or reduced-cost medical treatment is available in Hungary to European visitors on production of a valid European Health Insurance Card (EHIC). See page 10. Comprehensive travel insurance is still advised and is essential for all other visitors.

Pharmacies
A pharmacy (gyógyszetár or patica) sells both prescription and non-prescription medicines (bring your own medication if you need a specific product). Information about the nearest 24-hour facility is posted at all pharmacies.

Post offices
Buy stamps (bélyeg) at a post office (posta), news kiosk or tobacconist (dohanyaruds) or from a hotel. Post boxes are wall mounted and red with a calling-horn emblem.

Safe water
Although tap water is safe, you may find it causes mild upsets. Bottled mineral water and soda water are widely available and advised.

Telephones
The public phones take Ft10, Ft20, Ft50 and Ft100 coins or phone cards available from hotels, post offices, petrol stations, newsagents, kiosks and street vendors. The minimum charge for a call is Ft20.The country code for Hungary is 36. To call home from Hungary dial the international code (00) followed by the country code. To call the UK from Hungary dial 00 44.

Time
Hungary is on Central European Time, one hour ahead of GMT (GMT + 1). Daylight Saving Time comes into effect from the end of March to the end of October, CET + 1 (GMT + 2).

Emergency telephone numbers
Police **107**   Fire **105**   Ambulance **104**
International emergency number **112**

Toll charges in forints
For details of where to buy the motorway tax see page 88.

General	Car	Car towing caravan/ trailer
4-day vignette (May to September) **M1/M3/M5/M7**	1,530.00	1,530.00
4-day vignette (October to April) **M1/M3/M5/M7**	1,170.00	1,170.00
10-day vignette **M1/M3/M5/M7**	2,550.00	2,550.00
1 month **M1/M3/M5/M7**	4,200.00	4,200.00
1 year **M1/M3/M5/M7**	37,200.00	37,200.00

Driving in Iceland *(North Atlantic)*

The regulations below should be read in conjunction with the General motoring information on pages 18–21.

Drinking and driving

The maximum permitted level of alcohol in the driver's blood is 0.05 per cent. If it is more than 0.049 per cent, severe penalties include the withdrawal of your driving licence, a prison sentence and a fine of up to 160,000 króna.

Driving licence

The minimum age at which a UK licence holder may drive a temporarily imported car and/or motorcycle (over 50cc) is 17. All valid UK driving licences should be accepted in Iceland. This includes the older all-green-style UK licences (in Northern Ireland older paper-style with photographic counterpart) although the EC appreciates that these may be more difficult to understand and that drivers may wish to update them voluntarily before traveling abroad. Alternatively, older licences may be accompanied by an International Driving Permit (IDP).

Fines

On-the-spot fines may be imposed and collected by the traffic police. In some circumstances, payment may be made at a police station or the police officer will provide details of the official bank account into which the fine must be paid. Illegally parked cars may be towed away and a parking fine imposed.

Fuel

Unleaded petrol (95 and 98 octane) and diesel are available but not LPG. There is no leaded petrol (lead-substitute petrol is available as 98 octane). It is forbidden to import fuel in a spare can. Some credit cards are accepted at most filling stations; check with your card issuer for usage in Iceland before you travel.

Lights

The use of dipped headlights during the day is compulsory; a fine can be imposed for non-compliance.

Motorcycles

The use of dipped headlights during the day is compulsory. The wearing of crash helmets is compulsory for both driver and passenger.

Motor insurance

Third-party insurance is compulsory.

Passengers/children in cars

Children must be secured by either safety seats or safety belts. Children must not be placed on the front seat of a vehicle with an active air bag.

Seat belts

It is compulsory for front/rear-seat occupants to wear seat belts, if fitted.

Speed limits

The standard legal limits, which may be varied by signs, for **private vehicles without trailers** are: in built-up areas 50km/h (31mph), outside built-up areas 80km/h (49mph) on gravel roads and 90km/h (55mph) on asphalt roads. When **towing**, the limit on asphalt is 80km/h (49mph).

Additional information

- It is compulsory to carry a warning triangle, which must be used in conjunction with hazard warning lights.
- It is recommended that visitors equip their vehicle with first-aid kit, fire extinguisher and a set of replacement bulbs.
- Snow chains may be used when necessary.
- The use of spiked tyres is permitted between 15 November and 15 April.
- It is prohibited to drive outside marked roads or tracks in order to protect flora and fauna.
- Weather conditions can change rapidly; using a local phone you can dial 1777 between 7.30am and 10pm to obtain information about road and weather conditions.

Travel facts: Iceland

Embassy of Iceland in the UK
2a Hans Street, London SW1X 0JE
Tel: 020 7259 3999
There is currently no Icelandic tourist board in the UK, but the embassy can deal with enquiries.

Banking hours
Banks are generally open Monday to Friday 9.15am to 4pm. They may stay open later Thursday and Friday.

Credit/debit cards
Credit/debit cards are widely accepted.

Currency
Iceland uses the króna, plural krónur (kr). (International abbreviation: ISK). Notes are in denominations of 500, 1000, 2000 and 5000, and coins of 1, 5, 10, 50, 100.

Electricity
The power supply is 220/240 volts AC, 50Hz. Sockets accept two-round-pin plugs. UK visitors require a plug adaptor.

Health care
Free or reduced-cost medical treatment is available in Iceland to European visitors on production of a valid European Health Insurance Card (EHIC). See page 10. Comprehensive travel insurance is still advised and is essential for all other visitors.

Pharmacies
Most pharmacies (apótek) have English-speaking staff.

For 24-hour opening **tel: 118**.

Post offices
Post offices are found in the main communities around Iceland, and opening hours are generally Monday to Friday 8.30am to 4.30pm. Stamps can also be bought in most souvenir outlets where postcards are sold. Icelandic stamps are of particular interest to collectors.

Safe water
Cold tap water is some of the cleanest and best in the world (beware of the hot, which may come from natural thermal sources and smell faintly sulphurous). In the hills, clean spring water is usually safe to drink but avoid glacial meltwater.

Telephones
Public telephones (sími) are usually found outside the post office. They take coins (ISK10, 50 and 100) or phone cards – available from post offices/telephone stations. Iceland's country code is 354. To call home from here dial the international code (00) followed by the country code. To call the UK from Iceland dial 00 44.

Time
Iceland is on GMT all year. It does not go on to Daylight Saving Time. In the north of the island, the sun does not fully set in June; correspondingly, in January there may be only 3.5 hours of daylight in that region.

Emergency telephone number
Police, Fire and Ambulance **112**

Driving in Ireland (Republic of)

(Western Europe)

The regulations below should be read in conjunction with the General motoring information on pages 18–21.

For regulations covering Northern Ireland see Great Britain, pages 78–80.

Drinking and driving

If the level of alcohol in the bloodstream is more than 0.08 per cent, severe penalties, including a fine and/or imprisonment plus disqualification, can be imposed. Random breath testing is in force throughout Ireland.

Driving licence

The minimum age at which a UK licence holder may drive a temporarily imported car or motorcycle (exceeding 150cc) is 17.

Fines

There are on-the-spot fines for parking and speeding offences. Police are not authorised to collect fines – they will issue a notice that must be paid within 21 days. Wheel clamps are in use. In some areas parked cars can be towed away if causing an obstruction, and a significant fee is charged for release.

Fuel

Unleaded petrol (95 octane) and diesel are available. There is no leaded petrol. The availability of lead replacement petrol and LPG is extremely limited. Petrol in a can is permitted, but forbidden on board ferries. Credit cards are accepted at most filling stations; check with your card issuer for use in Ireland before travel.

Lights

Dipped headlights should be used in poor daytime visibility.

Motorcycles

The use of dipped headlights during the day is compulsory. The wearing of crash helmets is compulsory for both driver and passenger.

Motor insurance

Third-party insurance is compulsory.

Passengers/children in cars

Children under three years of age may not travel in a car (other than a taxi) unless they are placed in an appropriate child restraint. They can travel on the front seat of the car if they are in a rear-facing restraint system and the air bag is disabled. Children over three who are under 1.5m (4ft 11in) and weigh less than 36kg must use an appropriate child restraint when travelling in cars fitted with seat belts. If the car is not equipped with seat belts they must travel on the rear seats.

Seat belts

It is compulsory for front- and rear-seat occupants to wear seat belts, if fitted.

Speed limits

The standard legal limits, which may be varied by signs, for **private vehicles without**

trailers are: in built-up areas 50km/h (31mph), outside built-up areas 60–100km/h (37–62mph) according to road signs and 120km/h (75mph) on motorways.)

Additional information

- A warning triangle is compulsory for vehicles with an unladen weight exceeding 1,524kg (1.5 tonnes).
- The rule of the road is drive on the left, overtake on the right.
- Horns must not be used between 11.30pm and 7am.
- Distances are given in kilometres.

- Some level crossings have manual gates, which motorists must open and close.
- A GPS-based navigation system that has maps indicating the location of fixed speed cameras must have the 'fixed speed camera PoI (Points of Interest)' function deactivated.
- The use of radar detectors is prohibited; they can be confiscated by the Garda (Irish police).
- A barrier-free toll system now operates on the M50 Dublin. Number plates are recorded and the fee must be paid by 8pm the following day at any of the 'payzone' outlets. Further information can be found on **www.eflow.ie**

Travel facts and toll charges: Ireland

Irish Tourist Board
Nations House, 103 Wigmore Street
London W1U 1QS
Tel: 020 7518 0800
www.discoverireland.com
www.visitireland.com

Banking hours
Banks are generally open Monday to Friday 10am to 4pm. Some banks in small towns close 12.30 to 1.30pm. Banks open until 5pm one day a week (Thursday in Dublin).

Credit/debit cards
Credit and debit cards are accepted in major hotels, restaurants and large stores. Check first in small or rural establishments.

Currency
The monetary units in the Republic of Ireland is the euro (€); in Northern Ireland it is the pound sterling (£), see page 81. These are not interchangeable. Euro banknotes come in denominations of €500, €200, €100, €50, €20, €10 and €5; coins in denominations of €2 and €1 and 50, 20, 10, 5, 2 and 1 cents.

Electricity
The power supply in the Republic of Ireland is: 230 volts AC. Electrical sockets take either plugs with two round pins or three square pins.

Health care
Free or reduced-cost medical treatment is available in the Republic of Ireland to European visitors on production of a valid European Health Insurance Card (EHIC). See page 10. Comprehensive travel insurance is still advised and is essential for all other visitors.

Pharmacies
Prescription and non-prescription drugs and medicines are available from pharmacies.

Post offices
Opening hours are generally Monday to Friday 9am to 5.30/6pm, Saturday 9am to 1pm.

Safe water
Tap water in Ireland is safe to drink. Bottled mineral water is widely available.

Telephones
Public telephone boxes are being replaced by glass and metal booths. Lift the handset, insert the correct coins (10, 20 or 50 cents) or phone card and dial. The country code for Ireland is 353. To call home from the Republic dial the international code (00) followed by the country code. To call the UK from the Republic dial 00 44.

Time
Ireland observes Greenwich Mean Time (GMT), but from late March, when clocks are put forward one hour, until late October, Summer Time (GMT + 1) operates.

Emergency telephone numbers
Police, Fire, Ambulance and Coastal Rescue **999** or **112**

Toll charges in euros

Roads	Car	Car towing caravan/ trailer
M1 Toll Drogheda Bypass	1.90	1.90
M3 Toll Clonee – Kells	2.60	2.60
M4 Toll Kinnegad – Enfield – Kilcock	2.90	2.90
M6 Toll Galway – Ballinasloe	1.90	1.90
M7/M8 Portlaoise – Castletown/ Cullahill	1.80	1.80
M8 Toll Rathcormac – Fermoy	1.90	1.90
N18 Limerick Tunnel	1.80	1.80
N25 Waterford City Bypass	1.90	1.90

Bridges and tunnels

East Link Toll Bridge East of Dublin	1.70	1.70
M50 Dublin Port Tunnel (northbound, afternoon peak rate)	10.00	10.00
M50 Dublin Port Tunnel (southbound, morning peak rate)	10.00	10.00
West Link Toll Bridge on **M50** West of Dublin (peak time)	3.00	3.00

Driving in Italy and San Marino

(Southern Europe)

The regulations below should be read in conjunction with the General motoring information on pages 18–21.

Drinking and driving

If the level of alcohol in the bloodstream is 0.051 per cent or more, severe penalties, which include fines, confiscation of vehicle and imprisonment, can be imposed.

Driving licence

The minimum age at which a UK licence holder may drive a temporarily imported car and/or motorcycle (over 125cc or with a passenger) is 18. All valid UK driving licences should be accepted in Italy. This includes the older all-green-style UK licences (in Northern Ireland older paper-style with photographic counterpart) although the EC appreciates that these may be more difficult to understand and that drivers may wish to update them voluntarily before travelling abroad, if time permits. Alternatively, older licences may be accompanied by an International Driving Permit (IDP).

Fines

On-the-spot fines can be imposed. Fines for speeding offences are particularly heavy. The police can impose the fine and collect one quarter of the maximum fine; they must give a receipt for the amount paid. Fines for serious offences committed at night between 10pm and 7am are increased by one third; serious offences include speeding, going through a red light etc. Illegally parked vehicles can be clamped or towed away and a fine imposed.

Fuel

Unleaded petrol (95 octane and 98 octane), diesel *(gasolio)* and LPG are available. Leaded petrol is not available, but you can buy a lead-substitute additive. Carrying petrol in a can is permitted. Credit cards are accepted at most filling stations. Check with your card issuer for usage in Italy and San Marino before travel.

Lights

The use of dipped headlights during the day is compulsory outside built-up areas and during snow and rain or poor visibility. Rear fog lights may be used only when visibility is less than 50m or in case of strong rain or intense snow. Lights must be switched on in tunnels.

Motorcycles

The use of dipped headlights during the day is compulsory on all roads. The wearing of crash helmets is compulsory for both driver and passenger. The vehicle can be seized for non-compliance. It is prohibited to carry a child under four years of age on a moped or motorcycle. The registration certificate must state that the moped/motorcycle is designed to carry a passenger. Motorcycles under 150cc are not allowed on motorways.

Motor insurance

Third-party insurance is compulsory.

Motorways

See map, page 98. To join a motorway, follow the green signposts (vehicles that cannot exceed 40kmh/25mph and motorcycles under 150cc are prohibited). On the majority of toll motorways a ticket is issued on entry (do not enter in the yellow TELEPASS lanes) and the toll is paid on leaving the motorway. The entry ticket gives information about the toll charges, including the toll category of the vehicle. At the exit use either the white or blue lanes, return your ticket and pay. Blue lanes are self service and take credit cards or Viacard. White lanes are self service and take cash, credit cards or Viacard. White lanes with operators take cash, credit cards and pre-paid Viacard. Toll booths will not exchange traveller's cheques. If paying with cash ensure you have sufficient euros to meet the high toll charges. Credit cards are accepted at the majority of toll booths. Visit **www. autostrade.it** for further information.

It is usually possible to obtain services for a car and/or occupants every 30–50km (19–31 miles). Emergency telephones are sited every 2km (1.24 miles) on most motorways.

Passengers/children in cars

Children under 1.5m (4ft 11in) have to use a UNECE-approved child-restraint system. Rear-facing child restraints must not be used in a passenger seat equipped with an active passenger air bag.

Seat belts

It is compulsory for front- and rear-seat occupants to wear seat belts, if fitted.

Speed limits

The standard legal limits, which may be varied by signs, for **private vehicles without trailers** are: in built-up areas 50km/h (31mph), outside built-up areas 90km/h (55mph) on ordinary roads, 110km/h (68mph) on dual carriageways and 130km/h (80mph) on motorways.

Note: in wet weather lower speed limits of 90km/h (55mph) apply on dual carriageways and 110km/h (68mph) on motorways. Restrictions apply if vehicles have spiked tyres.

Additional information

- A warning triangle is compulsory for all vehicles with more than two wheels.
- The wearing of a reflective jacket/waistcoat is compulsory if the driver and/or passenger(s) exits a vehicle that is immobilised on the carriageway at night or in poor visibility. This does not apply to two-wheeled vehicles.
- Vehicles must be equipped with winter tyres or snow chains from 15 October until 15 April. Provinces can introduce their own legislation making the use of winter tyres or snow chains compulsory during winter conditions.
- It is recommended that visitors equip their vehicles with a set of replacement bulbs.
- Any vehicle with an overhanging load must display a **fully** reflectorised square panel 50cm x 50cm (20in x 20in) that is red and white diagonally striped; a fine may be imposed if the sign is not displayed. This also applies to vehicles such as cars/caravans carrying bicycles at the rear.
- Tolls are levied on the majority of motorways. See pages 99–100.
- In built-up areas the use of the horn is prohibited except in cases of immediate danger.
- The transportation or use of radar detectors is prohibited; violation of this regulation will result in a fine between of €708 and €2,834 and confiscation of the device.
- An experimental pollution charge is levied in the centre of Milan. Charges apply Monday

to Friday generally from 7.30am until 7.30pm. Drivers must purchase an eco-pass before entering the restricted zone. Tariffs vary according to the emissions of the vehicle. Full information can be found on **www.comune. milano.it/dseserver/ecopass/richiedere. html** (available only in Italian).

- Traffic is restricted in many historical centres/major towns known as *'Zone a Traffico Limitato'* or ZTLs; circulation is permitted only for residents. Entering such areas normally results in a fine by post.
- Either winter tyres or snow chains may be used on roads where chains are compulsory.

Toll charges in euros

Road	Car	Car towing caravan/ trailer	Road	Car	Car towing caravan/ trailer
E25 (A26)			**E45/E55 (A14)**		
Genova – Alessandria	4.30	5.50	Bologna – Taranto	42.50	54.90
Genova – Iselle			**E55 (A14)**		
(Swiss border)	12.50	16.00	Ancona – Pescara	8.70	11.20
E25 (A5)			Pescara – Bari	17.80	23.00
Santhià – Aosta	11.30	17.00	**E55 (A14)**		
E33 (A15)			Pescara – Taranto	21.60	23.20
Parma – La Spezia	10.90	15.20	**E55 (A23)**		
E35 (A1)			Udine – Tarvisio		
Milano – Bologna	12.00	15.50	(Austrian border)	6.00	7.70
Bologna – Firenze	6.50	8.30	**E62 (A7)**		
Firenze – Roma	14.60	18.80	Milano – Tortona	3.60	4.70
E35 (A8/A9)			Milano – Genova	8.00	9.80
Milano – Chiasso			**E62 (A8)**		
(Swiss border)	3.20	4.10	Milano – Varese	2.60	3.40
E35/E45 (A1)			**E64 (A4)**		
Milano – Napoli	45.10	58.30	Torino – Milano	9.60	12.10
E45 (A1)			Milano – Bréscia	5.60	7.10
Roma – Napoli	11.60	15.00	**E64/E70 (A4)**		
E45 (A3)			Milano – Venézia	15.70	20.40
Nápoli – Salerno	1.60	3.50	**E70 (A4)**		
E45/A14 Dir			Bréscia – Verona	2.90	3.80
Bologna – Ravenna	4.10	5.30	Verona – Padova	3.70	4.90
E45 (A18)			Padova – Venézia	2.70	3.60
Messina – Catania	Free	14.80	**E70 (A4)**		
E45 (A22)			Venézia – Trieste	7.00	9.20
Passo del Brennero			**E70 (A21)**		
– Trento	8.00	10.30	Torino – Alessandria	5.90	7.70
Trento – Verona	5.50	7.10	Alessandria – Piacenza	4.90	6.40
Verona – Modena	5.30	6.90	Torino – Piacenza	11.30	14.80
E45/E55 (A14)			Piacenza – Brescia	3.80	5.00
Bologna – Ancona	11.40	14.70			

Toll charges in euros *continued*

Road	Car	Car towing caravan/ trailer
E70 (A32)		
Torino – Tunnel del Fréjus (France)	9.80	17.60
E76 (A11)		
Firenze – Pisa	5.90	7.80
E80 (A10)		
Genova – Savona	2.40	3.00
Savona – Ventimiglia (French border)	11.50	21.70
E80 (A12)		
Genova – La Spezia	9.20	12.40
La Spezia – Livorno	6.60	9.30
Genova – Viareggio	11.40	15.60
Genova – Livorno	14.00	19.30
Livorno – Roma	8.30	11.00
E80 (A24)		
Roma – Téramo	12.40	14.80
E80 (A25)		
Roma – Pescara	13.60	17.40
E90 (A20)		
Messina – Palermo	10.40	30.60
E612/E25 (A5)		
Torino – Aosta	12.90	19.30
E717 (A6)		
Torino – Savona	10.40	14.70
E842 (A16)		
Napoli – Bari	15.70	20.20
E843 (A14)		
Bari – Táranto	3.80	5.00
A13 Bologna – Padova	5.60	7.20
Bologna – Ferrara	1.90	2.40
Ferrara – Padova	4.50	5.80

Road		Car	Car towing caravan/ trailer
A22	Passo del Brennero – Modena	18.80	24.20
A27	Venezia – Belluno	6.60	8.40
A30	Caserta – Salerno	3.30	4.30
A31	Vicenza – Trento	1.50	2.00

Bridges and Tunnels		Car	Car towing caravan/ trailer
E25	Tunnel Monte Bianco	35.10	46.40
E70	Tunnel dél Fréjus	35.10	46.40
	Tunnel Munt La Schera	10.00	20.00
	Tunnel du Grand-St-Bernard	23.60	36.50

General

For information on the Milan eco-pass see pages 96–97.

Travel facts: Italy and San Marino

Italian State Tourist Board
1 Princes Street
London W1B 2AY
Tel: 020 7408 1254
www.enit.it

Banking hours
Banks are generally open Monday to Friday 8.30am
to 1.30pm. Major banks may open Saturday and have
longer weekday opening hours.

Credit/debit cards
All major credit cards are widely accepted in Italy.
Check with your provider. Traveller's cheques can be
exchanged at most hotels and shops and at the foreign
exchange offices *(cambio)* in main railway stations and
at the airports.

Currency
The currency in Italy is the euro (€). Euro coins are
issued in denominations of 1, 2, 5, 10, 20 and 50 cents
and €1 and €2. Banknotes are issued in denominations
of €5, €10, €20, €50, €100, €200 and €500.

Electricity
The power supply is 220 volts AC, 50Hz. Plugs are two-
round-pin continental types; UK visitors will require
an adaptor.

Health care
Free or reduced-cost medical treatment is available
in Italy to European visitors on production of a valid
European Health Insurance Card (EHIC). See page 10.
Comprehensive travel insurance is still advised and is
essential for all other visitors.

Pharmacies
Prescription and other medicines are available from a
pharmacy *(una farmacia)*, indicated by a green cross.
Pharmacies usually open at the same time as shops
Tuesday to Saturday 8am to 1pm and 4pm to 8pm,
Monday 4pm to 8pm, and take it in turns to stay open
through the afternoon and into late evening.

Post offices
Post offices *(posta)* are usually open Monday to Friday
8.30am to 2pm, Saturday 8.30am to noon or 2pm. Post
boxes are red for normal post and blue for priority post
(posta prioritaria). Stamps *(francobolli)* can be bought
from post offices, bars, and tobacconists showing
a 'T' sign.

Safe water
Tap water is safe. So, too, is water from public drinking
fountains unless marked '*Acqua Non Potabile*'.

Telephones
Telecom Italia (TI) pay phones are on streets and in
bars, tobacconists and restaurants. Most take coins
or a phone card *(carta telefonica)*, bought from post
offices, shops or bars. Tear the corner off the card
before use. When calling within Italy, simply dial the
full number. Rome numbers all begin with 06. Dial 12 for
operator or directory enquiries. The country code for
Italy is 39. To call home from Italy dial the international
code (00) followed by the country code. To call the UK
from Italy dial 00 44.

Time
Italy is on Central European Time, one hour ahead of
Greenwich Mean Time (GMT +1). From late March,
when clocks are put forward one hour, until late
October, Daylight Saving Time (GMT + 2) operates.

Emergency telephone numbers
General emergencies **113** or **112**
Police **113** or **112**
Fire **115** or **112**
Ambulance **118** or **112**

Driving in Latvia *(Eastern Europe)*

The regulations below should be read in conjunction with the General motoring information on pages 18–21.

Drinking and driving

The maximum permitted level of alcohol in the bloodstream for drivers with more than two years' experience is 0.05 per cent. For drivers with less than two years' experience the maximum permitted level of alcohol in the bloodstream is 0.02 per cent. Penalties are severe if the levels are exceeded.

Driving licence

The minimum age at which a UK licence holder may drive a temporarily imported car and/or motorcycle (over 125cc) is 18.

Fines

The police can issue but not collect fines on the spot; the fines have to be paid or an appeal lodged within 30 days. Police control speeds closely and give fines for even the smallest of speeding offences.

Fuel

Unleaded petrol (95 and 98 octane), diesel and LPG are available. There is no leaded petrol, but petrol with lead substitute is available. Carrying petrol in a can is permitted (duty payable). Visa and MasterCard are accepted at most filling stations; check with your card issuer for usage in Latvia before travel. Cash payments are accepted only in the local currency.

Lights

The use of dipped headlights during the day is compulsory.

Motorcycles

The use of dipped headlights during the day is compulsory. The wearing of crash helmets is compulsory for both driver and passenger.

Motor insurance

Third-party insurance is compulsory.

Passengers/children in cars

A child less than 1.5m (4ft 11in) in height must use either a child-restraint system appropriate to height and weight or the lap strap of an adult seat belt.

Seat belts

It is compulsory for front- and rear-seat occupants to wear seat belts, if fitted.

Speed limits

The standard legal limits, which may be varied by signs, for **private vehicles without trailers** are: in built-up areas 50km/h (31mph), outside built-up areas 90km/h (55mph), dual carriageways 110km/h (68mph). When **towing a trailer or caravan**, the limit outside built-up areas and on dual carriageways is 80km/h (49mph). There are no motorways in Latvia. In some residential areas the speed limit is 20km/h (12mph).

Additional information

- A first-aid kit, fire extinguisher and warning triangle are compulsory for vehicles up to 3.5 tonnes. Winter tyres are compulsory from 1 December until 1 March.

- Spiked tyres are prohibited from 1 May until 1 October.
- It is recommended that visitors carry an assortment of spares for their vehicle, such as a fan belt, replacement bulbs and spark plugs.
- Latvia has very little signposting and very few road markings.
- The use of equipment that interferes with police equipment is prohibited.

Travel facts: Latvia

Latvia Tourism Bureaux
72 Queensborough Terrace
London W2 3SH
Tel: 020 7229 8271
www.latviatourism.lv
www.latviatravel.com

Banking hours
Banks and their retail branches are usually open
Monday to Friday 9am to 5 or 6pm; branches at
supermarkets close at 8 or 9pm on weekdays. Some
banks open 9am to 1pm on Saturday.

Credit/debit cards
Many transactions in Latvia are still dealt with in cash.
The most commonly used credit cards accepted in
Latvian hotels, larger shops, restaurants, cafés and
supermarkets are Eurocard, MasterCard, Visa, JCB,
Diners Club, American Express and Eurocheque. ATMs
can be found in cities and towns.

Currency
The Latvian national currency is the lat (LVL),
1 lat = 100 santimi. Bank notes are in denominations of
LVL500, 100, 50, 20, 10 and 5. Coins are in denominations
of LVL2 and 1, and 50, 20, 10, 5, 2 and 1 santimi.

Electricity
The electrical supply in Latvia is 220 volts AC, 50Hz.
Sockets take two-round-pin plugs.

Health care
Free or reduced-cost medical treatment is available
in Latvia to European visitors on production of a valid
European Health Insurance Card (EHIC). See page 10.
Comprehensive travel insurance is still advised and is
essential for all other visitors.

Pharmacies
There is an extensive network of pharmacies
throughout Latvia; some are at hospitals and health
centres, shopping malls, stations etc. Opening hours
vary; 24-hour pharmacies are denoted with the letter 'A'.

Post offices
Opening hours at post offices *(Pasts)* are Monday
to Friday 8am to 5 or 7pm and 8am to 4pm on
Saturday. Opening hours for sub-post offices in
small villages vary.

Safe water
Drinking water in major towns is generally safe, though
you may prefer to buy bottled mineral water.

Telephones
Public phone boxes can be found on the streets and in
train and bus stations, shopping malls etc., and contain
information about how to make calls within Latvia,
international country codes and local telephone books.
Public pay phones accept phone cards, credit cards or
coins. Phone cards are available from kiosks, shops,
post offices and petrol stations where the Lattelekom
sign is displayed. The country code for Latvia is 371.
To call home from Latvia dial the international code (00)
followed by the country code. To call the UK from Latvia
dial 00 44.

Time
Latvia is on Eastern European Time. It's two hours
ahead of Greenwich Mean Time (GMT + 2), but from late
March, when clocks are put forward one hour, to late
October, Summer Time (GMT + 3) operates.

Emergency telephone numbers
Police **02** or **112**
Fire **01** or **112**
Ambulance **03** or **112**

Driving in Lithuania *(Eastern Europe)*

The regulations below should be read in conjunction with the General motoring information on pages 18–21.

Drinking and driving

If the level of alcohol in the bloodstream is 0.04 per cent or more, severe penalties include a fine and/or withdrawal of your driving licence for up to 1.5 years.

Driving licence

The minimum age at which a UK licence holder may drive a temporarily imported car and/ or motorcycle is 18. UK licences that do not incorporate a photograph must be accompanied by photographic proof of identity e.g. a passport.

Fines

On-the-spot fines can be imposed (some fines may be paid at a local bank depending on the amount/traffic violation). Wheel clamps are in use.

Fuel

Leaded petrol is sold at Statoil petrol stations. Unleaded petrol (95 and 98 octane), diesel and LPG are available. Carrying petrol in a can is permitted (duty payable). Credit cards are accepted at filling stations; check with your card issuer for usage in Lithuania before travel.

Lights

The use of dipped headlights during the day is compulsory; there is a fine for non-compliance.

Motorcycles

The use of dipped headlights during the day is compulsory; a fine can be imposed for non-

compliance. The wearing of crash helmets is compulsory for both driver and passenger. A child under 12 cannot travel as a passenger.

Motor insurance

Third-party insurance is compulsory, but fully comprehensive insurance is recommended.

Passengers/children in cars

A child under 12 or under 1.5m (4ft 11in) cannot travel as a front-seat passenger unless using a child restraint appropriate to their age and size. Children under three years must be seated in a child seat appropriate to their age and size on the rear seats.

Seat belts

It is compulsory for front- and rear-seat occupants to wear seat belts, if fitted.

Speed limits

The standard legal limits, which may be varied by signs, for **private vehicles without trailers** are: in built-up areas 50km/h (31mph), other roads 70km/h (43mph), outside built-up areas 90km/h (55mph). On dual carriageways from 1 October to 30 March 100km/h (62mph) and from 1 April to 30 September a limit of 110km/h (68mph) applies. On motorways from 1 October to 30 March 110km/h (68mph) and from 1 April to 30 September a limit of 130km/h (80mph) applies between (i) Vilnius–Panevezys and (ii) Kaunas–Klaipeda. When **towing a trailer or caravan** with a combined weight less than 3.5 tonnes, the limit on all roads outside built-up areas, including motorways, is 90km/h (55mph) year-round. The police control speeds closely and give fines for even the smallest of speeding offences.

Additional information

- A first-aid kit, fire extinguisher and a warning triangle are compulsory.
- A reflective jacket must be worn by the driver exiting a vehicle at night in a breakdown situation. Therefore the jacket/waistcoat must be kept within the passenger compartment of the vehicle.
- Winter tyres are compulsory between 1 November and 1 April. Spiked tyres may also be used during this period.
- It is recommended that visitors carry an assortment of spares for their vehicle, for example, a fan belt, replacement bulbs and spark plugs.
- It is compulsory to call the police to the scene of an accident.

Travel facts: Lithuania

Lithuanian National Tourism Office
86 Gloucester Place
London W1U 6HP
(Not open to the public)
Tel: 020 7034 1222
www.lithuaniatourism.co.uk

Banking hours
Banks are generally open Monday to Friday 9am to 5pm; some banks also open Saturday 9am to 1pm. Currency can be exchanged at banks and bureaux de change. There are ATMs in most cities.

Credit/debit cards
Most major credit and debit cards are accepted in the main hotels, restaurants, shops and in some petrol stations. Check with your credit and debit card company for usage in Lithuania before you travel.

Currency
The official currency of the country is the Lithuania litas (LTL) which is divided into 100 centas. Banknotes come in denominations of LTL500, 200, 100, 50, 20, 10, 5, 2 and 1. Coins are in denominations of LTL5, 2 and 1, and the 50, 20, 10, 5, 2 and 1 centas. The litas is pegged to the euro. Cash payments will be accepted only in litas; however many shopping centres and other service outlets take credit cards.

Electricity
The electricity supply is 220 volts AC, 50Hz. European two-pin plugs are in use.

Health care
Free or reduced-cost medical treatment is available in Lithuania to European visitors on production of a valid European Health Insurance Card (EHIC). See page 10. Comprehensive travel insurance is still advised and is essential for all other visitors.

Pharmacies
Pharmacies in major cities will generally have regular prescription drugs readily available; there is usually at least one that is open 24 hours a day.

Post offices
In major towns, post offices *(pastas)* are open Monday to Friday 8am to 6pm, Saturday 8am to 3pm. Post boxes are yellow.

Safe water
It is advisable to drink bottled or filtered water.

Telephones
All public phones in Lithuania require telephone cards, which are available from the Central Post Office and kiosks. The cards are valid all over Lithuania. The country code for Lithuania is 370. To call home from Lithuania dial the international code (00) followed by the country code. To call the UK from Lithuania dial 00 44.

Time
Lithuania is on Eastern European Time. It's two hours ahead of Greenwich Mean Time (GMT + 2), but from late March, when clocks are put forward one hour, to late October, Summer Time (GMT + 3) operates.

Emergency telephone numbers
Police **02** or **112**
Fire **01** or **112**
Ambulance **03** or **112**

Driving in Luxembourg *(Western Europe)*

The regulations below should be read in conjunction with the General motoring information on pages 18–21.

Drinking and driving

If the level of alcohol in the bloodstream is 0.05 per cent or more, severe penalties can include fines and/or prison. The blood alcohol level for a young driver is 0.019 per cent.

Driving licence

The minimum age at which a UK licence holder may drive a temporarily imported car and/or motorcycle 18.

Fines

On-the-spot fines can be imposed. Unauthorised and dangerous parking can result in the car being impounded or removed.

Fuel

Unleaded petrol (95 and 98 octane) is available, along with diesel and LPG. It is forbidden to carry petrol in a can. Credit cards are accepted at filling stations, but check with your card issuer for usage in Luxembourg before you travel.

Lights

Side lights are required when parking where there is no public lighting. When visibility is below 100m (110 yards) due to fog, snow, heavy rain etc., dipped headlights must be used. It is compulsory to flash your headlights at night when overtaking outside built-up areas. In tunnels indicated by a sign, drivers must use their passing lights.

Motorcycles

The use of dipped headlights during the day is compulsory. The wearing of crash helmets is also compulsory for both driver and passenger. A child under 12 is not permitted to ride as a passenger.

Motor insurance

Third-party insurance is compulsory.

Passengers/children in cars

Children under three years of age must be seated in an approved restraint system. Children aged three to 18 years and/or under 1.5m (4ft 11in) must be seated in an appropriate restraint system. If they weigh over 36kg a seat belt can be used, but only on the rear seat of the vehicle. Rear-facing child-restraint systems are prohibited on seats with frontal air bags unless the air bag is deactivated.

Seat belts

It is compulsory for front- and rear-seat occupants to wear seat belts, if fitted.

Speed limits

The standard legal limits, which may be varied by signs, for **private vehicles without trailers** are: in built-up areas 50km/h (31mph), outside built-up areas 90km/h (55mph) and motorways 130km/h (80mph) except in rain or snow when the limit is 110km/h (68mph). When **towing a trailer or caravan** the limits are 75km/h (46mph) outside built-up areas and 90km/h

(55mph) on motorways. The speed limit for vehicles with spiked tyres is 70km/h (43mph).

Additional information

- It is compulsory for the driver and passengers to wear a reflective waistcoat when exiting a vehicle in a breakdown situation on a motorway or outside built-up areas, at night and in bad visibility.
- A warning triangle is compulsory for all vehicles with four or more wheels.
- All tyres on a car must be of the same type: either winter tyres (marked M&S on the sidewall) or summer tyres.
- The use of spiked tyres is permitted from 1 December until 31 March.
- Use of snow chains permitted, in case of snow or ice.
- Any vehicle immobilised on the motorway must use warning signals, a warning triangle and a flashing light at the rear.
- In built-up areas the use of the horn is prohibited except in case of immediate danger.

Travel facts: Luxembourg

Luxembourg Tourist Office
Sicilian House
Sicilian Avenue
London WC1A 2QR
Tel: 020 7434 2800
www.luxembourg.co.uk

Banking hours
Banks generally open from Monday to Friday 8.30am to 12 noon and 1.30pm to 4.30pm. Some banks open over lunch, and some stay open until 6pm. Some ATMs (e.g. near the Grand Ducal Palace) are open 24 hours.

Credit/debit cards
The use of credit/debit cards is becoming ever more common, but many retailers require a minimum sales amount before accepting them. American Express, Diners Club, MasterCard, Visa and others are all accepted, as well as Eurocheque cards.

Currency
The currency in Luxembourg is the euro (€). Euro coins are issued in denominations of 1, 2, 5, 10, 20 and 50 cents and €1 and €2. Banknotes are issued in denominations of €5, €10, €20, €50, €100, €200 and €500.

Electricity
The power supply in Luxembourg is 220 volts AC, 50Hz. Sockets accept two-round-pin plugs, so an adaptor is needed for most non-continental appliances.

Health care
Free or reduced-cost medical treatment is available in Luxembourg to European visitors on production of a valid European Health Insurance Card (EHIC). See page 10. Comprehensive travel insurance is still advised and is essential for all other visitors.

Pharmacies
Prescription medicines and advice can be obtained from a pharmacy *(pharmacie)* identified by a green cross. Information about the nearest 24-hour facility is posted at all pharmacies.

Post offices
Post offices are open Monday to Friday 9am to 12 noon, and 4.30 or 5pm. The Luxembourg-Ville main office (opposite the railway station) is open Monday to Friday 7am to 7pm, Saturday 6am to 12 noon. Smaller offices may open for only a few hours.

Safe water
Tap water is considered safe to drink and bottled mineral water *(eau minérale)* is widely available.

Telephones
Public telephones are found in most post offices, supermarkets, train or bus stations and close to major public buildings. Phone cards are available from post offices and most newsagents. Most coin-operated public phones have been phased out. The country code for Luxembourg is 352. To call home from Luxembourg dial the international code (00) followed by the country code. To call the UK from Luxembourg dial 00 44.

Time
Luxembourg is on Central European Time, one hour ahead of Greenwich Mean Time (GMT + 1). From late March, when clocks are put forward one hour, until late October, Daylight Saving Time (GMT + 2) operates.

Emergency telephone numbers
General emergencies **112**
Police **112** or **113**
Fire **112**
Ambulance **112**

Driving in Macedonia (Former Yugoslav Republic of Macedonia)

(South East Europe)

The regulations below should be read in conjunction with the General motoring information on pages 18–21.

Drinking and driving
If the level of alcohol in the bloodstream is 0.05 per cent or more, severe penalties, including a fine, imprisonment and/or suspension of driving licence, can be imposed. The limit is 0 per cent for newly qualified drivers.

Driving licence
The minimum age at which a UK licence holder may drive a temporarily imported car and/or motorcycle (exceeding 125cc) is 18.

Fines
On-the-spot fines can be imposed by the police. An official receipt should be obtained. The police can impound a vehicle that is wrongly parked and can detain a vehicle with worn tyres.

Fuel
Unleaded petrol (95 and 98 octane), diesel, Euro diesel and LPG are available. Carrying petrol in a can is permitted. Credit cards are accepted at some filling stations; check with your card issuer for usage in Macedonia before travel. Usually payment can be made only in the local currency.

Lights
The use of dipped headlights during the day is compulsory. Police can impose an on-the-spot fine for non-compliance.

Motorcycles
The use of dipped headlights during the day is compulsory. The wearing of crash helmets is also compulsory for both driver and passenger.

Motor insurance
Third-party insurance is compulsory; a Green Card is recognised.

Passengers/children in cars
A child under 12 is not permitted to travel in the front seat of a vehicle.

Seat belts
It is compulsory for front- and rear-seat occupants to wear seat belts, if fitted.

Speed limits
The standard legal limits, which may be varied by signs, for **private vehicles without trailers** are: in built-up areas 50km/h (31mph), outside built-up areas 80km/h (49mph) but 100km/h (62mph) on dual carriageways and 120km/h (74mph) on motorways. The limit when **towing** is 80km/h (49mph) on all roads outside built-up areas. Special speed limits apply to **newly qualified drivers, for private vehicles without trailers**: outside built up areas 60km/h (37mph), but 80km/h (49mph) on dual carriageways and 100 km/h (62mph) on motorways.

Macedonia

Additional information

- It is compulsory for visitors to equip their vehicle with a set of replacement bulbs (this does not apply if the vehicle is fitted with xenon, neon or LED lights), a first-aid kit and a 2kg ABC powder fire extinguisher. A warning triangle is compulsory; two triangles are required if towing a trailer. A warning triangle is not required for two-wheeled vehicles.
- It is compulsory to carry a reflective jacket, which must be kept within the vehicle (i.e. not in the boot) and worn by the driver before exiting the vehicle in the dark outside of towns and on motorways. It must be compliant with EN471.
- Snow chains must be carried to be used with all-year tyres from 15 November to 15 March, or winter tyres must be fitted on all wheels. Snow tyres must have a tread depth of 4mm.
- A person visibly under the influence of alcohol is not permitted to travel in a vehicle as a front-seat passenger.
- The authorities at the frontier must certify any visible damage to a vehicle entering Macedonia and a certificate obtained; this must be produced when leaving. A certificate must also be obtained if damage occurs while in Macedonia.
- Spiked tyres are prohibited.
- A GPS-based navigation system with maps indicating the location of fixed speed cameras must have the 'fixed speed camera POI (Points of Interest)' function deactivated.
- The use of radar detectors is prohibited.

Travel facts: Republic of Macedonia

Embassy of the Republic of Macedonia
Suite 2.1/2.2 Buckingham Court
75/83 Buckingham Gate
London SW1E 6PE
Tel: 020 7976 0535
www.exploringmacedonia.com

Banking hours
Banks are generally open Monday to Friday 8am to 7pm, Saturday 8am to noon or 1pm. Banks at airports, railway and bus stations are open longer hours. Money should be exchanged in official exchange offices (banks, post offices, hotels, tourist agencies) according to current exchange rates. When leaving Macedonia visitors can exchange MKDs back into foreign currency (at official places) only after presenting the evidence of exchange for denars when entering the country.

Credit/debit cards
Some major credit cards (Diners, American Express, Visa and MasterCard/EuroCard) and Eurocheques can be used for payment wherever a notice is displayed in hotels, shops, and restaurants, but acceptance throughout the country is limited. Check with your credit card provider. Credit card fraud is widespread in Macedonia so take care when making a purchase using this method. ATMs are widely available in Skopje, less so in other main towns, although the number is increasing, making the withdrawal of local currency much easier. Cash is the common form of payment.

Currency
The local currency is the Macedonian denar (MKD) which is divided into 100 deni. Banknotes come in denominations of Den5,000, 1,000, 500, 100, 50 and 10. Coins are in denominations of Den5, 2 and 1, and 50 deni. Euros are the easiest currency to exchange.
Note: You must declare all foreign currency on arrival.

Electricity
The electrical current is 220 volts AC, 50Hz.
Plugs have two round pins.

Health care
The UK has a reciprocal health-care agreement with Macedonia. If you're visiting Macedonia and need urgent or immediate medical treatment it will be provided at a reduced cost or, in some cases, free. The range of medical services available may be more restricted than under the NHS, therefore it is essential for all visitors to have comprehensive travel insurance. Visit **www.nhs.uk/NHSEngland/Healthcareabroad** for a country-by-country guide.

Pharmacies
You'll find a pharmacy in all bigger towns; service is good and prices moderate.

Post offices
Post offices are generally open Monday to Friday 7am to 7pm, Saturday 7am to 1pm.

Safe water
Mains water is normally chlorinated. Bottled mineral water is available. In rural areas it is recommended that all drinking water is boiled or you buy bottled water.

Telephones
All public telephones in Macedonia are card-operated and have instructions in English. Post offices have telephones where you pay in cash after you finish your call. Telephone cards worth Den150, 250 and 500 are for sale at post offices and kiosks. The country code for Macedonia is 389. To call home from Macedonia dial the international code (00) followed by the country code. To call the UK from Macedonia dial 00 44.

Time
Macedonia is on Central European Time, one hour ahead of GMT (GMT + 1). Daylight Savings Time comes into effect from end March to end October (GMT + 2).

Emergency telephone numbers
Police **192**
Fire **193**
Ambulance **194**
Road assistance **987**

Driving in Malta *(Mediterranean)*

The regulations below should be read in conjunction with the General motoring information on pages 18–21.

Drinking and driving

If the level of alcohol in the bloodstream is 0.08 per cent or more, severe penalties can be imposed, including a fine or imprisonment.

Driving licence

The minimum age at which a UK licence holder may drive a temporarily imported car and/or motorcycle is 18.

Fines

There are no on-the-spot fines, but if a fineable motoring or parking offence is committed, this may be settled prior to departure.

Fuel

Unleaded petrol (95 octane), lead replacement petrol 98 octane and diesel are available but not LPG. Carrying petrol in a can is permitted; however, it is forbidden aboard ferries and Eurotunnel. Credit cards are generally not accepted at filling stations; check with your card issuer for usage in Malta before travel.

Lights

Spot lights are prohibited. Lights should be switched on while travelling through tunnels.

Motorcycles

Helmets are compulsory for driver and passenger.

Motor insurance

Third-party insurance is compulsory; Green Cards are accepted.

Passengers/children in cars

Children under three cannot travel as front- or rear-seat passengers unless using a suitable restraint system. Children between three and 10 or under 1.5m (4ft 11in) in height travelling in front or rear seats must use a restraint system as appropriate, or an adult seat belt if a restraint system is unavailable.

Seat belts

It is compulsory for front- and rear-seat occupants to wear seat belts, if fitted.

Speed limits

The standard legal limits, which may be varied by signs, for **private vehicles with and without trailers** (under 3.5 tonnes combined weight) are: in built-up areas 50km/h (31mph), outside built-up areas 80km/h (49mph).

Additional information

- It is compulsory to carry a warning triangle.
- The rule of the road is drive on the left, overtake on the right.
- The use of the horn is prohibited in inhabited areas between 11pm and 6am.
- Parking in Valetta is extremely limited and there is a charge to enter the city.
- There is a park and ride system located on the outskirts of the city offering a free shuttle to the centre.
- Cars involved in a bumper-to-bumper accident need to contact the local warden service.

Travel facts: Malta

Malta Tourist Office
Unit C, Park House
14 Northfields
London SW18 1DD
Tel: 020 7292 4900
www.visitmalta.com
www.gozo.com
www.malta.com

Banking hours
Banks are normally open 8.30am to 12.30pm Monday to Friday and on Saturday up to 11.30am. Some banks work longer hours. Summer and winter opening hours may differ.

Credit/debit cards
Credit cards are accepted in the resorts and ATMs are common. In rural areas it's best to carry cash. Some filling stations, even in built-up areas, accept only cash. Traveller's cheques in sterling are widely accepted. Some establishments, typically those run by ex-pats and with strong links to the UK, will also accept sterling currency, though you may pay a slight premium.

Currency
The currency of Malta is the euro (€). Coins come in denominations of 1, 2, 5, 10, 20 and 50 cents, and €1 and €2. Notes come in denominations of €5, €10, €20, €50, €100, €200 and €500.

Electricity
The power supply is 240 volts AC, 50Hz. Sockets are the three-square-hole type taking square plugs with three square pins. Visitors from continental Europe should bring an adaptor.

Health care
Free or reduced-cost medical treatment is available in Malta to European visitors on production of a valid European Health Insurance Card (EHIC). See page 10. Comprehensive travel insurance is still advised and is essential for all other visitors.

Pharmacies
Pharmacies, usually known as chemists, are recognisable by a neon green cross sign. They sell most international drugs and medicines over the counter or by prescription. They open during normal shop hours, with a Sunday duty roster.

Post offices
Post office opening hours are Monday to Saturday 7.45am to 12.45pm. Closed Sunday. The post office at Castille Place, Valletta **(tel: 21 226224)** is open Monday to Friday 7.30am to 6pm, Saturday 8.15am to 12.30pm. On Gozo the post office at 129 Republic Street, Victoria **(tel: 21 556435)** is open later.

Safe water
Tap water is quite safe, although not very tasty. Water from fountains should be avoided as it may not come directly from the mains supply. Bottled 'table' water is widely available, at a reasonable cost, along with imported mineral water.

Telephones
Malta's public telephone boxes are either green, red or transparent booths. Few phones accept coins, most take a phone card *(telecard)* available for €5 and €10 from most newsagents, post offices and shops. The country code for Malta is 356. To call home from Malta dial the international code (00) followed by the country code. To call the UK from Malta dial 00 44.

Time
Malta is one hour ahead of Greenwich Mean Time (GMT + 1), but from late March, when clocks are put forward one hour, to late October, Summer Time (GMT + 2) operates.

Emergency telephone number
Police, Fire and Ambulance **112**

Driving in Montenegro *(South East Europe)*

The regulations below should be read in conjunction
with the General motoring information on pages 18–21.

Drinking and driving

If the level of alcohol in the bloodstream is 0.05
per cent or more or if a medical examination
shows that normal bodily functions are impaired,
severe penalties can be imposed including a
fine, imprisonment and/or suspension of the
driving licence.

Driving licence

The minimum age at which a UK licence
holder may drive a temporarily imported car
and/or motorcycle (exceeding 125cc) is 18.
We recommend that you obtain an International
Driving Permit to accompany your UK
driving licence.

Fines

Officials can issue an on-the-spot fine notice,
but cannot collect the payment. Fines vary
according to the gravity of the offence. Penalties
are higher if the motorist endangers other
people or causes an accident.

Fuel

Unleaded petrol (95 and 98 octane) and diesel
(dizel) are available. You can carry a small
amount of petrol in a can. Credit cards are
generally accepted; check with your card issuer
for usage in Montenegro before travel.

Lights

Dipped headlights are compulsory at all times.

Motorcycles

The use of dipped headlights is compulsory
at all times. The wearing of crash helmets is
compulsory for both driver and passenger.

Motor insurance

Third-party insurance is compulsory; a Green
Card is recognised.

Passengers/children in cars

A person visibly under the influence of alcohol
or child under 12 is not permitted to travel in a
vehicle as a front-seat passenger.

Seat belts

It is compulsory for front- and rear-seat
occupants to wear seat belts, if fitted.

Speed limits

The standard legal limits, which may be varied
by signs, for **private vehicles without trailers**
are: in built-up areas 50km/h (31mph), outside
built-up areas 80km/h (49mph) and 100km/h
(62mph) on fast roads.

Additional information

- It is compulsory for visitors to equip their
  vehicle with a set of replacement bulbs, a
  first-aid kit and a warning triangle (excluding
  motorcycles); two triangles are required if
  towing a trailer.
- The authorities at the frontier must certify
  any visible damage to a vehicle entering
  Montenegro and a certificate obtained; this

must be produced when leaving, otherwise you may experience serious difficulties. Every car entering the territory of Montenegro will be subject to an ecological tax, approximately €10. The eco tax is to be paid at the border and drivers will get a sticker for their vehicle (valid for one year) as proof of payment.

- It is compulsory for accidents resulting in serious injury or material damage to be reported to the police.

- Spiked tyres are prohibited. In winter, snow chains may be necessary on some roads.
- Vehicles entering a roundabout have right of way.
- Horns must not be used in built-up areas or at night except in cases of imminent danger.
- School buses must not be overtaken or passed when they stop for children to board or alight.

Travel facts: Montenegro

Montenegrin Embassy
Trafalgar House 11
Waterloo Place
London SW1Y 4AU
Tel: 020 7863 8806
http://montenegro.embassyhomepage.com
www.visitmontenegro.org
www.montenegro.org.uk

Banking hours
Banks are generally open Monday to Friday
8am to 7pm, Saturday 8am to 1pm.

Credit/debit cards
The most widely accepted cards are Visa, MasterCard,
Maestro and Diners. American Express cards are not
accepted in Montenegro. ATMs increasingly accept
international bank cards.

Currency
Although not a member of the EU, the currency in
Montenegro is the euro (€). Euro coins are issued in
denominations of 1, 2, 5, 10, 20 and 50 cents and €1 and
€2. Banknotes are issued in denominations of €5, €10,
€20, €50, €100, €200 and €500.

Electricity
The power supply is 220 volts AC, 50Hz. Two-round-pin
plugs are used.

Health care
Comprehensive travel insurance is essential for
all visitors.

Pharmacies
Medicines and basic medical supplies are largely
available from private pharmacies. Prescribed
medicines must be paid for.

Post offices
Postal services within Montenegro are
reasonably good.

Safe water
During the holiday season water shortages can affect
quality and the locals will often stop taking ice in drinks.
To avoid stomach upsets, drink bottled mineral water
and avoid ice in drinks.

Telephones
Public telephones take pre-paid cards, which can be
bought in post offices, operators' outlets or tobacco
shops/newsagents. The country code for Montenegro
is 382. To call home from Montenegro dial the
international code (00) followed by the country code.
To call the UK from Montenegro dial 00 44.

Time
Montenegro is on Central European Time, one hour
ahead of Greenwich Mean Time (GMT + 1). From late
March, when clocks are put forward one hour, until late
October, Daylight Saving Time (GMT + 2) operates.

Emergency telephone numbers
Police **92** or **112**
Fire Department **93** or **112**
Ambulance **94** or **112**

Driving in the Netherlands

(Western Europe)

The regulations below should be read in conjunction with the General motoring information on pages 18–21.

Drinking and driving

If the level of alcohol in the bloodstream is over 0.05 per cent, severe penalties including a fine, withdrawal of driving licence and imprisonment can be imposed. The lower limit of 0.02 per cent applies to new drivers for the first five years and moped riders up to the age of 24.

Driving licence

The minimum age at which a UK licence holder may drive a temporarily imported car and/or motorcycle is 18.

Fines

On-the-spot fines can be imposed. In the case of illegal parking the police can impose on-the-spot fines or tow the vehicle away. Vehicles can be confiscated in cases of particularly excessive speed and drink driving.

Fuel

Unleaded petrol (95 and 98 octane), diesel and LPG *(Autogas)* are available. There is no leaded petrol (lead-substitute petrol is available as 'super' 98 octane). Carrying petrol in a can is permitted but forbidden aboard ferries and Eurotunnel. Credit cards are accepted at most filling stations; check with your card issuer for use before travel.

Lights

The use of dipped headlights during the day is recommended. At night it is prohibited to drive with only side lights.

Motorcycles

The use of dipped headlights during the day is recommended. The wearing of crash helmets is compulsory on all motorcycles that are capable of exceeding 25km/h (15mph); this also applies to drivers and passengers of open micro cars without seat belts.

Motor insurance

Third-party insurance is compulsory.

Passengers/children in cars

Children up to the age of 18 and less than 1.35m (4ft 5in) in height cannot travel as a front- or rear-seat passenger unless using a suitable restraint system adapted to their size. Suitable child-restraint systems must meet the safety approval of ECE 44/03 or 44/04. If the vehicle is not fitted with rear seat belts, children under three are not permitted to travel in the vehicle. Children under three are permitted to travel in the front seats if using a rear-facing child seat with the air bag deactivated (if fitted). If the vehicle's front seats are not fitted with seat belts, only passengers measuring 1.35m (4ft 5in) or more may travel in the front seat.

The Netherlands

Seat belts

It is compulsory for front- and rear-seat occupants to wear seat belts, if fitted.

Speed limits

The standard legal limits, which may be varied by signs, for **private vehicles with and without trailers** (under 3.5 tonnes combined weight) are: in built-up areas 50km/h (31mph), outside built-up areas 80km/h (49mph) or 100km/h (62mph) and motorways 120km/h (74mph). There is no minimum speed on motorways.

Additional information

- A warning triangle or hazard warning lights must be used in case of an accident or breakdown (it is recommended that a warning triangle is always carried).

- Buses have the right of way when leaving bus stops in built-up areas.
- Trams have right of way except when crossing a priority road.
- Beware of large numbers of cyclists and skaters.
- Spiked tyres are prohibited.
- The use of a radar detector is prohibited; if you are caught using such a device by the police the radar detector will be confiscated and you will be fined €250.
- Horns should not be used at night and in moderation during the day.
- Parking discs can be obtained from local stores.
- When towing, the cable between the tower and the towed vehicle may not exceed 5m in length.

Road signs (a selection of standard and non-standard)

Residential zone

Parking for permit holders only

Disc parking zone

Park and ride

Maximum speed limit

Built-up areas

Travel facts and toll charges: the Netherlands

Netherlands Board of Tourism
PO Box 30783
London WC2B 6DH
Tel: 020 7539 7950
www.holland.com/uk

Banking hours
Most banks are generally open Tuesday to Friday from 9am to 4 or 5pm. On Monday banks open at 1pm. Banks are closed Saturday and Sunday.

Credit/debit cards
The major credit cards are widely accepted, but if in doubt, ask in advance. ATMs for cash advances can be found outside banks in all the major towns.

Currency
The currency in the Netherlands is the euro (€). Euro coins are issued in denominations of 1, 2, 5, 10, 20 and 50 cents and €1 and €2. Banknotes are issued in denominations of €5, €10, €20, €50, €100, €200 and €500.

Electricity
The power supply in the Netherlands is 220 volts AC. Hotels may have a 110-volt or 120-volt outlet for shavers, but travellers are advised to bring a converter and an adapter for two-round-pin plugs.

Health care
Free or reduced-cost medical treatment is available in the Netherlands to European visitors on production of a valid European Health Insurance Card (EHIC). See page 10. Comprehensive travel insurance is still advised and is essential for all other visitors.

Pharmacies
Prescription and non-prescription drugs and other medical products are sold in pharmacies (apotheeken), recognised by a green cross sign. Despite their name, drug stores (drogerijen) do not sell medicines, but toiletries and cosmetics. Pharmacies are open Monday to Friday from 8 or 9am to 5:30 or 6pm.

Post offices
Most PTT post offices (postkaantoren) are generally open Monday to Friday 9am to 5pm. Larger ones are also open on Saturdays between 9am and 12 noon or 1.30pm.

Safe water
Tap water is safe to drink. Bottled mineral water, often called by the generic name 'spa', after a popular Belgian label, is readily available.

Telephones
There are many types of public phones in the Netherlands, accepting coins or pre-paid or credit cards. As a general principle, the cheapest way to make calls either within the country or abroad is with a pre-paid card (available at tobacconists, supermarkets and bureaux de change); the most expensive method is from a hotel bedroom. The country code for the Netherlands is 31. To call home from the Netherlands dial the international code (00) followed by the country code. To call the UK from the Netherlands dial 00 44.

Time
The Netherlands is on Central European Time (GMT + 1). Dutch Summer Time (GMT+2) operates from lateMarch, when clocks are put forward one hour, until late October.

Emergency telephone numbers
Police **112**
Fire **112**
Ambulance **112**

Toll charges in euros Bridges and tunnels	Car	Car towing caravan/ trailer
Westerschelde Tunnel	4.70	7.00

Driving in Norway *(Northern Europe)*

The regulations below should be read in conjunction
with the General motoring information on pages 18–21.

Drinking and driving

If the level of alcohol in the bloodstream
exceeds 0.020 per cent, severe penalties can
include heavy fines and/or prison, and the
surrender of your driving licence.

Driving licence

The minimum age at which a UK licence holder
may drive a temporarily imported car is 18, for a
motorcycle up to 11kw the minimum age is 16,
11–25kw 18, and over 25kw it is 20.

Fines

On-the-spot fines for infringement of traffic
regulations can be imposed. Vehicles illegally
parked may be towed away.

Fuel

Unleaded petrol (95 and 98 octane) and diesel
are available; there is limited LPG. Petrol in a can
is permitted but not aboard ferries. Credit cards
are accepted at filling stations; check with your
card issuer for usage in Norway before travel.

Lights

The use of dipped headlights during the day
is compulsory.

Motorcycles

The use of dipped headlights during the day
is compulsory. The wearing of crash helmets is
compulsory for both driver and passenger.

Motor insurance

Third-party insurance is compulsory.

Passengers/children in cars

A child under four cannot travel as a front- or
rear-seat passenger unless seated in a child
restraint. Children over four must use a child-
restraint system or a seat belt.

Seat belts

It is compulsory for front- and rear-seat
passengers to wear seat belts, if fitted.

Speed limits

The standard legal limits, which may be varied
by signs, for **private vehicles with and
without trailers** are: in built-up areas 50km/h
(31mph), outside built-up areas 80km/h (49mph)
and up to 90km/h (55mph) or 100km (62mph)
on motorways.

Additional information

- A warning triangle is compulsory for all
  vehicles with more than two wheels.
- Reflective jackets are compulsory for
  residents and strongly recommended
  for visitors.
- We recommended that visitors equip their
  vehicle with a first-aid kit, fire extinguisher
  and a set of replacement bulbs.
- In addition to some road, bridge and tunnel
  tolls, city tolls are payable by motorists
  entering Bergen, Oslo, Stavanger and
  Trondheim, see panel opposite. The toll

charge needs to be paid prior to entering the 'zone'. The tolls can be paid at the nearest Esso station.

- Spiked tyres may be used between 1 November and the first Sunday after Easter. Cars with spiked tyres will be charged a fee by the municipalities of Oslo, Bergen and Trondheim, with stickers valid for one day, one month or a year. In the three northern counties of Nordland, Troms and Finnmark, spiked tyres are permitted from 15 October to 1 May.
- Snow chains may be used on all types of tyres. When there is snow or ice covering the roads, winter tyres or any tyres and snow chains must be used.
- A vehicle towing a caravan must be equipped with special rear-view mirrors.

- Trams always have right of way.
- The use of radar detectors is forbidden.
- We strongly recommended that a reflective jacket is carried in the vehicle and worn if the driver and/or passenger(s) need to exit a vehicle that is immobilised on the carriageway of all motorways and main or busy roads. We recommend that the jacket is carried in the passenger compartment of the vehicle (not the boot). The carriage/use of reflective jackets is compulsory for vehicles registered in Norway.
- When hiring a car in Norway, it is the hirer's responsibility to ensure that the vehicle comes complete with the compulsory equipment.

Toll charges in Norwegian kroner

Road		Car	Car towing caravan/ trailer	Bridges and tunnels	Car	Car towing caravan/ trailer
E6	Trondheim – Stjordal	25.00	50.00	Askim on **E18**	20.00	40.00
E18	Oslo – Drammen	20.00	40.00	Aust-Agder on **E18**	30.00	60.00
E18	Larvik – Porsgrunn	20.00	40.00	Folgefonntunnelen on **RV551**	65.00	130.00
E18	Kristiansaund	10.00	20.00	Moss on **E6**	16.00	36.00
				Nappstraumen Tunnel on **E10**	65.00	130.00
				Nordkapp on **E69**	145.00	460.00
A charge is made on the following ring roads				North Hordaland Tunnel **E39**	45.00	140.00
Oslo		25.00	75.00	Oslofjord Tunnel on **RV23**	55.00	120.00
Bergen		15.00	30.00	Oysand-Thamshamn on **E39**	30.00	60.00
Stavanger		13.00	26.00	Rennfast on **E39**	90.00	280.00
				Naustdal Tunnel on **RV5**	45.00	135.00
				Svinesundsforbindelsen on **E6**	20.00	100.00
				Trekantsambanet on **E39**	85.00	270.00
				Vestfold on **E18**	30.00	60.00
				Ostfold on **E18/E6**	20.00	40.00

Travel facts: Norway

Innovation Norway
Charles House
5 Regent Street
London SW1Y 4LR
Tel: 020 7389 8800
www.visitnorway.com

Banking hours
Banks are generally open from 8.15am to 3.30pm. They usually close half an hour earlier from mid-May to mid-August, but stay open until 5pm on Thursday all year. They are closed at weekends.

Credit/debit cards
The use of credits cards is widespread in Norway, and they are accepted almost everywhere. Eurocard/MasterCard, Visa, American Express and Diners Club are the most common. Check with your card provider about acceptability and available services.

Currency
Norway's currency is the krone (NOK), which is divided into 100 øre. The denominatoins of krone banknotes are NOK50, NOK100, NOK200, NOK500 and NOK1,000. There are coins of 50 øre and NOK1, NOK5, NOK10 and NOK20.

Electricity
Norway has a 220-volt AC power supply. Electrical sockets take plugs with two round pins. UK visitors will need an adaptor.

Health care
Free or reduced-cost medical treatment is available in Norway to European visitors on production of a valid European Health Insurance Card (EHIC). See page 10. Comprehensive travel insurance is still advised and is essential for all other visitors.

Pharmacies
A pharmacy *(apotek)* sells prescription medicines; many pharmacists speak English. Pharmacies are generally open Monday to Friday 9am to 4.30pm, Saturday 9am to 2pm. Information about the nearest late-night or 24-hour facility is posted at all pharmacies.

Post offices
Post offices are generally open Monday to Friday 8am to 5pm, Saturday 8am to 1pm; hours for rural post offices may vary. Buy stamps *(frimerker)* at a post office *(posten)*, a news-stand/tobacconist, such as Narvesen or MIX or from a hotel. Post boxes are red.

Safe water
Tap water is safe to drink throughout Norway. Bottled mineral water *(mineralvann)* is widely available.

Telephones
You can use cash or a telephone card *(telekort)* to make a call in Norway. Most phone booths have direct dialling for international calls. Use NOK1, NOK5, NOK10 and NOK20 coins (minimum charge NOK5). Greencard phones accept phone cards NOK40, NOK90 and NOK140, available from Narvesen and MIX kiosks. Some card phones accept credit cards. The country code for Norway is 47. To call home from Norway dial the international code (00) followed by the country code. To call the UK from Norway dial 00 44.

Time
Norway is on Central European Time, one hour ahead of Greenwich Mean Time (GMT + 1). From late March, when clocks are put forward one hour, until late October, Daylight Saving Time (GMT + 2) operates.

Emergency telephone numbers
Police **112**
Fire **110**
Ambulance **113**

Driving in Poland *(Central Europe)*

The regulations below should be read in conjunction with the General motoring information on pages 18–21.

Drinking and driving

The maximum level of alcohol permitted in the bloodstream is 0.02 per cent. If it is between 0.021 per cent and 0.05 per cent a heavy fine can be imposed and your driver's licence suspended. If over 0.05 per cent a fine is determined by a tribunal along with a prison sentence and suspension of the licence.

Driving licence

The minimum age at which a UK licence holder may drive a temporarily imported car and/or motorcycle (over 125cc) is 18. All valid UK driving licences should be accepted in Poland.

Fines

On-the-spot fines can be imposed. An official receipt should be obtained. The police are authorised to request foreign motorists to pay their fines in cash. Wheel clamps are in use. Illegally parked cars causing an obstruction may be towed away and impounded.

Fuel

Unleaded petrol (95 and 98 octane), diesel and LPG are available. There is no leaded petrol, but 95 octane petrol with lead-replacement additive is available. You can carry 10 litres of petrol in a can but not aboard ferries and Eurotunnel. Credit cards are accepted at most filling stations; check with your card issuer for usage in Poland before travel.

Lights

Dipped headlights or daytime running lights are compulsory for all vehicles at all times. A fine can be imposed for non-compliance.

Motorcycles

Dipped headlights or daytime running lights are compulsory for all vehicles at all times. The wearing of crash helmets is compulsory for both driver and passenger.

Motor insurance

Third-party insurance is compulsory.

Passengers/children in cars

A child under 12 and under 1.5m (4ft 11in) in height cannot travel as front- or rear-seat passenger unless using suitable restraint system adapted to their size. If a car is equipped with front-seat air bags it is prohibited to place a child in a rear-facing seat.

Seat belts

It is compulsory for front- and rear-seat occupants to wear seat belts, if fitted.

Speed limits

The standard legal limits, which may be varied by signs, for **private vehicles without trailers** are: in built-up areas 60km/h (37mph) from 11pm to 5am and 50km/h (31mph) from 5am to 11pm, outside built-up areas 90km/h (55mph), on express roads (2 x 1 lane) 100km/h (62mph) or (2 x 2 lanes) 110km/h (68mph) and 130km/h (80mph) on motorways. The minimum speed on motorways is 40km/h (24mph). Some residential zones have a limit of 20km/h (13mph).

Additional information

- A warning triangle is compulsory for all vehicles with more than two wheels.
- It is recommended that visitors equip their vehicle with a first-aid kit and a set of replacement bulbs. It is also recommended that a fire extinguisher is carried as this is compulsory for Polish-registered vehicles.
- The use of spiked tyres is prohibited. Snow chains may be used only on roads covered with snow.
- It is prohibited to carry and/or use a radar detector.
- The use of the horn is not authorised in built-up areas except to avoid an accident.

Travel facts and toll charges: Poland

Polish National Tourist Office
Westgate House
West Gate
London W5 1YY
Tel: 08700 675 010
www.poland.travel/en/
www.poland.pl

Banking hours
Banks are generally open Monday to Friday 8am to 5 or 7pm and Saturday 8am to 1.30pm. Hours are limited in smaller towns. Withdrawing cash from ATMs is convenient, but not all Polish ATMs take all cards. Inform your bank before you leave home that you intend making withdrawals in Poland.

Credit/debit cards
Card use is on the increase but Poland essentially still has a cash culture. Stickers on the doors and windows of businesses usually indicate which credit cards will be accepted.

Currency
The Polish currency is the zloty (Zl) = 100 groszy. Banknotes come in denominations of Zl10, Zl20, Zl50, Zl100 and Zl200 and coins of Zl1, Zl2 and Zl5 and 1, 2, 5 and 10 groszy. Euros can be used to pay for goods and services at a limited number of shops and hotels but expect exchange rates to be poor.

Electricity
The power supply is 220 volts AC, 50Hz. Sockets take two-round-pin continental-style plugs. Visitors from the UK require an adaptor.

Health care
Free or reduced-cost medical treatment is available in Poland to European visitors on production of a valid European Health Insurance Card (EHIC). See page 10. Comprehensive travel insurance is still advised and is essential for all other visitors.

Pharmacies
Major cities and most towns have several pharmacies (apteka), at least one of which will be open 24 hours.

Take adequate supplies of drugs you need on a regular basis as they may not be readily available.

Post offices
Stamps are bought at post offices and at some news kiosks. Post boxes are red and marked with the word 'Poczta'.

Safe water
Tap water is normally chlorinated and may taste unpleasant. Bottled mineral water is available.

Telephones
There are still many public telephone boxes operated by Telekomunikacja Polska at strategic points in every village, town and city. Telephone cards (karta telefoniczna) can be bought at post offices and news kiosks. There are no coin-operated telephones. The country code for Poland is 48. To call home from Poland dial the international code (00) followed by the country code. To call the UK from Poland dial 00 44.

Time
Poland is on Central European Time, one hour ahead of Greenwich Mean Time (GMT + 1). From late March, when clocks are put forward one hour, until late October, Daylight Savings Time (GMT + 2) operates.

Emergency telephone numbers
Police **997**
Fire Brigade **998**
Ambulance **999**

Toll charges in zlotys

Road		Car	Car towing caravan/ trailer
A4	Katowice – Kraków	16.00	27.00
A2	Wrzesnia – Konin	12.00	27.00
A2	Krzesiny – Wrzesnia	12.00	27.00
A2	Komorniki – Nowy Tomysl	12.00	27.00

Driving in Portugal *(South West Europe)*

The regulations below should be read in conjunction with the General motoring information on pages 18–21.

Drinking and driving

If the level of alcohol in the bloodstream is between 0.05 per cent and 0.08 per cent, a fine and withdrawal of the driving licence for a minimum of one month to a maximum of one year can be imposed; if more than 0.08 per cent, there is a fine and withdrawal of the driving licence for a minimum of two months up to a maximum of two years. The police are also empowered to test drivers for narcotics.

Driving licence

The minimum age at which UK licence holders may drive a temporarily imported car and/or motorcycle (over 50cc) is 17; however visitors under the age of 18 years may encounter problems even though they hold a valid UK licence. All valid UK driving licences should be accepted in Portugal. This includes the older all-green-style UK licences (in Northern Ireland older paper-style with photographic counterpart) although the EC appreciates that these may be more difficult to understand and that drivers may wish to update them voluntarily before travelling abroad, if time permits. Alternatively, older licences may be accompanied by an International Driving Permit (IDP).

Fines

On-the-spot fines can be imposed. An official receipt showing the maximum amount of the fine should be obtained. **Note:** Foreign motorists refusing to pay an on-the-spot fine will be asked for a deposit to cover the maximum

fine for the offence committed. If a motorist refuses to do this, the police can take the driving licence, registration document or, failing that, they can confiscate the vehicle. Wheel clamping and towing are in operation for illegally parked vehicles.

Fuel

Unleaded petrol (95 and 98 octane), diesel and LPG are available. There is no leaded petrol (lead replacement petrol is available as 98 octane). Carrying petrol in a can is permitted. Credit cards are accepted at most filling stations; check with your card issuer for use in Portugal before travel. **Note:** a tax of €0.50 is added to credit card transactions.

Lights

Dipped headlights must be used in poor daytime visibility and in tunnels.

Motorcycles

The use of dipped headlights during the day is compulsory. The wearing of crash helmets is compulsory. A child under seven is not permitted to ride as a passenger.

Motor insurance

Third-party insurance is compulsory.

Motorways

See Spain/Portugal motorway map on page 152.

Passengers/children in cars

Children under 12 and less than 1.5m (4ft 11in) in height cannot travel as front-seat passengers. They must travel in the rear in a special restraint system adapted to their size, unless the vehicle has only two seats, or is not fitted with seat belts. Children under three can be seated in the front passenger seat if using a suitable child restraint; however, the air bag must be switched off if using a rear-facing child-restraint system.

Seat belts

It is compulsory for front- and rear-seat occupants to wear seat belts, if fitted.

Speed limits

The standard legal limits, which may be varied by signs, for **private vehicles without trailers** are: in built-up areas 50km/h (31mph), outside built-up areas 90km/h (55mph) or 100km/h (62mph) and on motorways 120km/h (74mph). The minimum speed on motorways is 50km/h (31mph). Motorists who have held a driving licence for less than one year must not exceed 90km/h (55mph) or any lower speed limit.

Additional information

- It is a legal requirement to carry photographic proof of identity at all times.
- It is compulsory for residents to carry reflective jackets in their cars; this regulation is recommended for visitors (see below).
- A warning triangle is recommended as the use of hazard warning lights or a warning triangle is compulsory in an accident/breakdown situation.
- It is prohibited to carry and/or use a radar detector.
- Spiked tyres and winter tyres are prohibited. Snow chains may be used, where the weather conditions require.

- It is illegal to carry bicycles on the back of a passenger car.
- The wearing of reflective jacket/waistcoat is recommended if the driver and/or passenger(s) exits a vehicle that is immobilised on the carriageway on all motorways and main or busy roads. We recommend that the jacket is carried in the passenger compartment of the vehicle (not the boot). This is a compulsory requirement for residents.
- In built-up areas the use of the horn is prohibited during the hours of darkness except in the case of immediate danger.

Toll charges in euros

Road		Car	Car towing caravan/ trailer	Road		Car	Car towing caravan/ trailer
E1 (A1)	Lisboa – Porto	19.55	19.55	A13	Santo Estevao – Marateca (**E1/E90**)	8.90	8.90
E1 (A2)	Lisboa – VLA (Algarve)	18.40	18.40	A14	Figueira da Foz – Coimbra	2.20	2.20
E1 (A3)	Porto – Valença do Minho (Spain/Vigo)	7.85	7.85	A15	Obidos – Santarem (**E1**)	3.55	3.55
E82 (A4)	Porto – Amarante	3.65	3.65	A21	Malveria (**A8**) – Ericeira	0.55	0.55
A5	Lisboa – Cascais	1.25	1.25				
E90 (A6)	E1/E90 (Marateca) – Badajoz (Spanish border)	11.90	11.90				
A7	Vila do Conde – **A24**	7.85	7.85				
A8	Lisboa – Leiria	10.20	10.20				
A9	Alverca – Oeiras	2.95	2.95				
A10	A9 – Arruda dos Vinhos – **E1**	2.10	2.10				
A11	Braga – Guimaraes – **A4**	0.80	0.80				
A12	Setúbal – Ponte Vasco de Gama	1.95	1.95				

Bridges and tunnels

	Car	Car towing caravan/ trailer
Lisbon Tagus Bridge (Ponte 25 de Abril) on **A2** (tolls are payable in one direction only, when travelling north into Lisbon)	3.25	4.70
Vasco da Gama Bridge (Ponte Vasco da Gama) on **A12** (tolls are payable in one direction only, when travelling north)	5.40	8.05

Travel facts: Portugal

Portuguese National Tourist Office,
11 Belgrave Square
London SW1X 8PP
Tel: 0845 355 1212
www.visitportugal.com
www.portugal.org

Banking hours
Banks are open Monday to Friday from 8.30am to 3pm.
The national network of ATMs is identified by the
symbol MB (Multibanco), from which you can withdraw
cash 24 hours a day.

Credit/debit cards
Major credit cards are accepted in most resorts. In
rural areas it is advisable to have small denomination
notes to hand.

Currency
The currency in Portugal is the euro (€). Euro coins are
issued in denominations of 1, 2, 5, 10, 20 and 50 cents
and €1 and €2. Banknotes are issued in denominations
of €5, €10, €20, €50, €100, €200 and €500. **Note:** €200 and
€500 notes are not issued in Portugal, but those issued
elsewhere are valid.

Electricity
The native power supply is 220 volts AC, 50Hz. Sockets
take two-round-pin continental-style plugs. Visitors from
the UK require an adaptor.

Health care
Free or reduced-cost medical treatment is available in
Portugal to European visitors on production of a valid
European Health Insurance Card (EHIC). See page 10.
Comprehensive travel insurance is still advised and is
essential for all other visitors.

Pharmacies
Chemists *(farmácia)* are open Monday to Friday 9am
to 1pm and 2.30 to 7pm and Saturday 9am to 12.30pm.
Some open through lunch and the late-night duty
chemist is posted in pharmacy windows. Pharmacists
are highly trained and can sell some drugs that require
prescriptions in other countries. However, take
adequate supplies of any drugs you take regularly as
they may not be available.

Post offices
There is at least one post office *(correio)* in every town
and reasonably large village. They sell stamps *(selos)*
as do many places with *correios* signs. Opening hours
are Monday to Friday 8.30am to 6pm, Saturday 9am
to noon at main branches in cities, shorter hours in
provincial areas.

Safe water
Tap water is generally safe but not too pleasant.
Anywhere, but especially outside the main cities, towns
and resorts, it is advisable to drink bottled water *(água
mineral)*, either still *(sem gás)* or carbonated *(com gás)*.

Telephones
Most public telephones now accept coins and credit
cards or phone cards. Phone cards are available
from post offices, kiosks and shops displaying the
PT (Portugal Telecom) logo and can be used for
international calls. International calls are cheaper
between 9pm and 9am and at weekends. The country
code for Portugal is 351. To call home from Portugal dial
the international code (00) followed by the country code.
To call the UK from Portugal dial 00 44.

Time
Portugal is on Greenwich Mean Time (GMT), the same
as the UK, and one hour behind most of continental
Europe. During the summer, from the last Sunday
in March to the last Sunday in October, the time in
Portugal is GMT plus one hour (GMT + 1).

Emergency telephone numbers
Police **112**
Fire **112**
Ambulance **112**

Driving in Romania *(South East Europe)*

The regulations below should be read in conjunction
with the General motoring information on pages 18–21.

Drinking and driving

Drinking and driving is strictly forbidden. Nil
percentage of alcohol is allowed in the driver's
blood. The driving licence can be suspended
for a maximum of 90 days or a prison sentence
imposed for offenders.

Driving licence

The minimum age at which a UK licence holder
may drive a temporarily imported car and/or
motorcycle (for up to 90 days) is 18. Driving
licences issued in the UK that do not incorporate
a photograph must be accompanied by an
International Driving Permit (IDP).

Fines

Police can impose fines and collect them
on the spot; a receipt must be issued.
A vehicle that is illegally parked may be clamped
and removed. If a fine is paid within 48 hours
the amount is halved.

Fuel

Lead replacement petrol (95 and 98 octane),
unleaded petrol, diesel and LPG are available.
Carrying petrol in a can is permitted (must be
empty when leaving Romania). Tax is payable
on petrol and diesel in the vehicle tank when
leaving Romania. Credit cards are accepted at
many stations; check with your card issuer for
usage in Romania before travel. Payment is
usually made in local currency.

Lights

It is forbidden to drive at night if the vehicle
lighting is faulty. Additional headlamps are
prohibited. Dipped headlights must be used
outside built-up areas during the day.

Motorcycles

The use of dipped headlights during the day
is compulsory. The wearing of crash helmets
is compulsory for the driver and passenger of
machines of 50cc and above.

Motor insurance

A Green Card/third-party insurance is
compulsory. Drivers of vehicles registered
abroad who are not in possession of a valid
Green Card must take out short-term insurance
at the frontier.

Passengers/children in cars

A child under 12 cannot travel as a front-seat
passenger.

Seat belts

It is compulsory for front- and rear-seat
occupants to wear seat belts, if fitted.

Speed limits

The standard legal limits, which may be varied
by signs, for **private vehicles without trailers**
are: in built-up areas 50km/h (31mph), outside
built-up areas 90km/h (55mph), 100km/h
(62mph) on dual carriageways and 130km/h
(80mph) on motorways. There is no minimum

speed on motorways. **If towing** a 10km/h (6mph) reduction of the standard speed limit applies. A driver who has held a licence for less than one year is restricted to a speed limit of 20km/h (12mph) below the indicated speed. The speed limit for mopeds is 45km/h (28mph) inside and outside built-up areas.

Additional information

- A fire extinguisher, first-aid kit and a red warning triangle are compulsory (warning triangle not required for two-wheeled vehicles).
- It is against the law to drive a dirty car.
- If a temporarily imported vehicle is damaged before arrival in Romania, the importer must ask a Romanian customs or police officer to write a report on the damage so that the vehicle can be exported without problems. If any damage occurs inside the country a report must be obtained at the scene of the accident. Damaged vehicles may be taken out of the country only on production of this evidence.
- The use of the horn is prohibited between 10pm and 6am in built-up areas. *'Claxonarea interzisa'* – use of horn prohibited.
- Spiked tyres are prohibited.
- The use of snow chains is recommended for winter journeys to the mountains and may be compulsory in case of heavy snow.
- A road tax is levied on all motor vehicles for both residents and visitors. Road tax stickers *(rovinieta)* are available from border crossing points, petrol stations and post offices in Romania. The cost depends on the emissions category and period of use in Romania. Foreign drivers failing to purchase a *rovinieta* during their stay may incur a fine of between €3,000 and €4,000 when leaving the country. Proof of insurance and the vehicle registration document are required when purchasing the *rovinieta*.

Travel facts: Romania

Romanian National Tourist Office
22 New Cavendish Street
London W1G 8TT
Tel: 020 7224 3692
www.romaniatourism.com
www.romaniatravel.com

Banking hours
Banks are generally open Monday to Friday
9am to 2pm.

Credit/debit cards
Romania is largely a cash-only economy. American
Express, Diners Club, MasterCard and Visa are
accepted by an increasing number of hotels and some
restaurants and shops, but you are advised to use
cash due to the risk of credit card fraud. There are an
increasing number of ATMs *(bancomat)* throughout
the major cities. Do not expect to find ATMs in remote
areas or villages.

Currency
The monetary unit of Romania is the lei (RON), divided
into 100 bani. Notes are in denominations of Lei500, 100,
50, 10, 5 and 1. Coins are in denominations of bani 50,
10, 5 and 1. Foreign currencies may be exchanged at
banks or authorised exchange offices *(casa de schimb
or birou de schimb valutar)*. International airports and
larger hotels also offer currency exchange services. It
is illegal to change money on the black market.

Electricity
The electrical supply is 220 volts AC, 50Hz. Plugs are
of the two-pin type.

Health care
Free or reduced-cost medical treatment is available in
Romania to European visitors on production of a valid
European Health Insurance Card (EHIC). See page 10.
Comprehensive travel insurance is still advised and is
essential for all other visitors.

Pharmacies
Pharmacies *(farmacie)* in Bucharest are well stocked
and pharmacists may be able to suggest a medication
for certain complaints. Some pharmacies in the city are
open 24 hours a day.

Post offices
Post offices are generally open Monday to Friday 8am
to 7pm, Saturday 8am to 2pm. Bucharest main post
office is open 7.30am to 8pm. Airmail to Western Europe
takes one week.

Safe water
Mains water is normally chlorinated, and while
relatively safe, may cause abdominal upsets. You
are advised to drink bottled mineral water, which is
widely available.

Telephones
Public telephones are widely available and can be
used for direct international calls; most require a phone
card. Hotels often impose a high service charge for
long-distance calls. The country code for Romania is 40.
To call home from Romania dial the international code
(00) followed by the country code. To call the UK from
Romania dial 00 44.

Time
Romania is on Eastern European Time, which is two
hours ahead of Greenwich Mean Time (GMT + 2),
but from the last Sunday in March to the last Sunday
in October, when clocks are put forward one hour,
Summer Time (GMT + 3) operates.

Emergency telephone numbers
Police **955** or **112**   Fire **981** or **112**   Ambulance **961** or **112**

Charges in Euros

General	Car	Car towing caravan/ trailer
1-week *rovinieta* (road tax)	3.00	6.00
1-month *rovinieta* (road tax)	7.00	16.00
1-year *rovinieta* (road tax)	28.00	36.00

Driving in the Russian Federation

(Eastern Europe)

The regulations below should be read in conjunction with the General motoring information on pages 18–21.

Drinking and driving

The maximum level of alcohol in the blood for a driver is 0.03 per cent. Driving under the influence of narcotics is strictly prohibited.

Driving licence

An International Driving Permit (IDP) is compulsory for the holder of any type of UK driving licence. The minimum age at which a visitor may drive a temporarily imported car and/or motorcycle is 17.

Fines

On-the-spot fines can be imposed. Fines should be paid through a bank according to the ticket given by the policeman. Police can clamp or remove illegally parked vehicles.

Fuel

Leaded petrol is available, but it may be in short supply and low octane. Unleaded petrol (95 and 98 octane) is available, but it is advisable to keep your tank topped up whenever possible. It is not permitted to import fuel in a can, but once in the country it is advisable to carry spare fuel. Diesel *(solyarka)* and limited supplies of LPG are available. Credit cards are not widely accepted at filling stations; check with your card issuer for usage in the Russian Federation before travel.

Lights

The use of passing lights during the day is compulsory outside built-up areas; a fine is imposed for non-compliance.

Motorcycles

The wearing of crash helmets is compulsory when riding a scooter or motorcycle. A child under 12 is not permitted as a passenger. Motorcycles must use dipped headlights at all times.

Motor Insurance

Foreign motorists must take out short-term insurance cover at the border. Third-party insurance is compulsory, fully comprehensive insurance is recommended. If a motorist travels to Russia with a Green Card, they must ensure the code RUS is included on the document.

Passengers/children in cars

Children under 12 cannot travel as a front-seat passenger unless using a restraint system appropriate to their size.

Seat belts

It is compulsory for front- and rear-seat occupants to wear seat belts, if fitted.

Speed limits

Speed limits must be strictly adhered to. The standard legal limits, which may be varied by signs, for **private vehicles without trailers** are: in built-up areas 60km/h (37mph), outside built-up areas 90km/h (55mph) but 110km/h (68mph) on expressways. Motorists who have held a driving licence for less than two years must not exceed 70km/h (43mph). In some residential zones the speed limit is 20km/h (13mph) as signposted.

Additional information

- It is compulsory to carry a first-aid kit, fire extinguisher, warning triangle and a set of replacement bulbs.
- A road tax is payable at the frontier.
- In addition to the original vehicle registration document it is recommended that you carry an International Certificate for Motor Vehicles when visiting any Russian-speaking areas.

- State Traffic Inspectorate officials will stop vehicles to check documents, especially if vehicles are displaying foreign plates.
- We recommend that visitors carry an assortment of spares for their vehicle such as a fan belt and spark plugs.
- It is against the law to drive a dirty car, where the registration plate isn't legible.
- Use of the horn in towns is prohibited.
- It is forbidden to pick up hitch-hikers.
- Anti-radar equipment that interferes with specific radio frequencies to jam police signals is prohibited.
- It is necessary to pre-plan itineraries and book accommodation before departure.
- A visitor whose vehicle is involved in an accident or breakdown must contact the Militia; the police must always be called to the scene of an accident.
- Motorists should avoid driving at night if possible.

Travel facts: The Russian Federation

Russian National Tourist Office
70 Piccadilly
London W1J 8HP
Tel: 0207 495 7570
www.visitrussia.org.uk

Banking hours
Local banking hours are from Monday to Friday
9am to 5pm. Major banks are open Monday to Friday
9am to 8pm.

Credit/debit cards
Most hotels, restaurants and larger shops accept credit
and debit cards, including Visa and MasterCard, but
cash (in roubles) is often preferred. Smaller shops do
not accept cards. You'll find ATMs in most major cities.
Traveller's cheques are not widely accepted.

Currency
The official currency in Russia is the rouble with 100
kopeks in 1 rouble. Banknotes come in denominations
of 10, 50, 100, 500, 1,000 and 5,000 roubles; coins in
denominations of 1, 2, 5 and 10 roubles and 1, 2, 10,
50 kopecks. It is advisable to take US dollars or euros
(all notes should be in good condition) that can be
exchanged at banks, hotels and recognised exchange
kiosks. It is an offence to change money from street
traders. It is illegal to pay directly with dollars or euros.

Electricity
The power supply throughout Russia is 220 volts AC,
50Hz. The plug is two-pin European standard. Bring your
own converter as most places in Russia do not have
them.

Health care
The UK has a reciprocal health care agreement with
Russia. If you're visiting Russia and need urgent or
immediate medical treatment it will be provided at a
reduced cost or, in some cases, free. The range of
medical services available may be more restricted
than under the NHS, therefore it is essential for all
visitors to have comprehensive travel insurance.
Visit **www.nhs.uk/NHSEngland/Healthcareabroad** for
a country-by-country guide.

Pharmacies
It is advisable to take a supply of medicines that are
likely to be required during your stay in Russia (check
first that they may be imported legally). Pharmacies
can be identified by a large green cross.

Post offices
Post offices are generally open Monday to Friday 8am
to 6pm. Some also open on Saturday morning.

Safe water
Water quality varies throughout Russia. Do not drink tap
water – buy bottled water.

Telephones
Public telephones accept telephone tokens and cards
that can be purchased from news-stands, some stores
and many kiosks. The country code for Russia is 7. To
call home from Russia dial the international code (00)
followed by the country code. To call the UK dial 00 44.

Time
Both Moscow and St Petersburg are three hours ahead
of Greenwich Mean Time (GMT + 3). From late March to
late October they are three hours ahead of Greenwich
Mean Time (GMT + 3).

Emergency telephone numbers
Police **02**
Fire **01**
Ambulance **03**

From 2012 Russia will adopt the single European
emergency number **112**

Driving in Serbia *(South East Europe)*

The regulations below should be read in conjunction with the General motoring information on pages 18–21.

Drinking and driving
If the level of alcohol in the bloodstream is 0.03 per cent or more, or if a medical examination shows that normal bodily functions are impaired, severe penalties including a fine, imprisonment and/or suspension of the driving licence can be imposed. Nil percentage of alcohol is permitted in the driver's blood for motorcyclists, novice and professional drivers. Police can carry out random breath tests. All drivers involved in an accident will be tested for alcohol and narcotics. Drivers who refuse a test will be automatically imprisoned.

Driving licence
The minimum age at which a UK licence holder may drive a temporarily imported car and/or motorcycle (exceeding 125cc) is 18. We recommend that you obtain an International Driving Permit (IDP) to accompany your UK driving licence.

Fines
Fines are no longer payable on the spot. A ticket will be issued by the policeman and the fine must be paid at a post office or bank. Fines vary according to the gravity of the offence. Penalties are higher if the motorist endangers other people or causes an accident.

Fuel
Leaded (95 octane), diesel *(dizel)*, LPG and unleaded petrol (95 octane) are available. Carrying petrol in a can is permitted (duty payable). Credit cards are generally accepted; check with your card issuer for usage in Serbia before travel.

Lights
It is compulsory to use daytime running lights or dipped headlights during the day. A fine will be imposed for non-compliance.

Motorcycles
The wearing of crash helmets is compulsory for both driver and passenger on a motorcycle, moped, motorised tricycle or quadricycle. Passengers on motorcycles are not permitted to travel under the influence of alcohol. A child aged 12 or under is not permitted as a passenger.

Motor insurance
A Green Card is recognised, third-party insurance is compulsory. Green Cards must bear the new sign for Serbia (SRB), not the old sign (SCG). Insurance can be obtained at the border.

Passengers/children in cars
A person visibly under the influence of alcohol is not permitted to travel in a vehicle as a front-seat passenger. Children up to the age of three years old can travel in the front of a car on the condition that they are placed in a rear-facing child restraint adapted to their size and the air bag is deactivated.

Serbia

Seat belts

It is compulsory for front/rear-seat occupants to wear seat belts, if fitted.

Speed limits

The standard legal limits, which may be varied by signs, for **private vehicles without trailers** are: in built-up areas 50km/h (31mph), outside built-up areas 80km/h (49mph) but 100km/h (62mph) on dual carriageways and 120km/h (74mph) on motorways. The speed limit in school areas is 30km/h (18mph). When **towing a trailer or caravan** the speed limit on all roads outside built-up areas, including dual carriageways and motorways, is 80km/h (49mph).

Additional information

- It is compulsory to carry a first-aid kit (except mopeds); a spare bulb set; a warning triangle – two if towing a trailer (not required for two-wheeled vehicles).
- In winter, if weather conditions require, motor vehicles must be equipped with four radial tyres and carry snow chains or be fitted with winter/snow tyres marked M&S on the sidewalls with a minimum tread depth of 4mm. Snow tyres must be fitted on the driving wheels. We recommend that snow chains are carried as their use may become compulsory if the 'snow chains' sign is displayed.

- It is compulsory to use daytime running lights or dipped headlights during the day.
- It is compulsory to carry reflective jackets. Any person exiting a vehicle to walk on the road must wear the reflective jacket; therefore the jackets should be kept in the passenger compartment of the vehicle.
- It is compulsory to carry a spare wheel and a towing rope.
- You must have a European Accident Statement form (available from some insurers).
- The use or carriage of radar detectors is prohibited.
- Tolls are payable on most sections of motorway. See page 141.
- The authorities at the frontier must certify any visible damage to a vehicle entering Serbia and a certificate obtained; this must be produced when leaving, otherwise you may experience serious difficulties on leaving the country.
- Spiked tyres are prohibited.
- Vehicles entering a roundabout have right of way.
- Use of the horn is prohibited in built-up areas and at night except in cases of imminent danger.
- Do not overtake school buses that have stopped for children to board or alight.

Travel facts and toll charges: Serbia

Embassy of the Republic of Serbia
28 Belgrave Square
London SW1X 8QB
Tel: 020 7235 9049
www.serbianembassy.org.uk
www.serbia-tourism.org

Banking hours
Most banks are open Monday to Friday from 8am to 7pm and Saturday from 8am to 3pm. On Sunday a designated bank is usually open.

Credit/debit cards
Major credit cards such as Visa, MasterCard and Diners Club are accepted in most shops, hotels and restaurants in Serbia. Very few ATMs accept international bank cards. There are several money exchange machines in Belgrade (including one at the airport), which accept pounds Sterling, US dollars and euros, giving back dinars. Scottish and Northern Irish pound Sterling banknotes are not accepted.

Currency
The official currency in Serbia is the dinar (CSD) which is divided into 100 paras. Bank notes are in denominations of CSD5,000, 1,000, 200, 100, 50, 20 and 10 and coins in denominations of CSD20, 10, 5, 2 and 1 and 50 paras. Money should be exchanged through official exchange offices only.

Electricity
The electric current in Serbia 220 volts AC, 50Hz. Two-round-pin plugs are used.

Health care
Comprehensive travel insurance is essential for all visitors.

Pharmacies
Pharmacies are open Monday to Friday from 8am to 3pm and on Saturdays from 8am to 1pm. Each city has a pharmacy that is open on Sundays and throughout the night.

Post offices
Most post offices are open Monday to Friday from 8am to 7pm and on Saturday from 8am to 3pm. On Sunday there is usually a designated post office that maintains services.

Safe water
Mains water is normally chlorinated and, while relatively safe, may cause mild abdominal upsets. Bottled water is available.

Telephones
The country code for Serbia is 381. To call home from Serbia dial the international code (00) followed by the country code. To call the UK from Serbia dial 00 44.

Time
Serbia observes Central European Time (CET), which is one hour ahead of Greenwich Mean Time (GMT + 1), until late March to late October, when clocks are put forward one hour (GMT + 2).

Emergency telephone numbers
Police **92**
Fire **93**
Medical emergency **94**
Help on the road **987**
General information (hospitals, chemists on duty etc.) **9812**

Contact the Serbian Embassy for details of specific entry/exit requirements.

Toll charge in dinars

Road		Car	Car towing caravan/ trailer
E75	Beograd – Novi Sad	240.00	350.00
E75	Beograd – Nis	730.00	1,100.00
E75	Nis – Leskovac	190.00	280.00
E70	Beograd – Sid	70.00	100.00

Driving in Slovakia *(Central Europe)*

The regulations below should be read in conjunction with the General motoring information on pages 18–21.

Drinking and driving

Drinking and driving is strictly forbidden. Nil percentage of alcohol is allowed in the driver's blood. Penalties include a fine, withdrawal of licence and imprisonment.

Driving licence

The minimum age at which a UK licence holder may drive a temporarily imported car is 18, for a motorcycle (exceeding 50cc) it is 17.

Fines

On-the-spot fines (up to €600) can be imposed; an official receipt should be issued. Wheel clamps are in use and vehicles may be towed away.

Fuel

Unleaded petrol (95 octane), diesel *(nafta)* and LPG are available. There is no leaded petrol. Carrying petrol in a can is permitted. LPG can be used for road vehicles only on the condition that a safety certificate covers the equipment for its combustion. Credit cards are accepted at filling stations; check with your card issuer for usage in Slovakia before travel.

Lights

The use of dipped headlights during the day is compulsory. Any vehicle warning lights, other than those supplied with the vehicle as original equipment, must be made inoperative.

Motorcycles

The use of dipped headlights during the day is compulsory. The wearing of a crash helmet is compulsory when riding a machine over 50cc. It is forbidden for motorcyclists to smoke while riding their machine.

Motor insurance

Third-party insurance is compulsory.

Passengers/children in cars

No person under 1.5m (4ft 11in) in height or a child under 12 years may travel in a vehicle as a front-seat passenger. The use of child seats is compulsory for all children under 12 years of age or under 1.5m (4ft 11in).

Seat belts

It is compulsory for all occupants to wear seat belts, if fitted.

Speed limits

The standard legal limits, which may be varied by signs, for **private vehicles without trailers**, are: on motorways and expressways outside built-up areas 130km/h (80mph), motorways and expressways in built-up areas 90km/h (55mph). Other roads outside built-up areas 90km/h (55mph), other roads in built-up areas 50km/h (31mph). Drivers must not exceed a speed of 30km/h (18mph), 30m before a level crossing and while crossing over it. The minimum speed on motorways is 80km/h (49mph), 65km/h (40mph) on urban motorways.

Additional information

- A first-aid kit is compulsory.
- A warning triangle is compulsory (not required for two-wheeled vehicles).
- Winter tyres (M&S type) with a minimum tread depth of 3mm are compulsory when compacted snow or ice is on the road.
- Reflective jackets are compulsory for two- and four-wheeled vehicles on all roads outside built-up areas. Any person getting out of the vehicle as a result of a breakdown, puncture or accident must wear a reflective jacket. A fine of up to €60 will be imposed for non-compliance. Reflective jackets must comply with EU standard EN471.
- For vehicles under 3.5 tonnes a motorway tax (see page 144) is payable to travel on certain highways and motorways. A sticker must be displayed on the right-hand side of the windscreen of all vehicles (except motorcycles) as evidence of payment. Stickers may be purchased at border crossings and from selected filling stations and post offices for periods of one year, one month or one week. Fines are imposed for non-display. It is compulsory to remove stickers that are no longer valid.
- Radar detection equipment is strictly prohibited in Slovakia.
- The authorities at the frontier must certify any visible damage to a vehicle entering Slovakia.
- If any damage occurs inside the country with an estimated cost over €4,000 or where injury or fatality occurs, a police report must be obtained at the scene of the accident. Damaged vehicles may be taken out of the country only on production of this evidence.
- Drivers are advised by the Slovak police to be wary of people approaching their vehicle at border crossings and petrol stations near the border who may cause damage to tyres and then offer their assistance further along your route when the tyre becomes deflated.
- Spiked tyres are prohibited and snow chains may be used only where there is enough snow to protect the road surface.
- All foreign visitors are required to show proof of medical insurance cover on entry.
- Horns may be used only to warn of danger or to signify intention to overtake.

Travel facts: Slovakia

Slovakian Tourist Board
Slovak Tourist Centre
16 Frognal Parade
Finchley Road
London NW3 5HG
Tel: 020 7794 3263 or **0800 026 79432**
www.slovakia.travel/

Banking hours
Banks are usually open Monday to Friday from 8am to 4.30pm. In the largest shopping centres, the bank services are also available during weekends and holidays to 8pm.

Credit/debit cards
Major credit cards (American Express, Diners Club, MasterCard and Visa) and debit cards (Maestro and Visa Electron) are widely accepted in Slovakia

Currency
The euro (€) is the official currency of Slovakia. Coins are issued in denominations of 1, 2, 5, 10, 20 and 50 cents and €1 and €2. Notes are issued in denominations of €5, €10, €20, €50, €100, €200 and €500.

Electricity
The power supply in Slovakia is 220 volts AC, 50Hz. Sockets take two-round-pin plugs.

Health care
Free or reduced-cost medical treatment is available in Slovakia to European visitors on production of a valid European Health Insurance Card (EHIC). See page 10. Comprehensive travel insurance is essential for all visitors. All visitors must show proof of medical insurance cover on entry.

Pharmacies
Pharmacies *(apothéka)* are the only places to sell over-the-counter medicines. They also dispense many drugs *(leky)* normally available on prescription in other Western countries. Pharmacies are usually open from 7.30am to 4pm.

Post offices
Post offices are usually open Monday to Friday from 8am to 6pm and on Saturday to 1pm. Main post offices in larger towns or shopping malls are open daily to 8pm. Stamps *(známky)* for postcards and letters are available from post offices and some newspaper stands

Safe water
The tap water is normally be safe to drink in Slovakia. If in doubt, bottled mineral water is widely available.

Telephones
There is a network of public pay phones; most take phone cards (which can be purchased at most news-stands); some are coin operated. Some phones do not allow outgoing calls to international and mobile numbers (marked by an orange sticker with Slovak and English text). If you have any problems, dial 149 and ask for an English-speaking operator. The country code for Slovakia is 421. To call home from Slovakia dial the international code (00) followed by the country code. To call the UK from Slovakia dial 00 44.

Time
Slovakia is on Central European time (GMT + 1). Daylight Saving Time comes into effect on the last Sunday in March and ends on the last Sunday in October (GMT + 2).

Emergency telephone numbers
Police **112**
Fire **112**
Ambulance **112**

Charges in euros

General	Car
1 week (road tax)	4.90
1 month (road tax)	9.90
1 year (road tax)	36.50

Driving in Slovenia *(Central Europe)*

The regulations below should be read in conjunction
with the General motoring information on pages 18–21.

Drinking and driving

If the level of alcohol in the bloodstream is 0.05
per cent or more, severe penalties including a
fine or suspension of the driving licence can be
imposed. Nil percentage of alcohol is permitted
in the driver's blood if the licence has been held
for less than three years, the person is under 21
or employed as a professional driver. The driver
can still be fined for levels under 0.05 per cent
if unable to drive safely. These rules also apply
to narcotics.

Driving licence

The minimum age at which a UK licence
holder may drive a temporarily imported car
and/or motorcycle exceeding 125cc is 18. An
Internatioinal Driving Permit (IDP) is compulsory
for holders of driving licences not incorporating
a photograph.

Fines

On-the-spot fines must be paid in local currency.
Refusal to pay could result in your passport
being held. Illegally parked vehicles will be
towed away or clamped.

Fuel

Unleaded petrol (95 and 98 octane), diesel and
LPG are available. There is no leaded petrol (a
lead-substitute additive is available). Carrying
petrol in a can is permitted. Credit cards are
accepted at filling stations; check with your card
issuer for usage in Slovenia before travel.

Lights

The use of dipped headlights during the day
is compulsory.

Motorcycles

The use of dipped headlights during the day is
compulsory. The wearing of crash helmets is
also compulsory for both driver and passenger.
A child under 12 is not permitted as a
passenger.

Motor insurance

Third-party insurance is compulsory.

Passengers/children in cars

Children under 12 and under 1.5m (4ft 11in)
must use a restraint system suitable for their
age and size and are permitted to travel only
in the rear seats. Children over 12 may wear
normal seat belts.

Seat belts

It is compulsory for front- and rear-seat
occupants to wear seat belts, if fitted.

Speed limits

The standard legal limits, which may be varied
by signs, for **private vehicles without trailers**
are: in built-up areas 50km/h (31mph), outside
built-up areas 90km/h (55mph) but 100km/h
(62mph) on 'fast roads' (dual carriageways)
and 130km/h (80mph) on motorways. There
are areas with a restricted speed limit of
30km/h (18mph). The minimum speed on

motorways is 60km/h (37mph). When **towing a trailer or caravan** with a combined weight less than 3.5 tonnes, the limit on all roads outside built-up areas is 80km/h (49mph). Vehicles with snow chains must not exceed 50km/h (31mph). In bad weather and when visibility is reduced to less than 50m due to bad weather the maximum speed limit is 50km/h (31mph).

Additional information

- A reflective jacket is compulsory (not required for motorcycles). The reflective jacket(s)/waistcoat(s) should be kept in the vehicle and not in the boot as each person must wear one as soon as they leave their vehicle in an accident/breakdown situation. There is a fine for non-compliance.
- A warning triangle is compulsory (not required for two-wheeled vehicles); two are necessary if towing a trailer.
- Snow chains must be carried between 15 November and 15 March (and at other times in winter weather conditions) by private cars and vehicles up to 3.5 tonnes unless the vehicle fitted with four winter tyres. The minimum tyre tread depth is 3mm at times when snow chains/winter tyres are required.
- Warning triangle and/or hazard warning lights must be used in an accident/breakdown situation. At night if hazard lights fail, in addition to a warning triangle a yellow flashing light or position lights must mark the vehicle.
- A fire extinguisher, first-aid kit and set of replacement bulbs are recommended.
- Foreign drivers involved in an accident must call the police and obtain a written report. Keep this report as customs officials will ask to see it to allow exit.
- It is prohibited to overtake a bus transporting children when passengers are getting on/off.
- Use of the horn is prohibited in built-up areas or at night, except in cases of danger, injury or illness.
- A *vignette* system has been introduced that replaces tolls (see page 147). The *vignette* will have to be displayed when travelling on motorways and expressways and will be available to purchase from filling stations in Slovenia and in neighbouring countries. Vignettes (for vehicles up to 3.5 tonnes) are available for periods of one year, one month and seven days. The 1-year *vignette* is valid from 1 December to 31 January the following year. The minimum fine for non-display is €300. Visit **www.dars.si** for information.
- The use of spiked tyres is prohibited.
- Hazard warning lights must be used when reversing.

Travel facts: Slovenia

Slovenian Embassy
10 Little College Street,
London SW1P 3SJ
Tel: 020 7222 5400
www.slovenia.embassy-uk.co.uk

Banking hours
Banks are open Monday to Friday 9am to 12 noon and
2 to 5pm, some banks open on Saturday from 8.30am
to 11/12. Money can also be exchanged in exchange
offices, at hotel reception desks, tourist agencies, petrol
stations and larger supermarkets.

Credit/debit cards
Major cards accepted for payment are MasterCard,
Visa, American Express and Diners. ATMs are located
across the country.

Currency
The Euro (€) is the official currency of Slovenia. Coins
are issued in denominations of 1, 2, 5, 10, 20 and 50
cents and €1 and €2. Notes are issued in denominations
of €5, €10, €20, €50, €100, €200 and €500.

Electricity
The power supply is 220 volts AC, 50Hz. Sockets take
round plugs with two round pins.

Health care
Free or reduced-cost medical treatment is available in
Slovenia to European visitors on production of a valid
European Health Insurance Card (EHIC). See page 10.
Comprehensive travel insurance is still advised and is
essential for all other visitors.

Pharmacies
Prescription and over-the-counter medicines are
sold in pharmacies. A 24-hour service is available
in large towns.

Post offices
Post offices are generally open Monday to Friday 8am
to 6pm, Saturday 8am to 12 noon. Stamps can be bought
at bookstalls.

Safe water
Mains water is considered safe to drink. However,
bottled mineral water is available and is advised for the
first few weeks of the stay.

Telephones
Calls can be made with phone cards, which are sold
at post offices, newspaper kiosks and tobacco shops.
The country code for Slovenia is 386. To call home from
Slovenia dial the international code (00) followed by the
country code. To call the UK from Slovenia dial 00 44.

Time
Slovenia is on Central European time (GMT +1), Daylight
Saving Time comes into effect on the last Sunday in
March and ends on the last Sunday in October (GMT
+ 2).

Emergency telephone numbers
Police **113** or **112**
Fire **112**
Ambulance **112**

Charges in euros

General	Vehicles up to 3.5 tonnes
7-day *vignette*	15.00
1-month *vignette*	30.00
1-year *vignette*	95.00

Spain

- The wearing of reflective jacket/waistcoat is compulsory if the driver and/or passenger(s) exits a vehicle that is immobilised on the carriageway of all motorways and main or busy roads. However, it is not mandatory to carry a reflective jacket in the vehicle and Spanish police cannot fine a foreign motorist who does not carry one. Car-hire companies are not under legal obligation to supply them to persons hiring vehicles, so often don't.
- It is recommended that drivers who wear glasses carry a spare pair with them if this is noted on the driving licence.
- Apparatus with a screen that can distract a driver (such as television, video, DVD equipment) should be positioned where the driver is unable to see it. This excludes GPS systems. It is prohibited for the driver to touch or program the device unless parked in a safe place.
- The use of radar detectors is prohibited.
- In urban areas it is prohibited to sound the horn at any time, except in an emergency. Lights may be flashed instead of using the horn.
- The use of snow chains is recommended in snow conditions; police can stop vehicles not fitted with snow chains.
- In winter, spikes on spiked tyres must not exceed 2mm in length and must be used only on roads covered with snow or ice.
- In the case of a car towing a caravan/trailer exceeding 12m, there must be two yellow reflectors at the rear of the towed caravan or trailer.
- In some cities with one-way streets, vehicles must be parked on the side of the road where houses bear uneven numbers on uneven days of the month, and on the side of even numbers on even days.

Road signs (a selection of standard and non-standard)

Use dipped headlights

Motorway

Dual carriageway

Turning permitted

Limited parking zone

Water

Viewpoint

Travel facts: Spain

Spanish Tourist Office
22–23 Manchester Square
London W1M 5AP
Tel: 020 7486 8077
www.tourspain.co.uk

Banking hours
Banks are generally open Monday to Friday 8.30 or 9am to 1pm. Some banks open Saturday (October to May only) 8.30am to 1pm.

Credit/debit cards
All major credit cards are accepted in shops, restaurants and hotels throughout Spain. The most popular are Visa, MasterCard, American Express, Eurocheque, and to a lesser extent Diners.

Currency
The euro (€) is the official currency of Spain. Coins are issued in denominations of 1, 2, 5, 10, 20 and 50 cents and €1 and €2. Notes are issued in denominations of €5, €10, €20, €50, €100, €200 and €500.

Electricity
The power supply is 220 volts AC (in some bathrooms and older buildings it is 110/125 volts). Round two-hole sockets take two-round-pin plugs. British visitors will need an adaptor.

Health care
Free or reduced-cost medical treatment is available in Spain to European visitors on production of a valid European Health Insurance Card (EHIC). See page 10. Comprehensive travel insurance is still advised and is essential for all other visitors.

Pharmacies
Prescription and non-prescription drugs and medicines are available from pharmacies *(farmacias)* distinguished by a large green cross. They are able to dispense many over-the-counter drugs that would be available only on prescription in other countries.

Post offices
Post offices *(correos)* are generally open 8.30am to 2.30pm (1pm Saturday). In main centres they may open extended hours. Stamps *(sellos)* can also be bought at tobacconists *(estancos)*. Post boxes are yellow.

Safe water
Tap water is chlorinated and generally safe to drink; however, unfamiliar water may cause mild abdominal upsets. Bottled mineral water *(agua mineral)* is cheap and widely available. It is sold still *(sin gas)* and carbonated *(con gas)*.

Telephones
All telephone numbers throughout Spain consist of nine digits, and no matter where you call from, you must always dial all nine digits. Many public telephones *(teléfono)* take phone cards *(credifone)*, which are available from post offices and some shops for €6 or €12. The country code for Spain is 34. To call home from Spain dial the international code (00) followed by the country code. To call the UK from Spain dial 00 44.

Time
Spain is on Central European Time (GMT + 1); Daylight Saving Time comes into effect on the last Sunday in March and ends on the last Sunday in October (GMT + 2).

Emergency telephone numbers
Police **092** or **112**
Guardia Civil **062** or **112**
Fire **080** or **112**
Ambulance **061** or **112**

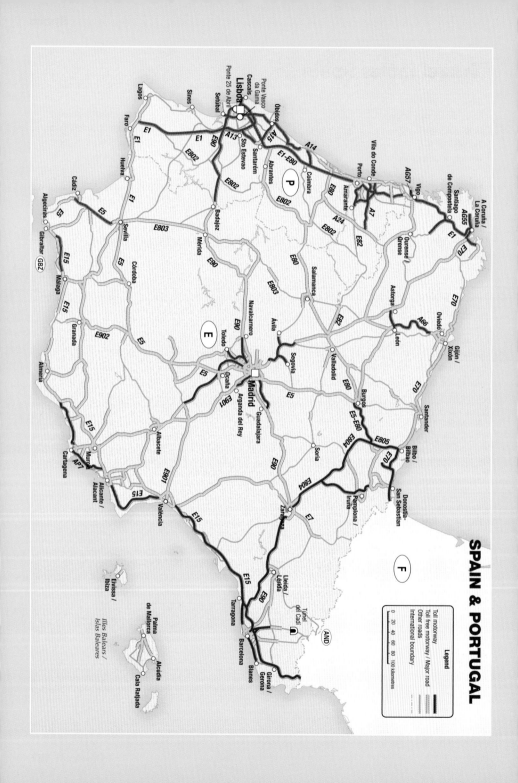

SPAIN & PORTUGAL

Legend

Toll motorway
Toll free motorway / Major road
Other roads
International boundary

0 20 40 60 80 100 kilometres

Toll charges in euros

Road		Car	Car towing caravan/ trailer
E1 (A9)	Santiago de Compostela – Vigo	7.35	7.35
E1 (A9)	La Coruna – Santiago de Compostela	5.15	5.15
E1 (A9)	Ferrol – La Coruña	3.60	3.60
E5 (A4)	Cádiz – Dos Hermanas (Sevilla)	5.90	5.90
E5 (A4) (R4)	Madrid – Ocaña	4.70	4.70
E5/E80 (A1)	Burgos – **E804** (Miranda de Ebro)	8.75	8.75
E9	Barclelona – Túnel del Cadí (Baga)	20.83	20.83
E15 (A7)	Barcelona – Tarragona	11.26	11.26
	Tarragona – València	22.00	22.00
	La Jonquera (French border) – Barcelona	12.56	12.56
	Málaga – Gibraltar	13.15	13.15
	València – Alacant	13.90	13.90
E70 (A8)	Bilbo – Irun (French border)	9.15	9.15
E90 (A2)	Zaragoza – Tarragona	16.25	16.25
E90 (R2)	Madrid – Guadalajara	7.00	7.00
E90 (R5)	Madrid – Navalcarnero	3.50	3.50
E804 (A68)	Zaragoza – Miranda de Ebro (**E5/E80**)	17.65	17.65
E805 (A68)	Miranda de Ebro (**E5/E80**) – Bilbo	8.80	8.80

Road		Car	Car towing caravan/ trailer
E901 (R3)	Madrid – Arganda del Rey	3.40	3.40
M12	Madrid (Barajas) Airport – **E5 (A1)** Alcobendas	1.75	1.75
A6	Madrid – Valladolid	9.35	9.35
A7	Cartagena – Alacant	3.15	3.15
A15	Pamplona – Irurtzun	1.90	1.90
	Pamplona – Tudela	12.05	12.05
A41	Madrid – Toledo	2.20	2.20
A51	Madrid – Ávila	8.10	8.10
A55	La Coruña – Carballo	2.30	2.30
A57	Vigo – Baiona	1.45	1.45
A61	Madrid – Segova	7.35	7.35
A66	León – Oviedo	10.60	10.60
A71	León – Astorga	3.85	3.85
AP53	Santiago de Compostela – Ourense	5.15	5.15
C32 (A19)	Barcelona – Blanes	3.97	3.97
C32	Barcelona Airport – Tarragona	11.26	7.57

Bridges and tunnels

Road		Car	Car towing caravan/ trailer
E9	Túnel del Cadí (French border)	11.00	11.00
	Tunels de Vallvidrera (Barcelona)	3.52	3.52

Driving in Sweden *(Northern Europe)*

The regulations below should be read in conjunction with the General motoring information on pages 18–21.

Drinking and driving

If the level of alcohol in the bloodstream is 0.02 per cent or more, severe penalties including fines, withdrawal of licence and/or prison can
be imposed.

Driving licence

The minimum age at which a UK licence holder may drive a temporarily imported car is 18. **Note:** UK driving licences that do not incorporate a photograph will not be recognised unless accompanied by photographic proof of identity e.g. a passport.

Fines

Police can impose but not collect fines on the spot for minor traffic offences. Fines must be paid at a bank within 2 to 3 weeks. Illegally parked vehicles may be towed away; the release charge is up to SEK1,400.

Fuel

Unleaded *(Blyfri)* petrol (95 and 98 octane) and diesel are available. There is very limited LPG. Carrying petrol in a can is permitted. Credit cards are accepted at filling stations; check with your card issuer for usage in Sweden before travel.

Lights

The use of dipped headlights during the day is compulsory. Fines will be imposed for inadequate lighting.

Motorcycles

The use of dipped headlights during the day is compulsory. The wearing of crash helmets is also compulsory.

Motor insurance

Third-party insurance is compulsory.

Passengers/children in cars

Children aged under 15 or under 1.35m (4ft 5in) must use an appropriate child restraint. There is only one exception in that they are permitted to travel unrestrained in the rear of a taxi if the correct child restraint is not available. A rear-facing baby seat may be used only if the air bag has been deactivated. A child aged 15 and over or 1.35m (4ft 5in) in height may use an adult seat belt. Children under three must use a child restraint appropriate for their weight, in any vehicle.

Seat belts

It is compulsory for front- and rear-seat occupants to wear seat belts, if fitted.

Speed limits

Speed limits are no longer based on the type of road, but on the quality and safety of the actual road itself. Speed limits may subsequently vary along the same road. It is therefore recommended that you pay particular attention to road signs. The lowest speed limits, which may be varied by signs, for **private vehicles**

without trailers are in built-up areas: 30km/h (18mph), outside built-up areas 70km/h (43mph), dual carriageways 100km/h (62mph) and motorways 110km/h (68mph). When **towing** the limit is 80km/h (49mph) on dual carriageways and motorways.

Additional information
- From 1 December to 31 March it is compulsory to use winter tyres (marked M&S) with a minimum tread depth of 3mm.
- A warning triangle, first-aid kit and fire extinguisher are recommended.
- Beware game (moose, deer, elk, etc.

– a yellow warning triangle with a red border, see below, depicts animals most common on a particular stretch of road), as animals constitute a very real danger on many roads.
- Spiked tyres (which must be fitted on all wheels) may be used from 1 October to 15 April. However, local authorities have the power to ban spiked/studded tyres on their roads. Snow chains may also be used if the weather or road conditions require.
- Congestion charges in Stockholm do not apply to foreign-registered vehicles.
- The use of radar detectors is strictly forbidden.

Road signs (a selection of standard and non-standard)

Elks

Additional stop sign

Slow lane

End of lane

Travel facts and toll charges: Sweden

Swedish Travel and Tourism Council (administration)
11 Montagu Place
London W1H 2AL
Tel: 020 7108 6168
www.visitsweden.com

Banking hours
Banks are generally open Monday to Friday 9.30am to 3pm (in some cities until 6pm), Saturday 8am to noon or 1pm. Banks are also open on Thursday until 4 to 5.30pm.

Credit/debit cards
Major credit cards are widely accepted at banks, hotels, stores and restaurants. Most shops and restaurants require an identity card when paying with a credit card. You can get cash with your Visa, MasterCard, Maestro or Cirrus card at any *'Bankomat'* or *'Minuten'* ATM.

Currency
Sweden's currency is the krona (SEK, SKr or Kr; plural kronor), which is divided into 100 öre. Bank notes are issued in values of SEK20, 50, 100, 500 and 1,000; coins 50 öre, 1SEK, 5 and 10.

Electricity
Sweden has a 220 volts AC, 50Hz power supply. Electrical sockets take two-round-pin plugs.

Health care
Free or reduced-cost medical treatment is available in Sweden to European visitors on production of a valid European Health Insurance Card (EHIC). See page 10. Comprehensive travel insurance is still advised and is essential for all other visitors.

Pharmacies
Prescription and non-prescription medicines are available from a pharmacy *(apotek)*. A 24-hour service is available in most cities.

Post offices
You'll find post offices in various shops, stores, kiosks and petrol stations. The opening hours differ according to the specific establishment. Buy stamps *(frimarken)* at a post office *(postkontoret)*, supermarket, news-stand *(nyhetsbyra)*, or kiosk displaying a blue-and-yellow post sign. Hours for rural post offices may vary. There are two different types of post boxes – the blue box is for local deliveries, the yellow box for national and international deliveries.

Safe water
Tap water is safe to drink, and bottled mineral water *(mineralvatten)* is widely available.

Telephones
You can use pre-paid phone cards or credit cards to make a call from a public phone *(telefon)* in Sweden. A telephone card *(telefonkort)* can be bought from news-stands, shops, hotels or magazine kiosks. Post offices do not have telephone facilities. The country code for Sweden is 46. To call home from Sweden dial the international code (00) followed by the country code. To call the UK from Sweden dial 00 44.

Time
Sweden is on Central European Time, which is one hour ahead of Greenwich Mean Time (GMT + 1). Daylight Saving Time (GMT + 2) is in effect from the last weekend in March to the last weekend in October.

Emergency telephone numbers
Police **112**
Fire **112**
Ambulance **112**

Toll charges in Swedish krona

Bridges and tunnels	Car	Car towing caravan/ trailer
Oresund Bridge (one way)	395.00	790.00

Driving in Switzerland and Liechtenstein *(Central Europe)*

The regulations below should be read in conjunction with the General motoring information on pages 18–21.

Drinking and driving

If the level of alcohol in the bloodstream is 0.05 per cent or more, severe penalties include a fine or prison. The police may request any driver to undergo a breath test or drugs test. Visiting motorists may be forbidden from driving in Switzerland for a minimum of two months.

Driving licence

The minimum age at which a UK licence holder may drive a temporarily imported car is 18, for a motorcycle (up to 50cc) it is 16, for a motorcycle (50cc or over) 18.

Fines

On-the-spot fines can be imposed in certain cases. Vehicle clamps are not used in Switzerland but vehicles causing an obstruction can be removed. Speeding fines are severe.

Fuel

Unleaded petrol (95 and 98 octane) and diesel *(gasoil)* are available. There is no leaded petrol (a lead-substitute additive is available). There is limited LPG availability (only eight outlets). Carrying petrol in a can is permitted. Credit card acceptance is variable, especially at night due to automatic pumps not recognising UK chip-and-PIN cards; check with your card issuer for usage in Switzerland and Liechtenstein before travel. Some automatic pumps accept banknotes.

Lights

The use of dipped headlights during the day is recommended for all vehicles. They are compulsory when passing through tunnels even if they are well lit. A fine will be imposed for non-compliance.

Motorcycles

The wearing of crash helmets is compulsory. The use of dipped headlights during the day is recommended.

Motor insurance

Third-party insurance is compulsory.

Passengers/children in cars

Vehicles registered outside Switzerland, i.e. visiting Switzerland, must comply with the requirements of their country of registration with regard to child-restraint regulations.

Seat belts

It is compulsory for front- and rear-seat occupants to wear seat belts, if fitted.

Speed limits

The standard legal limits, which may be varied by signs, for **private vehicles without trailers** are: in built-up areas 50km/h (31mph), outside built-up areas 80km/h (49mph), semi-motorways 100km/h (62mph) and 120km/h (74mph) on motorways. The maximum speed **with a trailer** on semi-motorways and motorways is 80km/h (49mph). The minimum speed on motorways is 80km/h (49mph). **Note:** Towing a car on the motorway is permitted only up to next exit at a maximum speed of 40km/h (24mph).

Additional information

- Snow chains are compulsory in areas indicated by the appropriate sign and they must be fitted on at least two drive wheels.
- Each motor vehicle must be equipped with a warning triangle, which must be kept within easy reach (not in the boot). This must be used in any breakdown/emergency situation.
- Hitch-hiking is prohibited on motorways and semi-motorways.
- The Swiss authorities levy an annual motorway tax and a vehicle sticker (costing CHF40 for vehicles up to 3.5 tonnes maximum total weight and known locally as a 'vignette') must be displayed in the prescribed manner by each vehicle (including motorcycles, trailers and caravans) using Swiss motorways and semi-motorways. The fine for non-display of the vignette(s) is the cost of vignette(s) plus CHF100. Motorists may purchase the stickers in the UK (telephone the Swiss Centre on **freephone 00800 100 20030** for information) or in Switzerland from customs offices at the frontier or service stations and garages throughout the country.
- Vehicles over 3.5 tonnes maximum total weight are taxed on all roads; coaches and caravans pay a fixed tax for periods of one day, 10 days, one month or one year but lorries are taxed on weight and distance travelled.

- A GPS-based navigation system that has maps indicating the location of fixed speed cameras must have the 'fixed speed camera PoI (Points of Interest)' function deactivated.
- Radar detectors are prohibited even if not switched on.
- All vehicles with spiked tyres are prohibited on motorways and semi-motorways except for certain parts of the A13 and A2.
- Snow tyres are not compulsory; however vehicles that are not equipped to travel through snow and which impede traffic are liable to a fine.
- Drivers who are involved in an accident who do not call the police must complete a European Accident Claim Form (available from some motor insurers).
- During daylight hours outside built-up areas drivers must sound their horns before sharp bends where visibility is limited; after dark this warning must be given by flashing headlights.
- In Switzerland, pedestrians generally have right of way. Some pedestrians may just step into the road when on crosswalks (crossings) and will expect your vehicle to stop.
- Blue-zone parking discs are available from many petrol stations, garages, kiosks, restaurants and police stations.

Travel facts and toll charges: Switzerland

Switzerland Tourism
30 Bedford Street
London WC2E 9ED
Tel: 020 7420 4900
www.MySwitzerland.com

Banking hours
Banks are generally open Monday to Friday from 8.30am to 4.30pm. Once a week they extend their hours. Check locally. They are closed Saturday, Sunday and public holidays. Many banks have ATMs, check with your local bank that your bank card is valid in Switzerland.

Credit/debit cards
The cards most used are Visa, MasterCard and American Express. Many Swiss banks have ATMs for cash advances with your credit card.

Currency
Switzerland's currency is the Swiss franc (CHF) issued in CHF1,000, CHF200, CHF100, CHF50, CHF20 and CHF10 notes, and 5CHF, 2CHF and 1CHF coins. There are 100 centimes in a franc and 20, 10 and 5 centime coins. Many prices are indicated in euros to aid comparing prices. Merchants may accept euros but are not obliged to do so. Change will likely be in Swiss francs.

Electricity
The power supply in Switzerland is 220 volts AC, 50Hz. Most power sockets take three-round-pin-plugs. The standard continental plug with two round pins may be used without a problem.

Health care
Free or reduced-cost medical treatment is available in Switzerland to European visitors on production of a valid European Health Insurance Card (EHIC). See page 10. Comprehensive travel insurance is still advised and is essential for all other visitors.

Pharmacies
Many prescription and non-prescription medicines are available from pharmacists.

Post offices
Post offices are usually open Monday to Friday from 7.30am to 12 noon and 1.45 to 6pm. Branches in shopping centres are usually open the same hours as the shopping centres. On Saturday, post offices in large cities are open from 7.30 to 11am.

Safe water
The tap water is safe to drink. Bottled mineral water is readily available.

Telephones
Public payphones take the Swiss phone card, *Taxcard*, on sale for CHF5, CHF10 and CHF20 at post offices, newsagents, railway stations, etc. The country code for Swizerland is 41. To call home from Swizerland dial the international code (00) followed by the country code. To call the UK from Swizerland dial 00 44.

Time
Switzerland is on Central European Time, which is one hour ahead of Greenwich Mean Time (GMT + 1), until late March to late October, when clocks are put forward one hour (GMT + 2).

Emergency telephone numbers
Police **117**   Fire **118**
Ambulance (not all areas) **144**

Toll charges in Swiss Francs
For details of where to buy the motorway tax *(vignette)* see page 158.

General	Car	Car towing caravan/ trailer
Annual *vignette* (includes use of Gotthard Tunnel and San Bernardino Tunnel)	40.00	40.00
Bridges and tunnels		
Munt La Schera Tunnel	15.00	20.00
Sankt Bernhard Tunnel	29.80	46.20

Driving in Turkey *(South East Europe)*

The regulations below should be read in conjunction
with the General motoring information on pages 18–21.

Drinking and driving

If the level of alcohol in the bloodstream is
0.05 per cent or more, severe penalties can be
imposed. For drivers of cars with caravans or
trailers the alcohol level in the bloodstream is nil.

Driving licence

The minimum age at which a UK licence holder
may drive a temporarily imported car and/or
motorcycle is 18. A UK driving licence is valid
for 90 days; licences that do not incorporate
a photograph must be accompanied by an
International Driving Permit (IDP).

Fines

On-the-spot fines can be imposed. Vehicles may
be towed away if causing an obstruction.

Fuel

Leaded (95 octane), unleaded petrol (95 and
97 octane) and diesel are available. LPG is
available in large centres. Carrying petrol in a can
(fireproof container) is permitted. Credit cards
are accepted at many filling stations; check
with your card issuer for usage in Turkey
before travel.

Lights

Dipped headlights should be used in poor
daytime visibility, and also after sunset in
built-up areas.

Motorcycles

The wearing of crash helmets is compulsory.

Motor insurance

Third-party insurance is compulsory. Foreign
insurance, e.g. UK insurance, is recognised
in the European part of Turkey, if the policy
covers Turkey. Visiting motorists driving vehicles
registered in the UK may use a valid Green
Card when driving in Turkey. The Green Card
must cover the whole of Turkey, i.e. both the
European Part and the Asian part (Anatolia).
Visiting motorists who are not in possession of
a valid Green Card or who are not in possession
of a valid UK insurance policy (validated for
the whole of Turkey) must take out short-term
insurance at the border or TTOK offices.

Passengers/children in cars

A child under 12 cannot travel as a front-
seat passenger.

Seat belts

It is compulsory for front-seat occupants to
wear seat belts, if fitted. It is compulsory for
rear-seat passengers to wear seat belts outside
built-up areas

Speed limits

The standard legal limits, which may be
varied by signs, for **private vehicles without
trailers** are: in built-up areas 50km/h (31mph),
outside built-up areas 90km/h (55mph) for cars,
70km/h (43mph) for motorcycles; motorways

120km/h (74mph) for cars and 80km/h (49mph) for motorcycles. The minimum speed on motorways is 40km/h (24mph). Speed limits are 10km/h (6mph) **less if the car is towing a trailer**.

Additional information

- It is compulsory to carry a first-aid kit and a fire extinguisher – these are not required for two-wheeled vehicles.
- It is compulsory for all vehicles to carry two warning triangles.
- The use of the horn is generally prohibited in towns from 10pm until sunrise.
- The use of spiked tyres is prohibited.
- It is recommended that winter tyres are used in snowy areas and snow chains are carried.
- In the event of an accident it is compulsory to call the police and obtain a report.

Travel facts and toll charges: Turkey

Turkish Tourist Office
29–30 St James's Street, 4th Floor
London SW1A 1HB
Tel: **020 7839 7778; www.gototurkey.co.uk**

Banking hours
Banks are generally open Monday to Friday 8.30am to 12 noon and 1.30 to 5pm. Some banks open weekends in tourist areas.

Credit/debit cards
Credit cards are widely accepted in hotels, restaurants and shops. However, it is advisable to carry cash for the smaller shops and cafés, particularly in rural areas. ATMs are found in convenient locations in cities, towns, resorts and the arrivals halls at most airports.

Currency
Turkey's currency is the Turkish lira (TL) divided into 100 kurus (Kr). Banknotes are issued in denominations of 1, 5, 10, 20, 50 and 100TL. Coins in 1, 5, 10, 25 and 50Kr and 1TL. Many shops and restaurants in the coastal resorts and big cities accept payment in foreign currency.

Electricity
The power supply in Turkey is 220 volts AC. Sockets take two-round-pin plugs but there are two sizes in use. Bring your own adaptor. Power cuts are frequent in rural areas but usually short lived.

Health care
Comprehensive travel insurance is essential for all visitors.

Pharmacies
Prescription and non-prescription drugs and medicines are available from pharmacies (eczane).

Post offices
Post offices (PTT) have a black-on-yellow logo. In major resorts and towns the main PTT will stay open for phone calls until midnight. Post offices are open Monday to Friday from 8am to 7 or 8pm and Saturday mornings. You can normally buy stamps with your postcards.

Safe water
Tap water is generally safe to drink, though it can be heavily chlorinated and taste unpleasant. Bottled mineral water is inexpensive and is sold either sparkling (maden suyu) or still (memba suyu).

Telephones
There are pay phones on many streets, and at PTT offices. Phone cards are sold at post offices and newsagents. Most phones also accept credit cards. The country code for Turkey is 90. To call home from Turkey dial the international code (00) followed by the country code. To call the UK from Turkey dial 00 44.

Time
Turkey is on Eastern European Time, which is two hours ahead of Greenwich Mean Time (GMT + 2), but from the last Sunday in March to the last Sunday in October, when clocks are put forward one hour, Summer Time (GMT + 3) operates.

Emergency telephone numbers
Police **155**   Fire **110**
Emergency (including ambulance) **112**

Toll charges in Turkish Lira

Road		Car	Car towing caravan/ trailer
E80 (O-3)	Edirne – Istanbul	8.50	15.25
E80/89 (O-4)	Istanbul – Ankara	17.00	30.50
E87 (O31)	Izmir – Aydin	3.50	6.50
E881 (O32)	Izmir – Cesme	2.25	5.00
E90 (O-21)	Pozanti – Tarus	3.50	7.75
E90 (O-52)	Adana – Sanliurfa	10.50	20.50
E91 (O-53)	Ceyhan – Iskenderun	3.50	7.00

Bridges and tunnels

Bosphorus and Fatih Sultan Mehmet Bridge (Istanbul) on **E80** Eastbound only	3.75	23.50

Driving in Ukraine *(Eastern Europe)*

The regulations below should be read in conjunction with the General motoring information on pages 18–21.

Drinking and driving

Drinking and driving is strictly forbidden. Nil percentage of alcohol is allowed in the driver's blood. Fines for driving under the influence of alcohol can be very high. The driving licence can be confiscated for a repeat offence.

Driving licence

An International Driving Permit (IDP) is compulsory for the holder of any type of UK driving licence. The minimum age at which a visitor may drive a temporarily imported car and/or motorcycle is 18.

Fines

Fines can be issued to foreign nationals on the spot; the police are permitted to demand immediate cash payment. If a visitor has not paid a penalty imposed before his departure or within 15 days, the offender's vehicle can be detained. The authorities can clamp or remove a vehicle that is parked illegally.

Fuel

Unleaded petrol (95 and 98 octane), diesel *(solyarka)* and LPG are available. Carrying petrol in a can is permitted. It is advisable to carry petrol in spare cans when undertaking a long journey. Credit cards are accepted at filling stations; check with your card issuer for usage in Ukraine before travel. Fuel is usually paid for in local currency.

Lights

Dipped headlights should be used in poor daytime visibility.

Motorcycles

The wearing of crash helmets is compulsory for both driver and passenger. Children under 12 and less than 1.45m (4ft 9in) in height are not permitted to travel as a passenger.

Motor insurance

Third party insurance is compulsory. Green Cards are accepted.

Passengers/children in cars

Children under 12 and less than 1.45m (4ft 9in) cannot travel as front-seat passengers.

Seat belts

It is compulsory for front-seat occupants to wear seat belts.

Speed limits

Signed speed limits must be strictly adhered to. The standard legal limits, which may be varied by signs, for **private vehicles without trailers** are: in built-up areas 60km/h (37mph), outside built-up areas 90km/h (55mph), major roads 110km/h (62mph), motorways 130km/h (80mph). In some residential zones the limit is 20km/h (13mph). Motorists who have held a driving licence for less than two years must not exceed 70km/h (43mph). When **towing a caravan or trailer** with a combined weight less than 3.5 tonnes, the limit on all roads outside built-up areas is 90km/h (55mph).

Additional information

- It is compulsory to carry a first-aid kit, a fire extinguisher and a warning triangle.
- A person temporarily taking a vehicle into the Ukraine must pay an ecological tax at the border. The amount varies according to the engine power.
- In addition to the original vehicle registration document, it is recommended that an International Certificate for Motor Vehicles also be carried if visiting any Russian speaking areas. State Traffic Inspectorate officials will stop vehicles to check documents, especially if they are displaying foreign plates.
- We recommend that visitors carry an assortment of spares such as fan belt, replacement bulbs and spark plugs.
- It is necessary to pre-plan itineraries and book accommodation before departure.
- During cold winters it is highly recommended that you use spiked tyres or snow chains.
- If a foreign-registered vehicle is involved in an accident it is compulsory to call the police.

Travel facts: Ukraine

Ukrainian Embassy
60 Holland Park
London W11 3SJ
Tel: 020 7727 6312
http://ukraine.embassyhomepage.com

Banking hours
Banks are usually open Monday to Friday 9am to 6pm.
Some banks open on Saturday.

Credit/debit cards
Some credit/debit cards, including MasterCard and
Visa, are accepted in large cities, but don't rely solely
on cards or traveller's checks. ATMs *(Bankomat)*
are located in public places such as shopping malls,
hotels, inside or next to banks, inside travel agencies or
ticket offices. Make sure your card logo is on the ATM
machine. Usually ATMs offer hryvnias. Instructions are
in Russian, Ukrainian or English.

Currency
The official currency of Ukraine is the hryvnia (Hrn),
also known as hryvnia or grivna. There are 100 Kopiyka
in a Hryvnia. There are banknotes for Hrn1, 2, 5, 10, 20,
50, 100, 200 and 500. There are coins for Hrn1, 2, and 5
and 1, 2, 5, 10, 25, and 50 kopiykas. US dollars and euros
are preferred foreign currency; they can be exchanged
at hotels, banks and airports. Make sure your foreign
banknotes are new-looking and crisp or they may not
be exchanged. Avoid changing money with private
individuals. The use of foreign currency is officially
forbidden in shops, bars and restaurants.

Electricity
The power supply is 220 volts AC, 50Hz in Ukraine. Plugs
and wall sockets are mostly the European two-pin style
or can be the old Soviet type which have narrower pins.

Health care
The UK has a reciprocal healthcare agreement with
Ukraine. If you're visiting Ukraine and need urgent or
immediate medical treatment it will be provided at a
reduced cost or, in some cases, free. The range of
medical services available may be more restricted than
under the NHS, therefore it is essential for all visitors to
have comprehensive travel insurance. Visit
www.nhs.uk/NHSEngland/Healthcareabroad for
a country-by-country guide.

Pharmacies
Take a supply of medicines that you are likely to need
during your stay as they may be difficult to obtain
locally. Check first that they may be legally imported.
In Kiev the pharmacy at Shevchenko Boulevard 36a,
opposite the University metro stop. is open seven days a
week from 8am to 9pm; English is spoken.

Post offices
Post offices are generally open 9am to 6pm. The main
post office in Kiev is located at Khreshchatik 22 and is
open 24 hours. You can make telephone calls and send
faxes here.

Safe water
Mains water is not considered safe to drink. You
are advised to buy bottled mineral water from
supermarkets. Be aware that some bottled water from
the smaller kiosks can be counterfeit.

Telephones
You can buy telephone cards for public pay phones in
post offices. The country code for the Ukraine is 380.
To call home from Ukraine dial the international code
(00) followed by the code. To call the UK from Ukraine
dial 00 44.

Time
Ukraine is in the Eastern European Time Zone (EET)
and is two hours ahead of Greenwich Mean Time
(GMT + 2). From the last Sunday in March to the last
Sunday in October it is three hours ahead of Greenwich
Mean Time (GMT + 3).

Emergency telephone numbers
Police **102**
Fire **101**
Ambulance **103**

Car tours

The Western Loire Valley

5 days 512km (319 miles)

Starting in Nantes, this tour soon leaves all Breton influences behind as it heads for the valleys of the Loire and the Sarthe. You will find some of France's finest *son et lumière* presentations here, one of the world's most famous motor-racing circuits, and the Pays Nantais and Anjou, which are packed with vineyards.

ITINERARY

NANTES • Clisson (27km/17 miles)
CLISSON • Cholet (36km/22.5 miles)
CHOLET • Doué-la-Fontaine (58km/36 miles)
DOUÉ-LA-FONTAINE • St-Hilaire (29km/18 miles)
ST-HILAIRE • Saumur (4km/2.5 miles)
SAUMUR • Baugé (44km/27 miles)
BAUGÉ • Le Lude (24km/15 miles)
LE LUDE • Le Mans Circuit (75km/47 miles)
LE MANS CIRCUIT • Le Mans (10km/6 miles)
LE MANS • Angers (106km/66 miles)
ANGERS • Nantes (99km/62 miles)

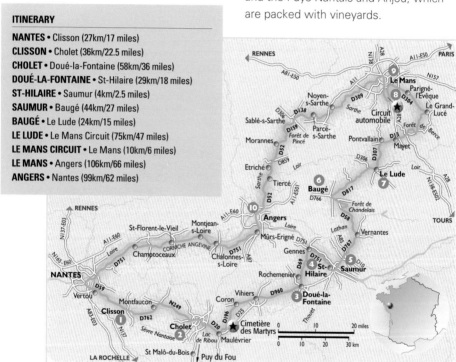

Leave Nantes for Clisson on the D59 through St-Fiacre. In Gorges go left of the D113 then take the D59 again into Clisson.

❶ **Clisson,** Loire Valley West
The Vendée Wars and the savage reprisals of the Revolutionary government army all but obliterated this little town. It was completely rebuilt, but not as it had been before: present-day Clisson is mostly a tribute to Palladian Italy, with colonnades, loggias and bell-towers of a style seen nowhere else in western France.

Look for the stabilised but unfurnished ruin of the 13th- to 15th-century castle, the

Clisson's impressive ruined 13th- to 15th-century castle sits majestically atop a rocky outcrop

15th-century market hall, the two medieval bridges contrasting with the soaring 19th-century road viaduct, and Italianate creations such as the Temple d'Amitié and the Church of Notre-Dame.

There are beautiful walks in the valleys of the Sèvre Nantaise and the Moine. Local wines may be tasted, but Clisson itself is the great attraction, especially its Italianate skyline and leafy riverside view.

Leave Clisson on the N149. Turn left as for Beaupréau on the D762 then go along the N249 and follow signs to Cholet.

❷ Cholet, Loire Valley West
Only 20 buildings were left standing in the brutal aftermath of the Vendée Wars of 1793–96.

A section of the Musée d'Art et de l'Histoire explains how the Vendée rising against the Revolutionary government's policies of mass conscription and the overthrow of all previous loyalties was at first successful, then viciously crushed. Other exhibitions are at the Musée Paysan with its old-style dairy and country house interiors in the leisure park by the Ribou lake.

This is a famous textile town, with a Musée du Textile illustrating the industry. Its trademark is the red-and-white handkerchief – the *mouchoir de Cholet* – whose design is rooted in another incident of the Vendée Wars. The town also has a shoe museum and at nearby Maulévrier there is a fine Oriental Garden that mirrors the Buddhist stages of human existence.

The Western Loire Valley

Leave Cholet on the D20 as for Poitiers. In Maulévrier turn left and right as for Vihiers, then left on the D196 through Chanteloup to Coron. Go right on the D960 to Doué-la-Fontaine.

❸ Doué-la-Fontaine, Loire Valley West
If you arrived in the middle of Doué without paying attention to its outskirts, you might shrug it off as an ordinary little town. It is far from that. The zoo, adapted from the cliffs, caverns and ditches of a disused limestone quarry, houses lions, tigers, birds of prey, deer, emus, rare snow panthers and 15 monkey enclosures. Naturoscope has displays relating to threatened species and the destruction of their habitats.

The Musée des Commerces Anciens features seven old-style shops and a rose-water distillery, in partly restored 18th-century stables.

Nobody is certain about the origins of Doué's arena, which is Roman in style but of a much later date. However, there is no doubt about the Moulin Cartier. Built in 1910, it was the last windmill raised in the region of Anjou (closed to visitors).

Leave Doué on the D69 to Gennes. Go right as for Saumur on the D751 through La Mimerolle and into St-Hilaire.

❹ St-Hilaire, Loire Valley West
Just before this village – a suburb of Saumur – the Musée du Champignon, in a cave system cut into the roadside cliffs, is more than simply an exhibition about mushrooms and how they are grown. The underground galleries were dug in medieval times, part of a network of more than 480km (300 miles) throughout the district, which produces 75 per cent of France's cultivated mushrooms.

Turn right in St-Hilaire for the École National d'Équitation. This is France's national riding academy, excellently housed and staffed. In the practice arena, in front of high wall mirrors, you may see members of the acadamy's Cadre Noire put their horses through the intricate, disciplined and stylish movements for which they are famous all over Europe. They also perform summer season shows.

Continue on the D751 into Saumur.

❺ Saumur, Loire Valley West
Straddling the Loire, this very appealing town is passionate about horses and the cavalry, wines, museums and exuberant outdoor displays. The Château de Saumur, overlooking the river, houses two separate collections. The Musée des Arts Décoratifs concentrates

The château at Saumur has been dubbed the 'castle of love'

on the decorative arts – ceramics, enamelware, carvings in wood and alabaster. Another, Musée du Cheval, celebrates centuries of horsemanship.

The cavalry has two separate exhibitions in the château, one recalling its mounted days, the other taking the story to more recent times with a comprehensive display of tanks and armoured cars.

Second only to Champagne, Saumur is famous for its sparkling wines. Several firms welcome visitors to their cellars. Notre-Dame de Nantilly, dating from the 12th century, houses a valuable collection of medieval and Renaissance tapestries.

And the old quarter of Saumur with its narrow streets and restored 17th-century houses adds to the attractions of a justifiably self-confident town.

Leave Saumur on the N147 as for Le Mans. At the roundabout take the second exit to Vernantes on the D767. In Vernantes, turn sharp left at the traffic lights as for Baugé, then right on the D58 as for Baugé through Mouliherne. In Le Guédéniau go right on the D186 as for Lasse. Turn left following 'Les Caves de Chanzelles' sign. At the roundabout in the forest take the fifth exit for Baugé. Rejoin the D58 and continue to Baugé.

❻ Baugé, Loire Valley West
Plenty of space has been left around Baugé's 15th-century castle, originally a hunting lodge of Good King René, Duke of Anjou. Holding displays of weapons, coins and ceramics, it stands beside public gardens dipping to an attractive riverside. The Convent of La Girouardière houses a venerated relic – a jewelled cross believed to contain a piece of the True Cross brought to France by a crusader

knight. Its unusual design was adopted as the Cross of Lorraine. Look also for Baugé's charming 17th-century Hospice-St-Joseph (not open to the public).

Sometimes an unfamiliar language may be seen or spoken here, describing Baugé, for instance, as *'bela kaj malmova urbeto'*: the Château de Grésillon, on your exit route from 'this fine old town', is an international Esperanto centre (not open to the public).

Leave Baugé on the D817, which becomes the D305. Do right on the D306 to Le Lude.

❼ Le Lude, Loire Valley West
Pride of this little town is the richly furnished château, rebuilt in Renaissance style after an English garrison was driven out – with heavy damage to the fabric – in 1427. The town's situation is most attractive, above balustraded gardens rising from the River Loir, whose waters eventually feed the larger Loire. Cultural life in Le Lude includes a number of special events and festivals featuring horticulture, theatre, music and children's activities.

Leave Le Lude on the D307 to Pontvallain. Go right on the D13 through Mayet and across the N138 to Le Grand-Lucé. Turn left at the give-way sign and left on the D304 as for Le Mans. Go under the bridge, then left following the 'Angers' sign, under another bridge and follow the 'Tours' signs along the N138. Go right at the roundabout on the D140 as for Arnage, then right on the D139 to the grandstands of the racing circuit.

❽ Le Mans Circuit, Loire Valley West
Prosaically, they may be the N138, D140 and D139, but these roads are also part of the great motor-racing circuit where the Le Mans 24-Hour

Race is held every June.

The N138 is the Mulsanne Straight, along which Jaguars, Porsches and Mercedes howl at speeds of over 320km/h (200mph).

There is a smaller but linked Bugatti Circuit. The two tracks play host to five major car and motorcycle events, plus a 24-hour truck race! You can watch test sessions from the main grandstands, which are informally open to the public on non-competition days.

An excellent motor museum also recalls that this was where Wilbur Wright, over from the United States, made the first powered flight in Europe in 1908.

Continue on the D139 into Le Mans.

❾ Le Mans, Loire Valley West

Many first-time visitors to Le Mans will find it familiar – if, that is, they have seen the films *Cyrano de Bergerac* or the 1997 version of *The Man in the Iron Mask*, which were shot here. It lies at the heart of a warren of cobbled medieval streets, lined with half-timbered buildings and attractive Renaissance mansions.

One of the loveliest of these houses is the Musée de la Reine Bérengère, a celebration of Sarthe history. Queen Bérengère was Richard the Lionheart's widow, and she built the Cistercian abbey outside the town. Art lovers should make for the Musée de Tessé, with its superb collection of paintings. In July, a lively street festival takes over the town.

Leave Le Mans on the D309 as for Sablé. In Parcé cross the river then go first right at the crossroads, left to Solesmes, then continue to Sablé-sur-Sarthe. Go straight across the D306 for Centre-Ville. At the roundabout take the last exit, then a side road right for

Pincé. This is the D159. Bear right on the C15 for 'Pincé par la Forêt'. Rejoin the D159, then follow the D18 and D52 through Morannes. Continue through Etriché and Tiercé. Go straight on along the N160 then right on the N23 to Angers.

❿ Angers, Loire Valley West

Here in the heart of Anjou lies a university town of parks, gardens and colourful floral decorations, with a grand Plantagenet castle rising in towers of banded stonework. The Cathédrale Saint Maurice is best approached by the Montée St-Maurice, a stairway climbing from the River Maine.

Angers is a tapestry town, and the longest tapestry in France, *La Tenture de l'Apocolypse*, completed in the late 14th century to show the Apocalypse, is on display in the castle. Many others, ancient and modern, are on show in the castle itself and in individual museums and galleries.

Fine Renaissance buildings survive, both around the cathedral and elsewhere. River cruises follow the Maine, and for the adventurous there are hot-air balloon flights to waft you high above the castles, vineyards and villages of Anjou.

Alternatively, visit the stunningly converted 13th-century abbey, now home to the monumental sculptures of David d'Angers (1788–1856).

Leave Angers through Les-Ponts-de-Cé on the N160. In Mûrs-Érigné, turn right to go through Chalonnes-sur-Loire and Champtoceaux on the D751 and return on the N249 to Nantes.

Right: The Cathedral of St-Julien, Le Mans

The Enchanting Mosel Valley

2/3 days 432km (267 miles)

Long before Rome was founded – legend says around 2050 BC – there was a settlement at Trier. The city blossomed under the Romans, but was later repeatedly attacked by invading Vandals. It is now a major tourist attraction. For spectacular views visit two of the area's most famous fortresses – Burg Eltz and the Felsenfestung Ehrenbreitstein (Rock Fortress).

ITINERARY

TRIER • Bernkastel-Kues (60km/37.5 miles)
BERNKASTEL-KUES • Traben-Trarbach (26km/16 miles)
TRABEN-TRARBACH • Cochem (52km/32 miles)
COCHEM • Burg Eltz (20km/12 miles)
BURG ELTZ • Koblenz (35km/22 miles)
KOBLENZ • Boppard (22km/13.5 miles)
BOPPARD • St Goar (15km/9 miles)
ST GOAR • Bingen (34km/21 miles)
BINGEN • Bad Kreuznach (13km/8 miles)
BAD KREUZNACH • Trier (155km/96 miles)

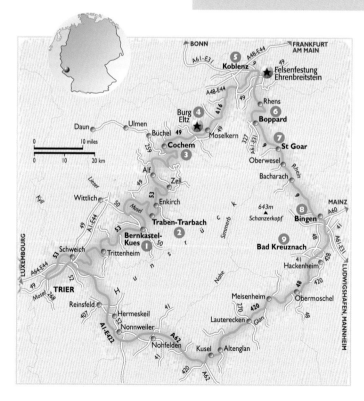

From Trier join the B53 northeast to Bernkastel-Kues, 60km (37.5 miles).

❶ Bernkastel-Kues, Rheinland-Pfalz
The square of this picturesque town is surrounded by timber-framed houses, with the fountain of St Michael in its centre, and the Rathaus (town hall) which was built in 1608. Fascinating but not quite so picturesque are the iron chains of the Pranger (stocks), the public punishment of the Middle Ages, preserved here. The parish church of St Michael dates from the 14th century and contains interesting works by a local sculptor, Hans Ruprecht Hoffmann. Bernkastel-Kues has a wine museum, and the excellent Bernkastler wine is well known.

South of Bernkasteler stands the ruin of the Landshut, the second fortress to be built on the same site, in 1280.

Continue on the B53 for 26km (16 miles) to Traben-Trarbach.

❷ Traben-Trarbach, Rheinland-Pfalz
A trip to the ruins of the fortress Grevenburg above Traben-Trarbach offers rewarding views over the town and the picturesque Mosel Valley. Between 1520 and 1734 the fortress was besieged six times and then blown up, so it is small wonder that only a fragment of a wall with window holes is left.

The little town of Zell, on the other side of the river, should not be missed. It appears to be built into the landscape with vineyards all around it. The 16th-century late Gothic palace in the town is now a hotel. Emperor Maximilian lived here at one time and it contains many treasures. Zeller Schwarze Katz (Black Cat) is a popular wine from the local grapes.

Cochem, with its romantic castle, the former Reichsburg, overlooking the Mosel

Continue on the B53, then the B49 to Cochem.

❸ Cochem, Rheinland-Pfalz

A real centre for tourism in the Mosel Valley is Cochem, which also lies in an important wine-growing area. The Reichsburg (imperial castle) was rebuilt in 1874, using plans from 1576. It affords splendid views over the Mosel Valley and its vineyards, which stretch from the river's edge up into the hills.

From Cochem continue on the B49/B416 and turn left at Moselkern for Burg Eltz.

❹ Burg Eltz, Rheinland-Pfalz

High above the wine-producing village of Moselkern stands the Burg or fortress of Eltz, one of the most rewarding attractions in the area. Numerous oriels and towers and a superb position made this fortress unconquerable for centuries. Even now, cars find the ascent difficult. The road stops at the Antonius Chapel, and the last few hundred metres have to be covered on foot or by shuttle bus. The knights

Castle ruins on the hillside above the village of St Goar

of Eltz were called the Eisenköpfe (Iron Heads), a tribute to their stubbornness as well as to the numerous skirmishes in which they took part. The guided tour around the fortress is accompanied by many entertaining stories and anecdotes.

From Burg Eltz return to Moselkern, then turn left on the B416 to Koblenz.

❺ Koblenz, Rheinland-Pfalz

Where the Mosel enters the mighty Rhine lies Koblenz. Its unique situation has made it a place of great importance from Roman times. Koblenz's name is derived from the Roman *castrum ad confluentes*, the 'camp at the confluence'. It is not known when the Romans actually established their outpost here, but it must have been before the reign of Emperor Tiberius (AD 14–37).

After almost total wartime destruction, part of the old centre of Koblenz has been meticulously restored. The actual point of land where the Mosel and Rhine meet is called the Deutsches Eck (German Corner), marked by a monument to German unity.

The Felsenfestung Ehrenbreitstein (Rock Fortress) dominates the Rhine and Mosel and is supposedly the largest fortress in Europe. It is best reached by chair-lift. The view from the fortress's terrace is spectacular, down to Koblenz and in the distance to the Eifel and Hunsrück mountain ranges. The fortress was always a thorn in the flesh of the French, and Napoleon destroyed it in 1801. It was subsequently rebuilt, but a clause in the Treaty of Versailles after World War I stated it must never again be used for military purposes. It now houses the Rhine Museum.

The former Kurfürstliches Schloss, or Residenzschloss as it is also known, was once the seat of Prince Wilhelm von Preussen and until 1918 it was owned by the Prussian kings. It now belongs to the state and is used for administrative purposes.

Schloss Stolzenfels, which was built in 1242, is a former royal castle. It was destroyed by the French in 1688 and rebuilt after 1836. Its interior (closed for renovation until 2011) is worth seeing, especially the large Rittersaal (Knights' Hall) and the King's Quarters.

From Koblenz take the B9 south for 22km (13.5 miles) to Boppard.

6 Boppard, Rheinland-Pfalz

At a bend in the Rhine lies Boppard, a very old settlement that the Celts called *Bandobriga*. Later the Romans erected fortifications here around AD 400, and parts of the 8m (26-foot) high walls can still be seen.

St Severuskirche (Church of St Severus) is late Romanesque. The Karmeliter-Kirche is interesting; it has no tower, which is very rare for a Gothic church. The Alte Burg (Old Castle), dating from the 14th century, now houses the Museum der Stadt Boppard.

Continue south on the B9 for 15km (9 miles) to St Goar.

7 St Goar, Rheinland-Pfalz

In the Middle Ages, many knights living in fortresses on narrow stretches of river supplemented their incomes by collecting tolls from passing ships – or just simply robbing them. They were the so-called Raubritter (robbing knights). One such fortress was 13th-century Burg Rheinfels, just before St Goar. This former royal castle is now a pleasant hotel.

The Stiftskirche in St Goar is a delightful mixture of styles. The church itself is 15th century, the crypt is Romanesque and the marble tombs are from the 16th and 17th centuries.

From St Goar continue south on the B9 to Bingen, 34km (21 miles).

8 Bingen, Rheinland-Pfalz

The Burg Klopp, which overlooks Bingen, was built on a Roman site with a deep well of 52m (170 feet), which probably goes back to the same period. The fortress was destroyed in 1689, and the remnants blown up in 1711, but between 1875 and 1879, it was totally rebuilt.

On an island in the river stands the Mäuseturm (Mice Tower). This stone construction dates from 1208 and replaced a wooden Roman tower erected in 8 BC under the Roman military leader Drusus. Legend has it that when Bishop Hatto was thrown into the tower as a punishment for his cruelties, he was eaten alive by mice.

From Bingen continue due south on the B48 to Bad Kreuznach, 13km (8 miles).

9 Bad Kreuznach, Rheinland-Pfalz

This sizeable spa lies on the River Nahe, and its thermal springs are used as the basis for well-organised treatments for rheumatism, gout and similar ailments. Unique to the town are the well-preserved Brücken-hauser (Bridge Houses). These date from the 15th century, and have been chosen as the town emblem. In the Römerhalle Museum, Roman mosaics and remains from the military camp are on view.

From Bad Kreuznach take the B48, then the B420 south to Kusel. Join the A62 northwest towards Nonnweiler. Continue on the A1/ E422 north to exit Moseltal, then southwest to Trier on the A602/B49, 155km (96 miles).

Cotswold Wool & Stone

2 days 99 miles (159km)

This is mainly a circuit of Cotswold countryside – a landscape of stone walls surrounding fertile fields and distinctive village architecture. The villages contain many fine churches, but the best known structure is the cross in the centre of Banbury. The family homes of two great men can also be seen: one Englishman in Blenheim and one American in Sulgrave.

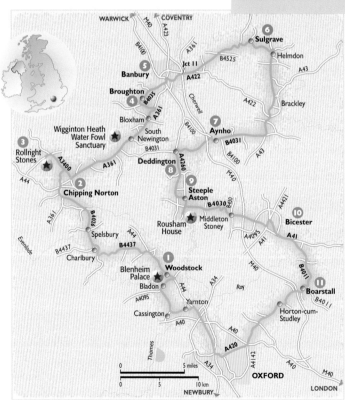

Right: Blenheim Palace sits in grounds landscaped by 'Capability' Brown

Leave Oxford on the A44 and turn left along an unclassified road towards Cassington. Turn right to Bladon on the A4095, then left on the A44 to Woodstock.

❶ Woodstock, Oxfordshire
You can stop off in Bladon, to visit the churchyard where Sir Winston Churchill, his wife and parents are buried, before continuing along the road to Blenheim, where he was born. Blenheim Palace was given to the Marlborough family by Queen Anne as a reward for the 1st Duke of Marlborough's victory over the French at Blenheim in 1704.

Just outside the park is the town of Woodstock, with its mellow stone buildings. Kings of England came here for the excellent hunting in the Forest of Wychwood, but modern visitors have gentler interests. A quiet hour can be spent in the Oxfordshire County Museum, in the town centre, where the history of the people and the changing landscape is conveyed in exhibitions ranging from the Stone Age to the present time.

From Woodstock take the A44 turning left on to the B4437 to Charlbury and then the B4026 to Chipping Norton.

❷ Chipping Norton, Oxfordshire
Gateway to the Cotswolds and a historic market town for the sheep farmers of the area, Chipping Norton has a wide main street that is a relic of those days (the name 'chipping' means market). There are many fine old stone buildings, including the church, market hall, pubs and big houses, but it is the fine wool church that dominates the town, one of over 40 in the Cotswolds. Paid for by the proceeds from sheep farming, it dates mainly from the 14th and 15th centuries, but much of its stonework has been restored. Another of the town's landmarks is the chimney of Bliss Tweed Mill, which is an important reminder of local industrial history.

Take the B4026, then go north along the A3400 for just over a mile (1.6km) and turn left along an unclassified road signed 'Little Rollright'.

❸ Rollright Stones, Oxfordshire
This Bronze Age circle, which dates from earlier than 1000 BC, was nearly as important as Stonehenge in the neolithic period. Nicknamed the 'King's Men', it measures a full 100 feet (30m) across. Over the road is the King Stone, a monolith, and near by, just along the road, is the group of stones called the Whispering Knights,

Cotswold Wool & Stone

at the site of a prehistoric burial chamber. The surrounding countryside is patterned with stone walls of weathered limestone.

Return to the A3400 and turn south before branching left on to the A361, then turn left in Bloxham along unclassified roads to Broughton.

❹ Broughton, Oxfordshire
Broughton Castle is a fortified manor rather than a castle, turned into an Elizabethan house of style by the Fiennes family in about 1600. Surrounded by a great moat lake, it is set in gorgeous parkland, and has a stone church near by. The present owners, Lord and Lady Saye and Sele, are descendants of the family that has lived here for centuries. Celia Fiennes, the 17th-century traveller and diarist, was a member of this family. William de Wykeham, founder of Winchester School and New College, Oxford, acquired the manor and converted the manor house into a castle. The medieval Great Hall is the most impressive room, and suits of armour from the Civil War are on show.

Drive 3 miles (5km) east along the B4035 to Banbury.

❺ Banbury, Oxfordshire
Banbury is a town of charm and character, with its interesting buildings and narrow medieval streets. Famous for the nursery rhyme 'Ride a cock horse to Banbury Cross', the town is also known for its spice cakes, which have been made here since the 16th century. The unusual church with its round tower replaced an older church demolished in the 18th century. There is still a weekly street market, which has been held regularly for over 800 years; there used to be a livestock market, too, but nowadays the

animals are taken to a site on the edge of town – it is Europe's largest cattle market.

Head east along the A422. After 2 miles (3km) turn left on to the B4525, then on to the unclassified road to Sulgrave.

❻ Sulgrave, Northamptonshire
The old manor in this attractive stone village was the home of ancestors of George Washington from 1539 to 1659, having been bought by Lawrence Washington, wool merchant and twice Mayor of Northampton. Not to be missed is the family coat of arms with its stars and stripes carved above the entrance porch; the most treasured possession inside is an original oil painting of George Washington.

Take the unclassified road through Helmdon, heading south to Brackley to join the A43, then shortly right on to the B4031 to Aynho.

❼ Aynho, Northamptonshire
This limestone village contains apricot trees from which, legend has it, fruit was paid as a toll to the Cartwrights, Lords of the Manor. They lived in the mansion in Aynhoe Park, and there are several memorials to them, including a Victorian marble cross in the church.

From Aynho go west along the B4031 for 3 miles (5km) to Deddington.

❽ Deddington, Oxfordshire
Dominating this village, which is built out of the honey-coloured local stone, is the church, with each of its eight pinnacles topped with gilded vanes. Adjacent Castle House was formerly the rectory, and parts of the building date from the 14th century. The area has many links with the days of the Civil War.

Drive southwards for 5 miles (8km) along the A4260 and then left on to an unclassified road to Steeple Aston.

⑨ Steeple Aston, Oxfordshire
Steeple Aston was winner of the Oxfordshire Best Kept Village Award in 1981 and 1983, and is still an eye-catching spot. The village inn, Hopcroft's Holt, had associations with Claude Duval, a French highwayman who worked in these parts. Just beyond Steeple Aston is the Jacobean mansion of Rousham House, built by Sir Robert Dormer in 1635 and still owned by the same family. William Kent improved the house in the 18th century by adding the wings and stable block. In the magnificent garden, the complete Kent layout has survived. There is a fine herd of rare Longhorn cattle in the park, and you should be sure not to miss the walled garden.

Another unclassified road leads south on to the B4030 in turn leading to the A4095 for the 9 miles (14km) to Bicester.

Broughton Castle is a gracious Elizabethan manor

⑩ Bicester, Oxfordshire
Little can be seen of the Roman town at Alchester, to the south of Bicester, but excavations show that people lived here from about the middle of the 1st century AD until the late Roman period. Bicester's church has elements of a 13th-century building.

Take the A41 and then the B4011 towards Thame. Turn sharp right to Boarstall.

⑪ Boarstall, Buckinghamshire
This tiny hamlet is the location of Boarstall Tower, an amazing stone gatehouse that was originally part of a massive fortified house. It dates from the 14th century and is now looked after by the National Trust, which also owns Boarstall Duck Decoy. This 18th-century decoy is in 13 acres (5 hectares) of natural old woodland. Attractions include a small exhibition hall, nature trail and bird hide.

Take unclassified roads via Horton-cum-Studley along the edge of Otmoor for the return to Oxford.

The Causeway Coast *2/3 days 163 miles (263km)*

Larne is a busy port, the terminus for the shortest sea crossing between Ireland and Britain. It marks the start of the scenic Antrim Coast Road, which was constructed in the 1830s to link the remote Glens of Antrim to the rest of Ulster. To the north is Carnfunnock Park, which has a maze in the shape of Northern Ireland.

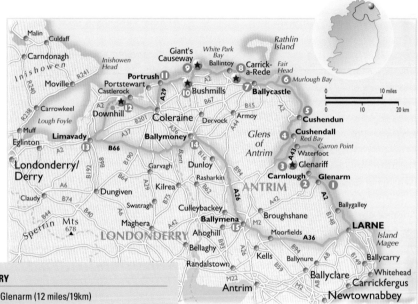

ITINERARY

LARNE • Glenarm (12 miles/19km)
GLENARM • Carnlough (3 miles/5km)
CARNLOUGH • Glenariff (14miles/22km)
GLENARIFF • Cushendall (7 miles/11km)
CUSHENDALL • Cushendun (6 miles/10km)
CUSHENDUN • Fair Head (10 miles/16km)
FAIR HEAD • Ballycastle (6 miles/10km)
BALLYCASTLE • Carrick-a-Rede (6 miles/10km)
CARRICK-A-REDE • Giant's Causeway (8 miles/13km)
GIANT'S CAUSEWAY • Bushmills (2 miles/3km)
BUSHMILLS • Portrush (6 miles/10km)
PORTRUSH • Downhill (12 miles/19km)
DOWNHILL • Limavady (11 miles/18km)
LIMAVADY • Ballymoney (20 miles/32km)
BALLYMONEY • Ballymena (19 miles/31km)
BALLYMENA • Larne (21 miles/34km)

Take the A2 coastal road north for 12 miles (19km) to Glenarm.

❶ Glenarm, Co Antrim
The Antrim Coast Road is so attractive that it is difficult to resist its magnetic lure, but leave it for a moment to sample the charm of Glenarm, a village that clings to the glen rather than to the coast. The neo-Tudor Glenarm Castle is the seat of the Earls of Antrim; its barbican and battlemented, buttressed walls of 1825 rise above the river just as it approaches the sea.

The village has twisting streets, pavements patterned in limestone and basalt, a market house with an Italianate campanile and Georgian houses and shops.

The forest, through the gateway at the top of the village, gives the first opportunity to walk up a delectable Antrim glen. This one is narrow and leafy with pathways and waterfalls.

Take the A2 to Carnlough.

❷ Carnlough, Co Antrim
Carnlough, at the foot of Glencloy, the least dramatic of the glens, has a good, safe beach. A railway used to carry lime from the kilns above the village to the harbour, over the bridge that spans the coast road. The bridge, the clock tower and the former town hall are made from great chunks of limestone. Frances Anne Vane Tempest Stewart, Countess of Antrim and Marchioness of Londonderry, was responsible for many major works, including Garron Tower, built in 1848, once a family home, now a boarding school. She is remembered in the town's main hotel, the Londonderry Arms, which was built in 1854 and has the feel of a coaching inn.

Take the A2, following signposts for Cushendall for 9 miles (14km) to Waterfoot. Turn left on to the A43 for 5 miles (8km) to Glenariff Forest Park.

❸ Glenariff, Co Antrim
The road obligingly provides a perfect route along this magnificent glen. The bay at its foot is 1 mile (1.6km) long and the chiselled sides draw in the fertile valley symmetrically to the head of the glen. There, the Forest Park allows easy exploration of the deep, wooded gorge with its cascades.

Between Red Bay and the pier are three caves. Nanny's Cave was inhabited by Ann Murray until her death, aged 100, in 1847. She supported herself by knitting and by selling poteen (an illicit distillation, pronounced *potcheen*), or 'the natural', as she called it.

Turn right to follow the B14 to Cushendall.

❹ Cushendall, Co Antrim
Cushendall sits on a pleasant, sandy bay below Glenaan, Glenballyemon and Glencorp and in the curve of the River Dall. The rugged peak of Lurigethan broods over the village, while the softer Tieveragh Hill is supposedly the capital of the fairies. Cushendall owes much to an East Indian nabob, Francis Turnley, who built the Curfew Tower in the centre as a 'place for the confinement of idlers and rioters'.

In a tranquil valley by the sea just north of the village is the 13th-century church of Layde. The MacDonnells of Antrim are buried here, as are Englishmen stationed in these lonely posts as coastguards, and one memorial stone mourns an emigré killed in the American Civil War in 1865 when he was only 18 years old.

Continue on the A2 for 3 miles (5km), then turn right on to the B92 for Cushendun.

❺ Cushendun, Co Antrim
The very decided character of Cushendun is a surprise. This is a black-and-white village, with an orderly square and terraces of houses that were designed to look Cornish. Lord Cushendun married a Cornish wife, Maud, and commissioned the distinguished architect Clough Williams-Ellis to create a streetscape with style.

A little salmon fishery stands at the mouth of the River Dun, the 'dark brown water'.

To the south is Cave House, locked in cliffs and approachable only through a long, natural cave. Castle Carra is to the north, the place where the clan quarrel between the O'Neills and the MacDonnells caused the treacherous murder of the great Shane O'Neill during a banquet in 1567.

At the north end of the village, turn on to the road signposted 'scenic route' for Ballycastle by Torr Head. After 9 miles (14km) turn right to Murlough Bay.

❻ Fair Head and Murlough Bay, Co Antrim
Paths from the cluster of houses known as Coolanlough cross the barren headland broken by three dark lakes – Lough Doo, Lough Fadden and Lough na Cranagh, which has a crannóg or lake dwelling. Fair Head itself is exposed and barren, a place inhabited by wild goats and choughs (red-legged crows). The careful walker can descend the cliff using the Grey Man's Path, which follows a dramatic plunging fissure.

By contrast, Murlough Bay is green and fertile, generous in contours and abundantly wooded. Tradition has it that the Children of Lir were transformed into swans to spend 300 years here. At the top of the road is a monument to the Republican leader Sir Roger Casement, and a row of lime kilns, which would have burned the stone for use in fertiliser, whitewash or mortar.

After 1 mile (2km) turn right for Ballycastle, then right again on to the A2 to Ballycastle.

❼ Ballycastle, Co Antrim
There are two parts to Ballycastle – the winding main street, which carries you up to the heart of the town, and Ballycastle by the sea, with its fine beach and tennis courts.

At the foot of the Margy River is Bonamargy Friary, founded by the Franciscans as late as 1500. The notorious Sorley Boy MacDonald is buried here. Elizabeth I found that he eluded all her attempts at capture, but in 1575, when he had sent his children to Rathlin Island for safety, he had to stand on the mainland helpless while they were murdered.

Ballycastle's museum illustrates the folk and social history of the Glens of Antrim.

At the harbour is a memorial to Guglielmo Marconi, who carried out the first practical test on radio signals between White Lodge, on the clifftop at Ballycastle, and Rathlin Island in 1898. You can travel by boat to Rathlin and savour the life of the 30 or so families who live and farm here. The island is a mecca for divers and birders. Robert the Bruce hid in a cave on Rathlin after his defeat in 1306. Watching a spider repeatedly trying to climb a thread to the roof, he was encouraged to 'try, and try again'. He returned to Scotland to fight on, and was successful at the Battle of Bannockburn.

From the shore follow the B15 coastal route west for Ballintoy, then turn right, following the signpost to Carrick-a-Rede and Larry Bane.

❽ Carrick-a-Rede, Co Antrim
A swinging rope bridge spans the deep chasm between the mainland and the rocky island of Carrick-a-Rede, and if you have a very strong heart and a good head, you can cross it. The bridge is put up each year by salmon fishermen, who use Carrick-a-Rede, 'the Rock in the Road', as a good place to net the fish in their path to the Bush and Bann rivers. The rope bridge is approached from Larry Bane, a limestone head that had once been quarried. Some of the quarry workings remain, and the quarry access

to the magnificent seascape provides some guaranteed birding. It is possible to sit in your car and spot kittiwakes, cormorants, guillemots, fulmars and razorbills, though you might have to use binoculars to catch sight of the puffins on Sheep Island further out to sea.

Just to the west is Ballintoy, a very pretty little limestone harbour, at the foot of a corkscrew road. A little farther west is the breathtaking sandy sweep of White Park Bay, accessible only on foot, and worth every step. Among the few houses that fringe the west end of the beach, tucked into the cliff, is Ireland's smallest church, dedicated to St Gobhan, patron saint of builders.

Take the B15 to join the A2 for Portrush, then turn right on to the B146 for the Giant's Causeway.

❾ Giant's Causeway, Co Antrim
Sixty million years ago, or thereabouts, intensely hot volcanic lava erupted through narrow vents and, in cooling rapidly over the white chalk, formed into about 37,000 extraordinary geometric columns and shapes – mostly hexagonal, but also with four, five, seven or eight sides. That is one story. The other is that a giant, Finn MacCool, fashioned it so that he could cross dry-shod to Scotland.

Generations of guides have embroidered stories and created names for the remarkable formations – the Giant's Organ, the Giant's Harp, the Wishing Chair, and Lord Antrim's Parlour. The Visitor Centre tells the full story of the fact and fiction, the folklore and traditions, and provides a bus service down the steep road to the Causeway.

One story absolutely based on fact is of the *Girona*, a fleeing Spanish Armada galleon, wrecked in a storm on the night of 26 October 1588. A diving team retrieved a treasure hoard from the wreck in 1967, now on display in the Ulster Museum in Belfast. The wreck still lies under cliffs in Port na Spaniagh, one of a magnificent march of bays and headlands on the Causeway.

The Giant's Causeway never fails to amaze and delight

The Causeway Coast

Near the Visitor Centre is the Causeway School Museum, a reconstructed 1920s schoolroom, complete with learning aids and toys of the era.

Take the A2 to Bushmills.

⑩ Bushmills, Co Antrim
This neat village is the home of the world's oldest legal distillery, which was granted its licence in 1608. The water from St Columb's rill, or stream, is said to give the whiskey its special quality, and visitors can discover something of its flavour on tours of the distillery.

The River Bush is rich in trout and salmon, and its fast-flowing waters not only supported the mills that gave the town its name, but generated electricity for the world's first hydroelectric

tramway, which carried passengers to the Giant's Causeway between 1893 and 1949.

Follow the A2 west to Portrush.

⑪ Portrush, Co Antrim
Portrush is a typical seaside resort, which flourished with the rise of the railways. It has three good bays, with broad stretches of sand, ranges of dunes, rock pools, white cliffs and a busy harbour.

Nearby Dunluce is one of the most romantic of castles today; a sprawling ruin clings perilously to the clifftop, presenting a splendid profile. The castle was a MacDonnell stronghold until half the kitchen fell into the sea on a stormy night in 1639.

All along the Antrim Coast Road, wonderful views unfold to delight the visitor

Take the A29 for Coleraine, then follow the A2 for Castlerock, then on to Downhill, a distance of 12 miles (19km).

⑫ Downhill, Co Londonderry
The feast of magnificent coastal scenery is given a different face at Downhill. Here Frederick Hervey, who was Earl of Bristol and Bishop of Derry, decided to adorn nature with man's art, by creating a landscape with eyecatching buildings, artificial ponds and cascades, in keeping with the taste of the time. He was a great 18th-century eccentric, collector and traveller, who gave his name to the Bristol hotels throughout Europe. Although nature has won back much of the Earl Bishop's ambitious scheme, the spirit of the place is strongly felt, and Mussenden Temple, a perfect classical rotunda, sits on a wonderful headland.

Nearby Benone Strand is one of the cleanest beaches in Europe.

From the A2 turn left on Bishop's Road for Gortmore, then after 8 miles (13km) turn right on to the B201, then left on to the A2 for Limavady.

⑬ Limavady, Co Londonderry
The Roe Valley was the territory of the O'Cahans, and O'Cahan's Rock is one of the landmarks of the nearby Roe Valley Country Park. One story says that it was here a dog made a mighty leap with a message to help relieve a besieged castle, giving this pleasant market town its name: 'The Leap of the Dog'.

The *Londonderry Air* was first written down here by Jane Ross, when she heard it being played by a street fiddler. Limavady was the birthplace of William Massey (1856–1925), Prime Minister of New Zealand from 1912 to 1925.

Take the A37 for Coleraine, then turn right on to the B66; follow signs for the B66 to Ballymoney.

⑭ Ballymoney, Co Antrim
A bustling town, Ballymoney recalls its farming past at Leslie Hill Open Farm, where visitors can travel through the park by horse and trap.

Take the A26 to Ballymena.

⑮ Ballymena, Co Antrim
Ballymena, the county town of Antrim, is a lively place with good shopping and a superb new museum, arts centre and civic complex all in one building, The Braid. As an introduction to the imaginative museum exhibitions, the lofty atrium contains a number of interactive installations providing a taster for the history galleries. The arts centre, with a 400-seat main hall and 77-seat studio theatre, hosts a full programme of drama, music, comedy and festivals, including the annual Ballymena Arts Festival and a Battle of the Bands contest. To the east the hump of Slemish Mountain rises abruptly from the ground. It was here that St Patrick worked when he was first brought to Ireland as a slave. In the southern suburbs is the 40-foot (12m) high Harryville motte and bailey – one of the finest surviving Anglo-Norman earthworks in Ulster.

Just to the west is 17th-century Galgorm Castle, a Plantation castle built by Sir Faithful Fortescue in 1618. Beyond is the charming village of Gracehill, founded by the Moravians in the 18th century.

Take the A36 for 21 miles (34km) and return to Larne.

Of Alps, Lakes & Plain *4 days 728km (452 miles)*

Lombardy is crossed by the huge River Po and studded with great lakes – Maggiore, Garda, Como, Iseo and Lugano. Since the Middle Ages it has been a prosperous commercial region. Milano (Milan) nowadays is the thriving economic capital of Italy but the traces of its cultural past are everywhere.

DRIVE ITINERARY

MILANO • Sacro Monte Varese (65km/40 miles)
SACRO MONTE VARESE • Lago Maggiore (32km/20 miles)
LAGO MAGGIORE • Como (76km/47 miles)
COMO • Lecco – around Lake Como (109km/68 miles)
LECCO • Bellagio (22km/14 miles)
BELLAGIO • Bergamo (61km/38 miles)
BERGAMO • Lago di Garda (78km/48 miles)
LAGO DI GARDA • Mantova (48km/30 miles)
MANTOVA • Cremona (66km/41 miles)
CREMONA • Pavia (136km/84 miles)
PAVIA • Milano (35km/22 miles)

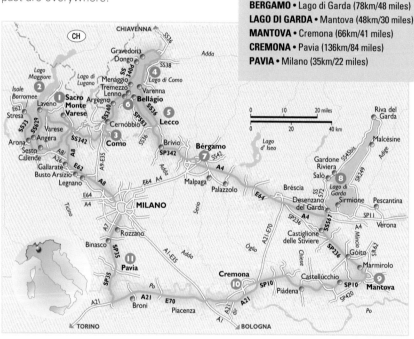

From Milano, take the A8 going north (via Legnano and Gallarate) – the latter about 38km (24 miles) – to Varese, about another 17km (10 miles). About 10km (6 miles) north of Varese lies Sacro Monte Varese.

❶ Sacro Monte Varese, Lombardia
The 'Sacred Mountain of Varese', with its narrow passages and ancient covered alleys, is only the backdrop for a pilgrimage route more famous nowadays for its art than for its saintly connections. It is said to have been founded by St Ambrose in thanks for Lombardy's

deliverance from the Arian heresy (the doctrine put forward by the 4th-century theologian Arius, that Christ is not one body with God).

From the bottom of the Sacro Monte to the top, about 800m (2,625 feet), is a cobbled route with 14 chapels at intervals along the Sacred Way, each one dedicated to the Mystery of the Rosary. The shrines are the work of Bernascone and each is filled with life-size terracotta figures, by Bussola, acting out some religious episode. At the top is the lavishly decorated Church of Santa Maria del Monte. The views from the Sacro Monte are wonderful and, to restore you after the climb, you will find cafés and restaurants in the town.

From Sacro Monte Varese, go back to Varese, then continue on the SS342 to Lago Maggiore, about 22km (14 miles).

❷ **Lago Maggiore,** Lombardia
Only the eastern shore of Lago Maggiore (Lake Maggiore) is in Lombardia. Its western shore is in Piedmont and its northern part in Switzerland. It would take days to drive around the lake seeing all that there is to look at. These are the highlights.

At Angera is the Borromeo fortress (open to the public), which contains well-preserved 14th-century frescos, a doll museum and a museum of children's clothing from the 18th century to the 1950s.

At Arona is another castle, this time ruined. Visit the Church of Santa Maria with, in the Borromeo Chapel, an altarpiece of 1511 by Ferrari.

Stresa is the largest resort on the lake. Full of Victorian-style hotels, it is also dotted with old-fashioned villas and luxurious gardens running down to the water's edge. Some gardens are open, including the Villa Pallavicino.

But the real gem of Maggiore is the Borromean islands. Isola Bella, perhaps the best known, is a huge private garden surrounding a palace (Palazzo Borromeo) – both open to the public. The gardens were laid out for Count Carlo III Borromeo in the 17th century by Angelo Crivelli. The elaborate complex includes white peacocks, grottos, fountains and statuary. Isola Madre is another of the islands, famous for its large botanical garden, which, with its palace, is well worth a visit. You can get a boat to either of these islands from Stresa.

Make for Varese from Stresa, take the SS33 to Sesto Calende at the foot of the lake, about 25km (16 miles), then follow signs to Varese, about 23km (14 miles). From Varese, take the SS342 to Como.

❸ **Como,** Lombardia
Como was the birthplace of the Roman writer Pliny the Elder. In fact you will see signs dotted around Lago di Como (Lake Como) pointing to the sites of the various villas the Pliny family owned here.

One of the most elegant towns on the lake, Como is a centre for the production of fine fabrics, and it has an interesting silk museum. There is a waterfront promenade, busy cafés, palm trees and parks. The Duomo (cathedral) dates mainly from the 15th century. The rose window on the façade is Gothic in style and there is excellent carving by the Rodari brothers of Maroggia, from about 1500.

Other relics of old Como include the churches of San Abbondio and San Fedele, which was once the cathedral, and the Porta Vittoria, the late 12th-century city gate. The Museum of Archaeology contains an enormous collection of pre-Roman and Roman finds. The History Museum shares the same building.

Como also has a good art gallery, with classical, abstractionist and futurist works. See also the Temple of Alessandro Volta, which has equipment used by the man who gave his name to the electric volt.

From Como, drive around the lake, starting on the SS340 up the left-hand side of the lake.

❹ Lago di Como, Lombardia

All around the lake you will see imposing villas and castles overlooking the water. Cernóbbio is a pretty town about 7km (4.5 miles) from Como. Here is the grand Hotel Villa D'Este, once the home of the English Queen Caroline.

At Tremezzo is the Villa Carlotta, once lived in by Princess Carlotta of Prussia, who laid out its gardens in the 1850s. You can visit this as well as the Villa Arconati, just a few kilometres outside Tremezzo, at Lenno. Farther on around the lake are Menaggio and Gravedona.

At nearby Dongo, Mussolini was captured by the partisans in 1945. On the other side of the lake, at Varenna, visit the Villa Monastero with its formal gardens and the Romanesque Church of San Giorgio. One really good way to see the lake – and admire the towns from a distance – is to take a boat trip around it. It is possible to take one that stops at a number of places, using it like a bus. Begin at Como.

Lecco lies at the foot of the eastern arm of Lake Como, from Como itself a direct distance of 29km (18 miles).

❺ Lecco, Lombardia

Lecco is in direct contrast to its illustrious neighbour Como. More industrial than prettier Como, Lecco's claim to fame is that it was the birthplace of Alessandro Manzoni, the great 19th-century Italian novelist. The Villa Manzoni, his former home, is now a museum – you will find it in Via Promessi Sposi, named after the writer's most famous novel, which, translated, means 'The Betrothed' (the street is also known as Via Amendola). While you are in town, visit the Duomo, with its 14th-century frescos in the style of Giotto, and the Ponte Azzone Visconti, a medieval bridge over the Adda river. Although much altered (it no longer has any towers) and enlarged, it still has much of its early character.

Take the SS583 up the western edge of Lecco's portion of Lake Como to Bellagio.

❻ Bellagio, Lombardia

Bellagio is one of the most beautiful points on Lake Como. Not only is it an interesting old town, but it is splendidly sited on a promontory overlooking the three arms of the lake. There is plenty to do here apart from just sitting in the sun enjoying the view. The 12th-century Basilica of San Giacomo has good carving in the apse. There is Villa Serbelloni, whose gardens can be visited, and Villa Melzi d'Eril, the gardens of which are open to the public. If time is short, the Villa Sebelloni gardens, supposed to stand on the site of the younger Pliny's villa 'Tragedia', are the more interesting.

Return to Lecco, then take the SS36 going south for about 15km (9 miles) until it cuts the SP342. Take the latter to Bergamo.

❼ Bergamo, Lombardia

Bergamo is divided into the Città Alta and the Città Bassa, the Upper City and the Lower City.

Right: The ornate Colleoni Chapel, dating from 1472, is one of Bergamo's most popular attractions

The former is the more interesting, as well as being the older. Its best monuments are in the Piazza Vecchia. In it is the late16th-century Biblioteca Civica (Civic Library), modelled on Venice's great library building, designed by Sansovino. Across the square, past Contarini's fountain surrounded by stone lions, is the 12th-century Torre Civica with its 15th-century clock that still tolls the curfew hour (10pm). Behind the 12th-century Palazzo della Ragione are the Duomo and the ornate Colleoni Chapel. You can just see the base of the latter through the pointed arched loggia beneath the Palazzo della Ragione. Built in 1476, the façade of the Colleoni Chapel is a mass of sculptured decoration and coloured marble. Inside is the tomb and a statue of Bartolomeo Colleoni, who controlled Venice's armed forces in the 15th century. The ceiling fresco is by Tiepolo.

The Church of Santa Maria Maggiore, in Piazza Duomo, is a fine Romanesque building. Also in the Upper City is the Cittadella (citadel), which contains the Natural History Museum, and the Museo Donizetti – this great composer was born in Bergamo, and you can visit the Teatro Donizetti in the Lower City. Between the Upper and Lower Cities is the Galleria dell'Accademia Carrara, a first-class collection of art, well worth taking in.

From Bergamo, take the A4 via Brescia to Lago di Garda, about 78km (48 miles) – at Desenzano del Garda at the foot of the lake.

❽ Lago di Garda, Lombardia

The most interesting ports of call around Lago (Lake) di Garda are Salò, Gardone Riviera, Riva del Garda, Malcesine and Sirmione. All are accessible by the steamer, and rather than drive around the lake, you could leave the car at Desenzano del Garda and go by boat. Salò

has a fine Gothic Duomo (cathedral) with a noteworthy Renaissance portal. At Gardone Riviera, most things to visit have something to do with Gabriele d'Annunzio (1863–1938), one of the greatest writers and poets of his generation. His villa, Vittoriale degli Italiani, was specially built for him and can be visited. The villa and grounds are filled with an extraordinary array of bits and pieces, like the great ornate organs in the music room, among which the writer chose to live. There is also a museum and a mausoleum in the villa's grounds.

At Riva del Garda, right at the northern tip of the lake, about 95 breathtaking kilometres (60 miles) away from Desenzano del Garda up the western edge of the lake, and actually in the Trentino region, is a 13th-century tower, the Torre Apponale, and a clutter of other ancient edifices of which the Palazzo Pretorio and the 12th-century Rocca (fortress) are the most interesting. The town's Museo Civico (Civic Museum) contains an interesting collection of armour and archaeological finds from the area, housed in the Rocca.

Malcesine, halfway down the eastern edge of the lake, is the proud possessor of the magnificent Castello Scaligero (Scaliger Castle), dramatically situated at the water's edge. But the castle at Sirmione is more remarkable. Also from the 13th century and one of the Scaligeri castles, its battlements and its dramatic situation half in the water make it possibly the most memorable sight on the Lago di Garda.

From Desenzano del Garda, take the SS567 for 11km (7 miles) to Castiglione delle Stiviere, at which branch on to the SP236 and continue on to Mantova, about 37km (23 miles).

⑨ Mantova, Lombardia

Mantova (Mantua) sits on a swampy, marshy bend in the Mincio River. Its claim to fame is that it was the seat of one of the most intellectually active and refined courts of the Italian Renaissance. The Gonzaga family were the rulers and they embellished the town with a remarkable Palazzo Ducale (Ducal Palace) that still contains some of their art collection. The neo-classical rooms have a set of early 16th-century Flemish tapestries and the duke's apartments have a fine collection of classical statuary. Here you will see Rubens' vast portrait of the Gonzaga family. The Camera degli Sposi in the Castel di San Giorgio is world famous for its brilliant frescos by Mantegna, finished in 1474. Apart from a series of portraits of the family, there are others of their favourite dwarfs. In the Casetta dei Nani, the House of the Dwarfs, you can see the miniature rooms where the latter were once thought to have lived. The Palazzo del Té is another Gonzaga palace built by Giulio Romano in 1527 for Federico II Gonzaga's mistress. The Sala dei Giganti, the Room of the Giants, is its masterpiece: huge frescoed fighting giants seem to bring down the ceiling. The Basilica of Sant'Andrea, designed by Leon Battista (1472), houses a chalice of Christ's blood, a relic once much venerated by the Gonzaga.

Take the SP10 for 66km (41 miles) to Cremona.

⑩ Cremona, Lombardia

You cannot come to Cremona and not visit the Museo Stradivariano (Stradivarian Museum). The modern violin was developed in this city in 1566, and one of the great masters of violin-making here – though much later – was Antonio Stradivarius. The town hall has a valuable collection of violins, including instruments by Stradivari, Amati and Guarneri. There is also the Museo Civico (civic museum) in which much space is devoted to Roman Cremona. The Duomo (cathedral) has five wonderful 17th-century Brussels tapestries as well as a series of frescos by local artists. The tall bell-tower of the cathedral can also be visited, and there are fine views from the top. Among the town's most interesting churches is Sant' Agostino, with a *Madonna and Saints* by Perugino, who was once Raphael's teacher.

From Cremona, take the A21 via Piacenza for 33km (20 miles) as far as the Casteggio turning, 82km (51 miles), for the SP35 to Pavia, a further 21km (13 miles).

⑪ Pavia, Lombardia

Pavia was at one time an important Roman city *(Ticinum)*. Little remains, though the municipal museums in Castello Visconteo contain finds from Roman times and early Pavia. On an upper floor you will find the picture gallery with works by, among others, Bellini and Van der Goes, the latter one of the most important of the Flemish Renaissance painters.

The most noteworthy monument to visit is the Certosa di Pavia, a remarkable, highly decorative Renaissance monastery complex, just on the outskirts of town. A tour will take in the vestibule, the cloisters and the church with Gothic, Renaissance and baroque decoration.

Back in the town, Leonardo was partially responsible for the design of the Duomo, begun in 1488, and in addition to the cathedral, there are about six other churches worth seeing.

Take the SP35 back to Milano, about 35km (22 miles).

Roman Relics & Golden Beaches

2/3 days 597km (373 miles)

Barcelona's hills, Montjuïc and Tibidabo, are great places for entertainment. Museums, from modern to Romanesque art, and the Olympic Stadium are on Montjuïc, which rises above the city's brilliantly redeveloped seafront. Tibidabo has a funfair and stunning panoramic views. Below lies the amazing Gaudí creation of Parc Güell.

ITINERARY

BARCELONA • Sitges (40km/25 miles)

SITGES • Vilanova i la Geltrú (6km/4 miles)

VILANOVA I LA GELTRÚ • Calafell (14km/9 miles)

CALAFELL • Tarragona (31km/19 miles)

TARRAGONA • Cambrils de Mar (18km/11 miles)

CAMBRILS DE MAR • Peñiscola (112km/70 miles)

PEÑISCOLA • Tortosa (62km/39 miles)

TORTOSA • Lleida (128km/80 miles)

LLEIDA • Monestir de Poblet (53km/33 miles)

MONESTIR DE POBLET • Montblanc (8km/5 miles)

MONTBLANC • Monestir Santes Creus
(35km/22 miles)

MONESTIR SANTES CREUS • Barcelona
(90km/56 miles)

Leave Barcelona from the Plaça Espanya and take the C31 southwest to Sitges.

❶ Sitges, Barcelona
Sitges is a traditional resort that lured Spanish families long before it became an international tourist centre. As well as its splendid sandy beach and shallow waters, Sitges is a picturesque little town with great charm. The local church, with its rose-coloured façade, adds to the picture. The Cau Ferrat Museum, once home of the writer and artist Santiago Rusinyol (1861–1931), houses a collection of his paintings, together with works by El Greco, Picasso, Utrillo and others.

Take a minor road southwest for 6km (4 miles) to Vilanova i la Geltrú (Vilanueva y Geltrú).

❷ Vilanova i la Geltrú, Barcelona
This is an industrial town and a resort, with a fine sandy beach and picturesque fishing harbour. It has two museums of interest: the Museu Municipal Romàntic Casa Papiol, which is housed in an elegantly furnished town house and devoted to life in the early 1800s, and the Biblioteca Museu Balaguer, which is noted for its fine collection of antiquities and Catalan paintings.

Continue down the C31 coast road to Calafell.

❸ Calafell, Barcelona
The small fishing village of Calafell is another favourite summer resort with a long sandy beach, suitable for a quiet stop and a look at the Romanesque parish church and the ruins of the 12th-century castle.

This quiet corner of Tortosa is typical of the historic towns in the region

Continue on the C31 to El Vendrell and join the N340 to Tarragona.

❹ Tarragona, Tarragona
The route passes through El Vendrell, the birthplace of the famous Spanish cellist Pablo Casals (1876–1973).

The old Roman town of Tarragona was founded by Publius Cornelius Scipio during the Second Punic War of 218 BC. A stroll along the attractive tree-lined Rambla Nova leads to the observation platform '*Balcó del Mediterrani*', which offers a sweeping view of the coast. Below is the harbour and the Parc del Miracle, where you can see the remnants of a 2nd- or 3rd-century BC Roman amphitheatre, once the venue for combats between man and beast. The Museu National Arqueològic has mosaics, ceramics and antiquities from the region. A climb from the centre of town takes you to the cathedral, which was built between the 12th and 14th centuries. It shows a harmonious blending of Romanesque and Gothic styles, with a fine façade and lovely rose window in the centre. The Passeig Arqueologic is a pleasant shaded walk along the foot of the massive city ramparts, which extend for some 1,000m (1,100 yards) and up to 10m (33 feet) in parts.

The Museu y Necrópolis Paleocristina, on the outskirts of the town, has a fine display of tombs, mosaics and jewellery. Adjoining it is an old Christian cemetery dating back to the 3rd century.

Continue on the N340 south to Cambrils de Mar.

❺ Cambrils de Mar, Tarragona
Cambrils de Mar is a picturesque little port with a maritime tradition. The harbour is dominated by an ancient church tower, originally a Roman defence fortification.

The port becomes a hive of activity when the fishing fleet comes in, and has a reputation for good eating.

Continue south down the coastal road (N340) for 112km (70 miles) to Peñiscola.

❻ Peñiscola, Castellón
This is a veritable jewel of a place, rising like a fortress from a rocky peninsula that juts out to sea. The town was taken from the Moors in 1233 by King Jaime I. Its main feature is the castle, an impressive structure built by the Knights Templars. Later, the deposed antipope, Benedict XIII (Pope Luna), took refuge in the castle and spent his last years here until his death in 1422. The castle offers magnificent views of the coastline. Within the surrounding walls is the old town, a labyrinth of tiny winding streets – strictly for pedestrians only.

Drive inland to join the AP7 north, turning off after 46km (29 miles) on the C42 to Tortosa.

❼ Tortosa, Tarragona
The episcopal town of Tortosa holds a commanding position over the delta of the River Ebre. The cathedral was begun in 1347 and built over a long period of time. The naves are 14th-century Gothic, while the façade and the chapel to the Mare de Deu de la Cinta (the Virgin), patron saint of the city, are baroque.

Other buildings of note in the town are the 14th-century Palau Episcopal and the Colegio de Sant Lluis, which was founded in 1544 by Emperor Charles V for converts from the Moorish faith, and has an elegant courtyard with some fine decoration. Many splendid old palaces from the 15th and 16th centuries can be seen, as well as remains of the city walls.

Take the C12 north to Maials, then on to Lleida (Lérida).

❽ Lleida, Lleida/Lérida
Originally an Iberian settlement, Lleida came under the Romans in the 2nd century BC and was the scene of numerous battles and sieges over the years. It was the birthplace of Enrique Granados (1867–1916), famed for his classical guitar compositions.

Enclosed within the city walls is the Seu Vella (old cathedral), which is dominated by a tall 14th-century octagonal tower. Built between the 12th and 15th centuries, it shows the transition from Romanesque to Gothic. During the 18th century the cathedral was used as a garrison and has been undergoing restoration for some years. It has a fine Gothic cloister, noted for its tall, graceful arches.

Lleida also has a new cathedral. The Seu Nova was built in the 18th century in neo-classical style, and was the first of its kind in Catalunya. Other sights of interest include the 13th-century town hall; the Palau de la Paeria and the churches of Sant Llorenc and Sant Martín. The 15th-century former hospital of Santa María one of the best-preserved examples of Gothic architecture in Catalunya, houses the Museo Diocesano, which exhibits archaeological finds. Lleida is an excellent centre for excursions into the Pyrenees.

Take the N240 southeast towards Tarragona. Shortly after going under the AP2 (motorway) turn right to the Monestir de Poblet.

⑨ Monestir de Poblet, Tarragona
Tucked away on the lower slopes of the Prades Mountains, the Monastery of Santa María de Poblet was founded in 1149 by Ramón Berenguer IV as a token of thanks to God for the regaining of Catalunya from the Moors. The following year 12 Cistercian monks, sent from Fontfroide (near Narbonne in France), began building the monastery, which is a fine example of Cistercian art.

The monks benefited from the patronage of the Aragón kings, for whom the monastery became a favourite stopping place for royal journeys. The lovely Gothic cloister and adjoining chapter house contain a number of abbots' tombstones in the pavement.

Rejoin the N240 and continue for 8km (5 miles) to Montblanc.

⑩ Montblanc, Tarragona
Montblanc is an impressive sight, with its massive medieval ramparts and towers and narrow entrance gates. Overlooking the town is the Church of Santa María, begun in the 14th century and never fully completed.

Continue on the N240 southeast to Valls. Turn left on to the C51, then left again on a minor road, crossing the AP2 to Santes Creus.

⑪ Monestir Santes Creus, Tarragona
The Santes Creus monastery rises grandly over the forest around it. It is a fine example of the Cistercian style and is, like Poblet, among Catalunya's most important monasteries.

Founded in 1157, the monastery was occupied by Cistercian monks from France. It enjoyed the favour of the Kings of Aragón but, like Poblet, it suffered damage during the wars of the 19th century, and is also under restoration. The church is 12th-century Romanesque and contains the royal tombs of former kings of Catalunya including that of Pedro III.

Return south to the AP2 and join the AP7 back to Barcelona, 90km (56 miles).

The Monestir de Poblet is one of the largest Cistercian abbeys in Spain

Historischer Sta

Schwerdtners Ka

Kleiner Hafen & G
Am Mühlenwehr

Strubels Stübche

tkern

nfahrten

sthaus

Useful words
and phrases

Dutch: words and phrases

For clarity we have put the English phrase in light type, foreign language terms in dark type and their phonetic pronunciation in light italic.

Asking for directions

Excuse me, could I ask you something?
Pardon, mag ik u iets vragen?
Pardon, makh ik oo eets frakhen?

I've lost my way
Ik ben de weg kwijt
Ik ben de vekh kwayet

Is there a...around here?
Weet u een...in de buurt?
Vayt oo an...in de boo-ert

Is this the way to...?
Is dit de weg naar...?
Is dit de vekh naar...?

Could you tell me how to get to...
by car/on foot?
**Kunt u me zeggen hoe ik naar...
moet rijden/lopen?**
*Kunt-oo me zekhen hoo ik naar...
moot rayeden/loapen?*

What's the quickest way to...?
Hoe kom ik het snelst in...?
Hoo kom ik het snel-ste in...?

How many kilometres is it to...?
Hoeveel kilometer is het nog naar...?
Hoofayl keelomayter is het nokh naar...?

Could you point it out on the map?
Kunt u het op de kaart aanwijzen?
Kunt oo het op de kaart aan-wayezen?

Ask the speaker to point to what
they are saying

Ik weet het niet, ik ben hier niet bekend
I don't know, I don't know these parts

U zit verkeerd
You're going the wrong way

U moet terug naar...
You have to go back to...

Daar wijzen de borden u verder
From there on just follow the signs

Daar moet u het opnieuw vragen
When you get there, ask again

Useful words

rechtdoor
straight on

linksaf
turn left

rechtsaf
turn right

afslaan
turn

volgen
follow

oversteken
cross

de kruising
intersection

de straat
the street

het verkeerslicht
the traffic light

de tunnel
the tunnel/ underpass

**het verkeersbord
'voorrangskruis-ing'**
the 'give-way' sign

het gebouw
the building

op de hoek
at the corner

de rivier
the river

het viaduct
the fly-over

de brug
the bridge

**de
spoorwegovergang/
de spoorbomen**
the level crossing/the
crossing barriers

het bord richting...
the sign pointing to...

de pijl
the arrow

Road traffic signs

afrit
exit

alle richtingen
all directions

andere richtingen
other directions

centrum
town centre

doodlopende weg
dead end (cul-de-sac)

doorgaand verkeer gestremd
road closed

doorgaand verkeer
through traffic

eenrichtingsverkeer
one-way traffic

einde snelheidsbeperking
end of speed limit

fabrieksuitgang
works exit

fietsers
cyclists

fietspad
cycle path

gevaar
danger

gevaarlijke bochten
dangerous bends

helling
incline

ijzel
black ice

inrijden verboden
no entry

kruising
junction

langzaam
slow

links houden
keep left

maximum snelheid
maximum speed

ondergrondse parkeergarage
underground car park

ontsteek uw lichten
switch on lights

oversteekplaats voetgangers
pedestrian crossing

overweg
level crossing

parkeerplaats
parking/layby (out of town)

parkeerzone (parkeerschijf verplicht)
zone parking (disc must be shown)

rechts houden
keep right

rijbaan voor bus
bus lane

slecht wegdek
irregular road surface

slipgevaar
slippery road

snelheid verminderen
reduce speed

snelweg
motorway

stapvoets
drive at walking pace

steenslag
loose chippings

tegenliggers
oncoming traffic

uitgang
exit/way out

uitrit
exit

uitrit vrijlaten
keep exit free

verboden in te halen
no overtaking

verboden linksaf te slaan
no left turn

verboden rechtsaf te slaan
no right turn

verminder snelheid
reduce speed

verplichte rijrichting
compulsory route

voetgangers
pedestrians

voorangsweg
major road

voorrang verlenen
give way

voorsorteren
get in lane

wachtverbod
no waiting

weg afgesloten
road closed

wegomlegging
diversion

wegversmalling
road narrows

werk in uitvoering
roadworks

zachte berm
soft verge

ziekenhuis
hospital

French: words and phrases

For clarity we have put the English phrase in light type, foreign language terms in dark type and their phonetic pronunciation in light italic.

Asking for directions

Excuse me, could I ask you something?
Pardon, puis-je vous demander quelque chose?
pahrdawn, pwee jhuh voo duhmohnday kehlkuh shoaz?

I've lost my way
Je me suis égaré(e)
jhuh muh swee zaygahray

Is there an... around here?
Connaissez-vous un...dans les environs?
konehssay voo zuhn... dohn lay zohnveerawn?

Is this the way to...?
Est-ce la route vers...?
ehs lah root vehr...?

Could you tell me how to get to...?
Pouvez-vous me dire comment aller à...?
poovay voo muh deer komohn tahlay ah...?

What's the quickest way to...?
Comment puis-je arriver le plus vite possible à...?
komohn pwee jhuh ahreevay luh plew veet pohseebl ah...?

How many kilometres is it to...?
Il y a encore combien de kilomètres jusqu'à...?
eel ee yah ohnkor kohnbyahn duh keeloamehtr jhewskah...?

Could you point it out on the map?
Pouvez-vous me l'indiquer sur la carte?
poovay voo muh lahndeekay sewr lah kahrt?

☞ Ask the speaker to point to what they are saying

Je ne sais pas, je ne suis pas d'ici
I don't know, I don't know my way around here

Vous vous êtes trompé
You're going the wrong way

Vous devez retourner à...
You have to go back to...
Là-bas les panneaux vous indiqueront la route
From there on just follow the signs

Là-bas vous demanderez à nouveau votre route
When you get there, ask again

Useful words

tout droit	**le panneau 'cédez lapriorité'**
straight ahead	the 'give-way' sign
à gauche	**l'immeuble**
left	the building
à droite	**à l'angle, au coin**
right	at the corner
tourner	**la rivière, le fleuve**
turn	the river
suivre	**l'autopont**
follow	the fly-over
traverser	**le pont**
cross	the bridge
le carrefour	**le passage à niveau**
the intersection	the level crossing
la rue	**la barrière**
the street	boom
le feu (de signalisation)	**le panneau direction...**
the traffic light	the sign pointing to...
le tunnel	**la flèche**
the tunnel	the arrow

Road traffic signs

carrefour dangereux
dangerous crossing

chaussée à gravillons
loose chippings

chaussée déformée
uneven road surface

chaussée glissante
slippery road

circulation alternée
alternate priority

danger
danger

danger priorité à droite
priority to vehicles from right

descente dangereuse
steep hill

déviation
diversion

fin d'allumage des feux
end of need for lights

fin de...
end of...

fin de chantier
end of roadworks

interdiction de dépasser
no overtaking

interdiction de klaxonner
no horns

interdiction de stationner
no parking

interdiction sauf riverains
access only

limite de vitesse
speed limit

passage à niveau
level crossing

passage d'animaux
animals crossing

passage pour piétons
pedestrian crossing

péage
toll

poids lourds
heavy goods vehicles

rappel
reminder

remorques et semi-remorques
lorries and articulated lorries

sens unique
one-way traffic

serrez à droite
keep right

sortie
exit

sortie de camions
factory/works exit

taxis
taxi rank

travaux (sur...km)
roadworks ahead

véhicules lents
slow traffic

**véhicules transportant des
   matières dangereuses**
vehicles transporting dangerous substances

verglas fréquent
ice on road

virages sur...km
bends for...km

vitesse limite
maximum speed

zone bleue
parking disc required

zone piétonne
pedestrian zone

German: words and phrases

For clarity we have put the English phrase in light type, foreign language terms in dark type and their phonetic pronunciation in light italic.

Asking for directions

Excuse me, could I ask you something?
Verzeihung, dürfte ich Sie etwas fragen?
fair tsaioong, duerfter ikh zee etvass frargen?

I've lost my way
Ich habe mich verlaufen/(with car) mich verfahren
ikh harber mikh fairlowfen/mikh fairfahren

Is there a(n)... around here?
Wissen Sie, wo hier in der Nähe ein(e)...ist?
vissen zee, vo heer in dayr nayher ain(er)...ist?

Is this the way to...?
Ist dies die Strasse nach...?
ist dees dee shtrasser nakh...?

Could you tell me how to get to the... (name of place) by car/on foot?
Können Sie mir sagen, wie ich nach... (name of the place) fahren/gehen muss?
koenen zee meer zargen, vee ikh nakh ... fahren/gayhen muss?

What's the quickest way to...?
Wie komme ich am schnellsten nach...?
vee kommer ikh am shnellsten nakh...?

How many kilometres is it to...?
Wieviel Kilometer sind es noch bis...?
veefeel kilomayter zint ez nokh biss...?

Could you point it out on the map?
Können Sie es mir auf der Karte zeigen?
koennen zee ez meer owf dayr karter tsaigen?

☞ Ask the speaker to point to what they are saying

Ich weiss nicht, ich kenne mich hier nicht aus
I don't know, I don't know my way around here

Da sind Sie hier nicht richtig
You're going the wrong way

Sie müssen zurück nach...
You have to go back to...

Sie fahren über die...Strasse
You take...Street

Sie fahren über die...Strasse drüber
You cross over...Street

Da sehen Sie schon die Schilder
From there on you will see the signs

Da müssen Sie noch mal fragen
When you get there, you will have to ask again

Useful words

geradeaus
straight

nach links/links abbiegen
left/turn left

nach rechts/ rechts abbiegen
right/turn right

abbiegen
turn

folgen
follow

überqueren
cross

die Kreuzung
the intersection

die Strasse
the street

die (Verkehrs)ampel
the traffic light

das Gebäude
the building

an der Ecke
at the corner

der Fluss
the river

die Brücke
the bridge

die (Bahn)schranken
the level crossing/the boomgates

das Schild Richtung...
the sign pointing to...

der Pfeil
the arrow

Road traffic signs

abbiegen
turn

Anlieger frei
residents only

Auffahrt
slip road/approach to house

Auflieger schwenkt aus
trailer may swing out

Ausfahrt
exit

Autobahndreieck
motorway merging point

Baustelle
roadworks ahead

bei Nässe/Glätte
in wet/icy conditions

Durchgangsverkehr (verboten)
(no) throughway

Einbahnstrasse
one-way street

Einfahrt
entry/access

Ende der Autobahn
end of motorway

Frostaufbrüche
frost damage

Gefahr
danger

gefährlich
dangerous

Gegenverkehr
oncoming traffic

gesperrt (für alle Fahrzeuge)
closed (for all vehicles)

Glatteis
ice on road

Kurve(nreiche Strecke)
bend/dangerous bends

Licht einschalten/ ausschalten
switch on lights/end needs for lights

LKW
heavy goods vehicle

Naturschutzgebiet
nature reserve

Nebel
beware fog

Parkscheibe
parking disk

PKW
motorcar

Radfahrer kreuzen
cyclists crossing

Rasthof-stätte
services

Rastplatz bitte sauberhalten
please keep picnic area tidy

Rollsplit
loose chippings

Schleudergefahr
danger of skidding

Seitenstreifen nicht befahrbar
soft verges

Seitenwind
cross wind

Spurrillen
irregular road surface

Standstreifen
hard shoulder

Starkes Gefälle
steep hill

Stau
traffic jam

Stauwarnanlage
hazard lights

Steinschlag
falling stones

Talbrücke
bridge over a valley

Überholverbot
no overtaking

Umleitung
diversion

Unbeschränkter Bahnübergang
unguarded level crossing/ dangerous crossing

Verengte Fahrbahn
narrow lane

Vorfahrt beachten
give way

Vorfahrtsstrasse
major road

Wasserschutzgebiet
protected reservoir area

zurückschalten
to change back

Greek: words and phrases

For clarity we have put the English phrase in light type, foreign language terms in dark type and their phonetic pronunciation in light italic.

Asking for directions

Excuse me, could I ask you something?
Συγγνώμη, μπορώ να σας ρωτήσω κάτι;
sighnómi, boró na sas rotíso káti?

I've lost my way
'Εχασα το δρόμο
échasa to dhrómo

Is there a(n)...around here?
Ξέρετε κανέα...εδώ κοντά
xérete kanéna...edhó kondá?

Is this the way to...?
Αυτός είναι ο δρόμος για...;
aftós íne o dhrómos ya...?

Could you tell me how to get to...
 (name of place)
Μπορείτε να μου πείτε πώς μπορώ να
 πάω σε...;
boríte na moo píte pos boró na páo se...?

What's the quickest way to...?
Ποιός είναι ο πιο σύντομος δρόμος για...;
pyos íne o pyo síndomos dhrómos ya ...?

How many kilometres is it to...?
Πόσα χιλιόμετρα είναι ακόμα ως...;
pósa hilyómetra íne akóma os...?

Could you point it out on the map?
Μπορείτε να το δείξετε στο χάρτη;
boríte na to dhíxete sto chartí?

☞ Ask the speaker to point to what
 they are saying
Δεν ξέρω, δεν είμαι από δω
I don't know, I don't know my way
 around here

Πήρατε λάθος δρόμο
You're going the wrong way

Πρέπει να γυρίσετε σε...
You have to go back to...

Εκεί θ' ακολουθήσετε τις πινακίδες
From there on just follow the signs

Εκεί θα ξαναρωτήσετε
When you get there, ask again-

Useful words

ίσια
straight ahead

αριστερά
left

δεξιά
right

στρίβω
turn

ακολουθώ
follow

περνάω το δρόμο
cross the road

η διασταύρωση
the intersection

ο δρόμος/η οδός
the street

το φανάρι
the traffic light

το τούνελ
the tunnel

η πινακίδα
 διασταύρωση
 προτεραιότητας
the `give way' sign

το κτίριο
the building

στη γωνιά
at the corner

το ποτάμι
the river

η ανισόπεδη
 διασταύρωση
the fly-over

Road traffic signs

ΑΠΑΓΟΡΕΥΕΤΑΙ Η ΠΡΟΣΠΕΡΑΣΗ
no overtaking

ΑΠΑΓΟΡΕΥΕΤΑΙ Η ΣΤΑΘΜΕΥΣΗ
no parking

ΑΡΓΑ
slow

ΑΥΤΟΚΙΝΗΤΟΔΡΟΜΟΣ
road suitable for cars

ΑΦΥΛΑΚΤΗ ΔΙΑΒΑΣΗ
unmanned crossing

ΔΕΥΤΕΡΕΥΩΝ ΔΡΟΜΟΣ
minor road

ΔΙΑΧΩΡΙΣΜΟΣ
road divides

ΔΙΟΔΙΑ
toll

ΔΩΣΕΤΕ ΠΡΟΤΕΡΑΙΟΤΗΤΑ
give way

ΕΘΝΙΚΗ ΟΔΟΣ (ΜΕ ΔΙΟΔΙΑ)
motorway (with toll)

ΕΙΣΟΔΟΣ
entrance

ΕΛΑΤΤΩΣΑΤΕ ΤΑΧΥΤΗΤΑ
reduce speed

ΕΛΕΥΘΕΡΗ ΚΥΚΛΟΦΟΡΙΑ
clearway

ΕΠΑΡΧΙΑΚΗ ΟΔΟΣ
minor road

ΕΠΙΚΙΝΔΥΝΗ ΔΙΑΣΤΑΥΡΩΣΗ
dangerous junction

ΕΠΙΚΙΝΔΥΝΗ ΚΑΤΩΦΕΡΕΙΑ
steep hill

ΕΠΙΚΙΝΔΥΝΗ ΣΤΡΟΦΗ
dangerous bend

ΕΞΟΔΟΣ
exit

ΕΞΟΔΟΣ ΟΧΗΜΑΤΩΝ
exit for heavy goods vehicles

Η ΤΑΧΥΤΗΤΑ ΕΛΕΓΧΕΤΑΙ ΜΕ ΡΑΝΤΑΡ
radar speed checks

ΚΑΤΟΛΙΣΘΗΣΕΙΣ
loose chippings

ΚΕΝΤΡΟ
centre

ΚΙΝΔΥΝΟΣ
danger

ΚΛΕΙΣΤΗ ΟΔΟΣ
road closed

ΚΥΚΛΟΦΟΡΙΑ ΑΠΟ ΑΝΤΙΘΕΤΗ ΚΑΤΕΥΘΥΝΣΗ
oncoming traffic

ΜΟΝΟΔΡΟΜΟΣ
one-way street

ΝΟΣΟΚΟΜΕΙΟ
hospital

ΟΔΟΣ ΠΡΟΤΕΡΑΙΟΤΗΤΑΣ
road with priority over vehicles entering from side roads

ΠΑΡΑΚΑΜΠΤΗΡΙΟΣ
diversion

ΠΕΖΟΔΡΟΜΟΣ
pavement

ΠΕΡΙΜΕΝΕΤΕ
wait

ΠΡΟΣΟΧΗ
look out!

ΠΡΟΣ ΠΑΡΑΛΙΑ
to the beach

ΣΤΑΘΜΟΣ ΠΡΩΤΩΝ ΒΟΗΘΕΙΩΝ
first-aid post

ΣΤΕΝΩΜΑ ΟΔΟΣΤΡΩΜΑΤΟΣ
road narrows

ΣΤΡΟΦΕΣ
bends

ΤΕΛΟΣ ΑΝΑΓΟΡΕΥΜΕΝΗΣ ΖΩΝΗΕ
end of forbidden zone

ΥΨΟΣ ΠΕΡΙΟΡΙΣΜΕΝΟ
restricted height

ΧΩΜΑΤΟΔΡΟΜΟΣ
packed-earth road

Italian: words and phrases

For clarity we have put the English phrase in light type, foreign language terms in dark type and their phonetic pronunciation in light italic.

Asking for directions

Excuse me, could I ask you something?
Mi scusi, potrei chiederLe una cosa?
Mee skoozee potray keeaydayrlay oonah kozah?

I've lost my way
Mi sono perso/a
Mee sono payrso/ah

Is there a(n)...around here?
Sa se c'è un/una... da queste parti?
Sah say chay oon/oonah...dah kwaystay pahrtee?

Is this the way to...?
E' questa la strada per...?
Ay kwaystah lah strahdah payr...

Could you tell me how to get to....?
Mi può indicare la strada per...?
Mee pwo eendeekahray lah strahdah payr...?

What's the quickest way to...?
Qual'è la strada più diretta per...?
Kwahlay ay lah strahdah peeoo deerayttah payr...?

How many kilometres is it to...?
A quanti chilometri è...?
Ah qwahntee keelomaytreeay....?

Could you point it out on the map?
Me lo può indicare sulla mappa?
May lo pwo eendeekahray soollah mahppah?

☞ Ask the speaker to point to what they are saying

Non lo so, non sono di questa città/regione
I don't know, I don't know my way around here

Ha sbagliato strada
You're going the wrong way

Deve ritornare a...
You have to go back to...

Là, deve seguire le indicazioni
From there on just follow the signs

Là, chieda di nuovo
When you get there, ask again

Useful words

Vada dritto
Go straight ahead
Giri a sinistra
Turn left
Giri a destra
Turn right
Volti a destra/sinistra
Turn right/left
Segua
Follow
Attraversi
Cross
l'incrocio
the intersection/crossroads
la strada
the road/street
il semaforo
the traffic light
la galleria
the tunnel
il cartello/segnale stradale di 'dare la precedenza'
the 'give way' sign
il palazzo
the building
all'angolo
at the corner
il fiume
the river
il viadotto
the flyover
il ponte
the bridge
il passaggio a livello
the level crossing
le indicazioni per...
the signs pointing to....
la freccia
the arrow

Road traffic signs

accendere i fari (in galleria)
switch on headlights (in the tunnel)

alt
stop

altezza limitata a...
maximum headroom...

area/stazione di servizio
service station

attenzione
beware

autocarri
heavy goods vehicles

banchina non transitabile
impassable verge

caduta massi
beware, falling rocks

cambiare corsia
change lanes

chiuso al traffico
road closed

corsia di emergenza
emergency lane

curve
bends

deviazione
detour

diritto di precedenza a fine strada
right of way at end of road

disco orario (obbligatorio)
parking disk (compulsory)

divieto di accesso
no entry

divieto di sorpasso/di sosta
no overtaking/no parking

galleria
tunnel

incrocio
intersection/crossroads

(isola/zona) pedonale
traffic island/ pedestrian precinct

lasciare libero il passo/ passaggio
do not obstruct

lavori in corso
roadworks

pagamento/ pedaggio
toll payment

parcheggio a pagamento/ riservato a...
paying car park/parking reserved for...

parcheggio custodito
supervised car park

passaggio a livello
level crossing

passo carrabile
driveway

pericolo(so)
danger(ous)

pioggia o gelo per km....
rain or ice for...kms

precedenza
right of way

rallentare
slow down

senso unico
one way

senso vietato
no entry

soccorso stradale
road assistance (breakdown service)

sosta limitata
parking for a limited period

strada deformata/ in dissesto
broken/uneven surface

strada interrotta
road closed

strettoia
narrowing in the road

tenere la destra/sinistra
keep right/left

traffico interrotto
road blocked

transito con catene
snow chains required

uscita
exit

velocità massima
maximum speed

vietato l'accesso/ai pedoni
no access/no pedestrian access

vietato l'autostop
no hitch-hiking

vietato svoltare a destra/ sinistra
no right/left turn

zona disco
disk zone

zona rimozione (ambo i lati)
tow-away area (both sides of the road)

Portuguese: words and phrases

For clarity we have put the English phrase in light type, foreign language terms in dark type and their phonetic pronunciation in light italic.

Asking for directions

Excuse me, could I ask you something?
Desculpe, posso-lhe fazer uma pergunta?
deshcoolp possoo lher fazair ooma pergoonta?

I've lost my way
Perdi-me
perdee muh

Is there a...around here?
Conhece um...perto daqui?
coonyes oom...pairtoo dakee?

Is this the way to...?
É este o caminho para...?
eh esht oo cameenyoo parra...?

Could you tell me how to get to the... (name of place) by car/on foot?
Poderia dizer-me como devo fazer para ir para...a pé/de carro?
pooderia dizair muh como dayvoo fazair parra eer parra...ah peh/duh cahroo?

What's the quickest way to...?
Como é que chego o mais depressa possível a...?
como eh kuh chaygoo oo mysh depressa posseevel ah...?

How many kilometres is it to...?
Quantos quilómetros faltam ainda para chegar a...?
cuarntoosh keelometroosh faltam ayeenda parra sheggar ah...?

Could you point it out on the map?
Poderia indicar-me aqui no mapa?
pooderiah eendiccar muh akee noo mappa?

☞ Ask the speaker to point to what they are saying

Não sei, não conheço isto aqui
I don't know, I don't know my way around here

Está enganado
You're going the wrong way

Tem de voltar a...
You have to go back to...

Aí as placas indicam-lhe o caminho a seguir
From there on just follow the signs

Aí deve perguntar de novo
When you get there, ask again

Useful words

em frente
straight ahead

à esquerda
left

à direita
right

cortar
turn

seguir
follow

atravessar
cross

cruzamento
intersection

estrada
street

semáforo
traffic light

placa de trânsito
`cruzamento com prioridade'
`give-way' sign

rio
river

passagem de nível; cancelas
level crossing

placa indicando o caminho à...
sign pointing to...

ponte
bridge

seta
arrow

Road traffic signs

aberto
open

animais cruzando
animals crossing

auto-estrada (com portagem)
motorway (with tolls)

bermas baixas
low hard shoulder

bifurcação
road fork

centro da cidade
city centre

circule pela direita
keep right

circule pela esquerda
keep left

cruzamento perigoso
dangerous crossroads

cuidado
caution

curva a...quilómetros
road bends in... km

curva perigosa
dangerous bend

dê passegem
give way

desvio
diversion

devagar
slow down

espere
wait

estacionamento
parking

estacionamento proibido
no parking

estrada em mau estado
irregular road surface

estrada interrompida
no through road

estrada nacional
main road

excepto
except

fechado
closed

fim de...
end of...

fim de obras
end of roadworks

gelo
ice on road

neve
snow

nevoeiro
fog

obras
roadworks

passagem de nivel (sem guarda)
level crossing (unmanned)

perigo
danger

portagem
toll

posto de primeiros socorros
first-aid post

saída
exit

sentido único
one-way street

vedado ao trânsito
road closed

veículos pesados
heavy vehicles

velocidade máxima
maximum speed

via de acesso
access only

Russian: words and phrases

For clarity we have put the English phrase in light type, foreign language terms in dark type and their phonetic pronunciation in light italic.

Asking for directions

Excuse me, could I ask you something?
Извините, можно вас спросить?
Eezvineetyeh, morzhna vuss sprusseet?

I've lost my way
Я заблудился (заблудилась)
Ya zubloodeelsya (zubloodeelas)

Is there a(n)... around here?
Вы не знаете, здесь поблизости...?
Vy nyeh znah-yetyeh, zdyess publeezusti...?

Is this the way to...?
Это дорога в...?   *Eto durrorga v...?*

Could you tell me how to get to the... (name of place) by car/on foot?
Вы не подскажете, как доехать/ дойти до...?
Vy nyeh pudskarzhityeh, kukk duh-yekhat/ duytee dor...?

What's the quickest way to...?
Как можно быстрее доехать до...?
Kukk morzhna bystrayeh duh-yekhat dor...?

How many kilometres is it to...?
Сколько километров до...?
Skorlka keelumyetruff dor...?

Could you point it out on the map?
Покажите на карте, пожалуйста
Pukkuzheetyeh nah kartyeh, puzharlooysta

☞ Ask the speaker to point to what they are saying

Я не знаю, я не отсюда
I don't know, I don't know my way around here

Вы едете в неправильном направлении
You're going the wrong way

Вам нужно вернуться в...
You have to go back to...

Вы увидите, там будет написано
From there on just follow the signs

Там вам придётся снова спросить
When you get there, ask again

Useful words

прямо
straight ahead

налево
left

направо
right

повернуть
turn

последовать
follow

перейти
cross

перекрёсток
the intersection

улица
the street

светофор
the traffic lights

туннель
the tunnel

знак "уступите дорогу"
the 'give-way' sign

здание
the building

на углу
at the corner

река
the river

путепровод
the fly-over

мост
the bridge

железнодорожный переезд/шлагбаум
level crossing/barrier

указатель направления...
the sign pointing to...

стрелка
the arrow

Road traffic signs

Russia uses international traffic signs, but there are two special forms:

 means STOP

 means END OF RESTRICTION

Берегитесь автомобиля!
watch out for cars

велосипедисты
cyclists

внимание, впереди ведутся работы
road works ahead

(внимание) пешеходы
watch out for pedestrians

встречное движение
oncoming traffic

въезд запрещён
no entry

ГАИ
traffic police

движение в один ряд
single-file traffic

держитесь правой стороны
keep to the right

камнепад
falling rocks

обгон запрещён
no overtaking

обочина
kerb

объезд
diversion

ограничение скорости
speed limit

одностороннее движение
one-way traffic

опасно
dangerous

опасный поворот
dangerous bend

остановка автобуса
bus stop

остановка запрещена
no stopping

переход
crossing

плохая дорога
bad surface

светофор через сто метров
lights ahead 100 metres

стоп
stop

стоянка запрещена
no parking

сужение дороги
road narrows

такси
taxi

таможня
customs

Spanish: words and phrases

For clarity we have put the English phrase in light type, foreign language terms in dark type and their phonetic pronunciation in light italic.

Asking for directions

Excuse me, could I ask you something?
Perdone, ¿podría preguntarle algo?
pehrdohneh, pohdreeah prehgoontahrleh ahlgoh?

I've lost my way
Me he perdido
meh eh pehrdeedoh

Is there a(n)...around here?
¿Sabe dónde hay un(a)...por aquí?
sahbeh dohndeh ay oon(ah)...pohr ahkee?

Is this the way to...?
¿Se va por aquí a...?
seh bah pohr ahkee ah...?

Could you tell me how to get to the... (name of place) by car/on foot?
¿Podría decirme cómo llegar a... (en coche/a pie)?
pohdreeah dehtheermeh kohmoh lyehgahr ah... (ehn kohcheh/ah pyeh)?

What's the quickest way to...?
¿Cómo hago para llegar lo antes posible a...?
kohmoh ahgoh pahrah lyehgahr loh ahntehs pohseebleh ah...?

How many kilometres is it to...?
¿Cuántos kilómetros faltan para llegar a...?
kwahntohs keelohmehtrohs fahltahn pahrah lyehgahr ah...?

Could you point it out on the map?
¿Podría señalarlo en el mapa?
pohdreeah sehnyahlahrloh ehn ehl mahpah?

☞ Ask the speaker to point to what they are saying

No sé, no soy de aquí
I don't know, I don't know my way around here

Por aquí no es
You're going the wrong way

Tiene que volver a...
You have to go back to...

Allí los carteles le indicarán
From there on just follow the signs

Vuelva a preguntar allí
When you get there, ask again

Useful words

todo recto
straight ahead

a la izquierda
left

a la derecha
right

doblar
turn

seguir
follow

cruzar
cross

el cruce
the intersection

la calle
the street

el semáforo
the traffic light

el túnel
the tunnel

el stop
the `give-way' sign

el edificio
the building

en la esquina
at the corner

el río
the river

el viaducto
the fly-over

el puente
the bridge

el paso a nivel/las barreras
the level crossing/ the boom gates

el cartel en dirección de...
the sign pointing to...

la flecha
the arrow

Road traffic signs

a la derecha
right

a la izquierda
left

abierto
open

altura máxima
maximum height

arcenes sin afirmar
soft verges

žatención, peligro!
danger

autopista de peaje
toll road

autovía
motorway

bajada peligrosa
steep hill

calzada resbaladiza
slippery road

cambio de sentido
change of direction

cañada
animals crossing

carretera comarcal
secondary road

carretera cortada
road closed

carretera en mal estado
irregular road surface

carretera nacional
main road

ceda el paso
give way

cerrado
closed

cruce peligroso
dangerous crossing

curvas en...km
bends for...km

despacio
drive slowly

desprendimientos
loose rocks

desvío
diversion

dirección prohibida
no entry

dirección única
one-way traffic

encender las luces
switch on lights

espere
wait

**estacionamiento
  reglamentado**
limited parking zone

excepto...
except for...

fin de...
end of...

hielo
ice on road

niebla
beware fog

obras
roadworks ahead

paso a nivel (sin barreras)
level crossing (no gates)

paso de ganado
cattle crossing

peaje
toll

peatones
pedestrian crossing

precaución
caution

prohibido adelantar
no overtaking

prohibido aparcar
no parking

puesto de socorro
first aid

salida
exit

salida de camiones
factory/works exit

substancias peligrosas
dangerous substances

travesía peligrosa
dangerous crossing

zona peatonal
pedestrian zone

Turkish: words and phrases

For clarity we have put the English phrase in light type, foreign language terms in dark type and their phonetic pronunciation in light italic.

Asking for directions

Excuse me, could I ask you something?
Özür dilerim, size bir şey sorabilir miyim?
urzewR dileRim, sizeh biR shey soRabiliR miyim?

I've lost my way
Yolumu kaybettim
yoloomoo kíbet-tim

Is there a(n)...around here?
Bu civarda bir...var mı?
boo jivaRda biR...vaR muh?

Is this the way to...?
...giden yol bu mu?
...giden yol boo moo?

Could you tell me how to get to the... (name of place) by car/on foot?
Bana...arabayla/yaya nasıl gidebileceğimi söyleyebilir misiniz?
bana...aRabíla/ya-ya nasuhl gidebileje:imi suhyleyebiliR misiniz?

What's the quickest way to...?
...en çabuk nasıl gidebilirim?
...en chabook nasuhl gidebiliRim?

How many kilometres is it to...?
...kaç kilometre kaldı?
...kach kilometReh kalduh?

Could you point it out on the map?
Haritada gösterebilir misiniz?
haRitada gursteRebiliR misiniz?

☞ Ask the speaker to point to what they are saying

Bilmiyorum, buralı değilim
I don't know, I don't know my way around here

Yanlış yoldasınız
You're going the wrong way

...geri dönmelisiniz
You have to go back to...

Oradan levhaları takip ediniz
From there on just follow the signs

Oraya varınca tekrar sorun
When you get there, ask again

Useful words

doğru
straight ahead
sola
left
sağa
right
dönmek
turn
takip etmek
follow
karşıya geçmek
cross
kavşak
the intersection
sokak
the street
trafik ışıkları
the traffic lights
tünel
the tunnel

'yol ver' işareti
the `give-way' sign
bina
the building
köşede
at the corner
ırmak/nehir
the river
bağlantı yolu
the fly-over
köprü
the bridge
hemzemin geçit
the level crossing/the boom gates
...giden yolu gösteren levha
the sign pointing to...

Road traffic signs

Beklemek yasaktır
no waiting

Bozuk yol
poor road surface

D (durak)
D (bus stop)

Dikkat
caution

Dur
stop

Gümrük
customs

H (hastane)
H (hospital)

Havaalanı
airport

Jandarma
gendarmerie

Park etmek yasaktır
no parking

Polis
police

Şehir merkezi
city centre

Tamirat
roadworks

Tek yön
one way

Tünel
tunnel

Viraj
bend

Yangın tehlikesi
danger of fire

Yavaş
slow

Useful information

Channel Tunnel maps

The Eurotunnel shuttle service for cars, cars towing caravans and trailers, motorcycles, coaches and HGV vehicles runs between terminals at Folkestone in Kent and Calais/Coquelles in France.

It takes just over one hour to travel from the M20 motorway in Kent, via the Channel Tunnel, to the A16 autoroute in France. The service runs 24 hours a day, every day of the year.

Liquefied petroleum gas (LPG)

An LPG-fuelled car will not be allowed through the Eurotunnel, even if you can prove the tank has been disconnected or emptied. If you are travelling by ferry, check with the operator before you book.

Travel information

For the latest ticket and travel information call the Eurotunnel Call Centre (**tel: 08443 353535**) or visit **www.eurotunnel.com**

There are up to three departures per hour at peak times, with the journey in the tunnel from platform to platform taking just 35 minutes. Travellers pass through British and French frontier controls on departure, saving time on the other side of the Channel.

Each terminal has plenty of parking, ATMs, bureaux de change, restaurants, toilet facilities, a 24-hour information point and a variety of shops. In Calais/Coquelles, the Cité de l'Europe contains numerous shops, restaurants and a hypermarket.

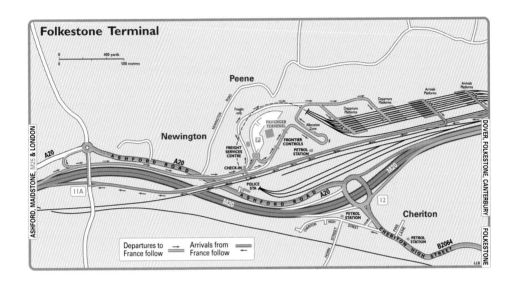

Folkestone Terminal

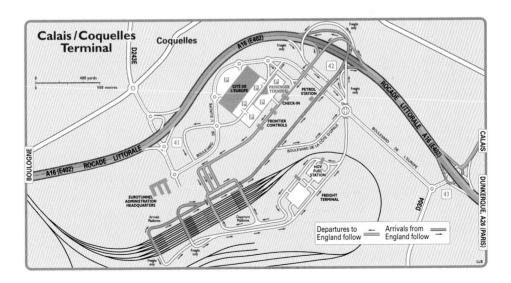

Calais / Coquelles Terminal

Road distance chart

City labels (diagonal headers, in order): Amsterdam, Athina, Barcelona, Belfast, Beograd, Berlin, Bern, Birmingham, Bordeaux, Bratislava, Brussel/Bruxelles, Bucureşti, Budapest, Dublin, Edinburgh, Frankfurt am Main, Genève, Göteborg, Hamburg, Helsinki/Helsingfors, Istanbul, København, Köln, Kyïv, Lisboa, Ljubljana, London, Luxembourg, Madrid, Manchester

Frankfurt am Main–Ljubljana = 804 km

```
2760
1557 2520
1312 3520 2265
1718 1044 1981 2816
655  2288 1863 1868 1247
838  1971 944  1725 1363 922
738  3285 1691 582  2244 1295 1152
1091 3049 552  1815 2007 1634 852  1241
1225 1618 1866 2324 577  671  938  1750 1879
206  2568 1355 1148 1673 763  637  574  883  1181
2181 1106 2597 3279 619  1646 1893 2706 2613 977  2136
1398 1429 1897 2497 388  864  1111 1923 2053 194  1353 788
1088 3455 2041 164  2594 1644 1502 358  1585 2101 925  3057 2274
1190 3557 2143 305  2695 1746 1603 460  1686 2203 1026 3159 2376 468
445  2323 1323 1545 1281 565  423  971  1150 788  400  1744 961  1321 1422
908  2372 778  1683 1331 1072 165  1109 687  1088 706  1946 1261 1457 1561 573
1178 3131 2479 2412 2090 823  1637 1839 2185 1514 1307 2490 1708 2187 2290 1214 1787
463  2602 1763 1696 1561 294  910  1123 1470 985  591  1961 1178 1471 1574 487  1059 728
2580 3590 3788 3792 2641 1959 2847 3220 3551 2208 2687 2483 2252 3567 3670 2489 2996 982  2192
2649 1092 2913 3748 935  2179 2294 3175 2929 1509 2605 681  1320 3522 3626 2213 2261 3022 2493 3164
920  2873 2220 2153 1832 564  1378 1580 1927 1255 1048 2231 1449 1928 2031 955  1528 269  469  1123 2764
265  2506 1342 1352 1464 575  585  778  1062 972  208  1928 1145 1126 1230 192  735  1141 425  2500 2396 882
2016 1994 3093 3228 1322 1398 2190 2655 2988 1251 2123 888  1123 3003 3106 1884 2340 2211 1681 1595 1569 1952 1935
2296 3787 1237 3019 3188 2838 2150 2446 1202 3090 2905 3804 3103 2793 2897 2355 1989 3397 2681 4764 4119 3138 2273 4199
1241 1572 1455 2294 530  999  836  1721 1471 435  1153 1146 443  2069 2173 804  803  1916 1203 2623 1462 1656 987  1565 2661
533  2910 1486 766  2039 1090 947  193  1030 1546 370  2502 1719 541  645  766  905  1634 918  3015 2970 1375 574  2450 2243 1537
386  2355 1149 1355 1469 762  431  782  946  1010 213  1965 1183 1129 1233 240  500  1326 610  2687 2401 1066 188  2081 2159 956  582
1800 3145 614  2523 2573 2343 1535 1950 706  2458 1599 3189 2489 2298 2402 1859 1374 2901 2185 4268 3505 2642 1778 3684 619  2046 1750 1662
868  3415 1821 461  2374 1425 1282 138  1365 1881 705  2837 2054 310  339  1101 1240 1969 1253 3350 3305 1710 909  2785 2578 1872 323  911  2082
1236 2567 505  2003 1526 1541 623  1429 654  1419 1034 2141 1441 1778 1881 1003 422  2158 1442 3467 2457 1899 1025 2564 1711 999  1230 832  1096 1560
1077 1218 977  1963 1026 1033 350  1390 985  919  876  1642 942  1737 1841 662  317  1833 1120 2959 1958 1574 823  2064 2182 499  1190 669  1568 1520 5
1742 2448 2878 2955 1513 1124 1938 2381 2714 1178 1850 1341 1125 2729 2833 1620 2088 1938 1408 1183 2023 1678 1662 557  3927 1593 2181 1817 3307 2387 2
2449 2864 3584 3661 2084 1830 2644 3088 3420 1885 2556 1758 1831 3435 3539 2326 2794 2643 2114 1116 2440 2385 2368 871  4364 2300 2888 2523 4138 3218 3
827  1990 1370 1880 949  585  442  1297 1278 466  739  1421 639  1655 1759 390  591  1502 789  2511 1880 1242 573  1718 2576 435  1107 521  1961 1437 1
1859 597  1555 2746 1483 1693 1132 2173 1704 1376 1658 2099 1399 2521 2624 1444 1085 2586 1874 3563 2415 2327 1606 2521 2761 956  1973 1476 2146 2303 1
1490 3443 2790 2723 2402 1134 1949 2150 2497 1826 2118 2801 2019 2498 2601 1525 2098 315  1039 1030 3333 580  1446 2522 3710 2248 1963 1516 3636 3214 2
525  2465 1039 1248 1800 1068 592  659  583  1340 324  2295 1513 1023 1126 604  529  1626 910  2993 2732 1367 502  2428 1796 1287 475  407  1300 805  7
2094 4028 1076 2818 2986 2637 1948 2244 1000 2889 1893 3602 2902 2592 2696 2153 1788 3196 2480 4563 3918 2936 2072 3997 300  2459 2044 1956 531  2375 15
891  1946 1709 2045 904  341  769  1471 1601 328  902  1304 522  1820 1923 510  919  1186 657  2178 1836 927  693  1389 2814 664  1272 731  2300 1602 13
1618 2807 2825 2830 1766 996  1885 2257 2590 1333 1725 1676 1378 2604 2708 1527 2035 1760 1230 800  1448 1183 1347 2357 1501 1537 1029 3803 1748 2057 1724 3307 2387 2
1658 1190 1354 2545 1282 1493 932  1972 1503 1175 1457 1898 1198 2320 2423 1243 884  2386 1673 3363 2214 2126 1405 2321 2560 755  1772 1275 1945 2102 8
2180 3190 3388 3393 2241 1558 2447 2819 3152 1809 2288 2084 1853 3167 3271 2089 2597 2284 1793 387  2765 2063 2099 1196 4365 2223 2619 2286 3869 2950 30
1727 1121 1990 2826 303  1389 1372 2252 2007 707  1682 824  539  2600 2704 1290 1339 2402 1644 2791 1113 2143 1474 1601 3196 539  2052 1478 2581 2383 15
2277 3998 998  3000 2957 2838 2157 2467 1183 2842 2076 3573 2873 2775 2878 2299 1759 3378 2662 4763 3889 3119 2255 4068 403  2437 2227 2128 510 2557 14
2139 654  2402 3237 424  1668 1783 2664 2418 998  2094 598  809  3012 3115 1702 1750 2512 1982 3061 781  2253 1885 1485 3608 951  2464 1890 2993 2794 19
2095 735  2358 3193 380  1624 1739 2620 2375 954  2050 372  765  2968 3071 1658 1707 2468 1938 2854 555  2209 1841 1259 3564 907  2420 1846 2949 2750 19
1534 3488 2835 2768 2446 1175 1993 2195 2541 1870 1663 2846 2064 2543 2646 1570 2143 481  1084 505  3378 624  1497 2566 3755 2293 1995 1681 3259 2325 25
1920 3105 3127 3132 2063 1298 2187 2559 2892 1631 2027 1973 1675 2907 3011 1829 2337 2062 1532 90  2654 1803 1839 1326 4105 2046 2359 2026 3609 2689 28
2333 454  2597 3432 619  1862 1978 2858 2613 1193 2288 656  1004 3207 3310 1896 1945 2707 2177 3139 642  2447 2080 1543 3802 1145 2658 2085 3188 2989 21
2103 735  2366 3201 606  1765 1748 2628 2383 1083 2058 886  915  2976 3163 1666 1715 2778 2020 3167 1069 2518 1849 1773 3572 915  2428 1854 2957 2758 19
3071 4692 4371 4304 3743 2715 3529 3731 4078 3311 3199 3586 3355 4114 4182 3106 3679 1949 2620 1360 4267 2160 3033 2698 5291 3829 3531 3217 4795 3861 40
1897 3363 363  2604 2322 2202 1283 2030 803  2206 1695 2957 2378 2482 1663 1123 2819 2012 2418 3253 2560 1686 3433 894  1795 1830 1492 342  2160 8
1636 2550 2776 2849 1509 1018 1836 2280 2575 2608 1077 1744 1384 1121 2623 2727 1518 1986 1733 1203 1142 2066 1474 1555 738 3821 1492 2075 1715 3325 2406 24
1202 2097 2342 2414 1056 584  1402 1841 2174 643  1309 1240 668  2189 2293 1084 1552 1397 868  1566 1922 1138 1121 815  3387 1057 1641 1281 2891 1971 20
1148 1664 1789 2246 622  629  861  1673 1802 66  1103 1022 240  2021 2125 711  1010 1473 943  2246 1554 1214 895  1319 3016 378  1473 933  2380 1804 13
1326 1435 1586 2424 394  988  968  1852 1603 417  1281 1009 347  2199 2302 889  936  2001 1243 2604 1325 1741 1073 1470 2793 135  1647 1074 2177 1982 11
```

Map of Europe with city labels:

Tromsø · Oslo · Stockholm · Helsinki · Sankt-Peterburg · Moskva · Göteborg · Tallinn · Riga · København · Vilnius · Minsk · Belfast · Edinburgh · Dublin · Manchester · Birmingham · London · Amsterdam · Hamburg · Warszawa · Kyïv · Bruxelles · Köln · Berlin · Luxembourg · Frankfurt a. M. · Paris · Praha · München · Wien · Bratislava · Bordeaux · Bern · Budapest · Genève · Ljubljana · Zagreb · Porto · Marseille · Milano · Beograd · București · Lisboa · Sarajevo · Madrid · Roma · Skopje · Sofiya · İstanbul · Barcelona · València · Napoli · Tiranë · Thessaloniki · Sevilla · Athina

Distances (in kilometres) are calculated by the shortest or quickest route and should be considered to be approximate.
The calculation includes any part of the journey taken by car ferry.

Distance chart (diagonal headers: Milano, Minsk, Moskva, München, Napoli, Oslo, Paris, Porto, Praha, Riga, Roma, Sankt-Peterburg, Sarajevo, Sevilla, Skopje, Sofiya, Stockholm, Tallinn, Thessaloniki, Tiranë, Tromsø, València, Vilnius, Warszawa, Wien, Zagreb):

```
48  Minsk
55  704  Moskva
02  1524 2231 München
'9  2534 3240 1109 Napoli
44  2248 2954 1813 2898 Oslo
'4  2154 2861 852  1643 1937 Paris
81  3724 4430 2375 2559 3506 1589 Porto
59  1149 1855 375  1483 1498 1031 2611 Praha
96  472  931  1548 2655 2072 2016 3601 1260 Riga
'8  2333 3040 908  237  2697 1417 2358 1281 2456 Roma
58  784  716  2110 3164 2325 2574 4164 1778 562  2963 Sankt-Peterburg
34  1664 2370 958  1492 2713 1779 2995 1046 1917 1291 2392 Sarajevo
52  3853 4559 2346 2530 3690 1771 650  2684 3802 2329 4364 2968 Sevilla
46  1934 2356 1370 1903 2823 2191 3406 1324 2187 936  2662 470  3377 Skopje
02  1713 2130 1326 1859 2779 2147 3363 1281 2047 1317 2455 558  3333 227  Sofiya
89  2293 2656 1858 2943 537  1964 3551 1541 910  2743 906  2756 3736 2867 2823 Stockholm
98  770  1043 1850 2957 2374 2314 3903 1562 302  2757 357  2214 4103 2484 2344 595  Tallinn
41  1997 2414 1565 2098 3018 2385 3601 1519 2381 1164 2740 698  3572 228  284  3062 2678 Thessaloniki
10  2040 2644 1334 640  3089 2155 3371 1422 2293 816  2768 385  3342 288  514  3133 2660 393  Tiranë
25  2286 2219 3394 4479 1616 3500 5089 3077 2064 4279 1502 3894 5272 4164 3957 1605 1859 4242 4346 Tromsø
16  3217 3924 1710 1895 3130 1375 879  2048 3166 1694 3728 2328 644  2743 2699 3175 3538 2936 2706 4744 València
47  181  863  1424 2432 2044 2030 3620 1046 291  2231 743  1660 3752 1929 1756 2089 658  2040 2111 2245 3116 Vilnius
13  541  1247 990  1998 1709 1596 3185 612  692  1797 1167 1207 3317 1476 1433 1753 1059 1671 1659 2669 2682 435  Warszawa
'1  1216 1923 388  1318 1784 1233 2814 285  1371 1117 1847 758  2765 1043 999  1829 1739 1237 1225 3398 2179 1115 681  Wien
'2  1472 2178 554  1089 2312 1406 2591 645  1730 887  2205 400  2562 815  771  2356 2097 1008 862  3926 1926 1473 1039 359  Zagreb
```

Mountain passes

It is best not to attempt to cross mountain passes at night, and daily schedules should make allowances for the comparatively slow speeds inevitable in mountainous areas.

Gravel surfaces (such as dirt and stone chips) vary considerably; they are dusty when dry, slippery when wet. Where known to exist, this type of surface has been noted. Road repairs can be carried out only during the summer, and may interrupt traffic. Precipitous road sides are rarely, if ever, totally unguarded; on the older roads, stone pillars are placed at close intervals. Gradient figures take the mean figure on hairpin bends, and may be steeper on the inside of the curves, particularly on the older roads.

Gradients conversion table

All steep hill signs show the grade in percentage terms. The following conversion table may be used as a guide:

30% = 1 in 3	14% = 1 in 7
25% = 1 in 4	12% = 1 in 8
20% = 1 in 5	11% = 1 in 9
16% = 1 in 6	10% = 1 in 10

Before attempting late-evening or early-morning journeys across frontier passes, check the times of opening of the frontier controls. A number close at night; for example, the Timmelsjoch border is closed between 8pm and 7am and during the winter.

Always engage a low gear before either ascending or descending steep gradients, and keep well to the right-hand side of the road and avoid cutting corners. Avoid excessive use of brakes. If the engine overheats, pull off the road, making sure that you do not cause an obstruction, leave the engine idling, and put the heater controls (including the fan) into the maximum heat position. Under no circumstances should you remove the radiator cap until the engine has cooled down. Do not fill the coolant system of a hot engine with cold water.

Always engage a lower gear before taking a hairpin bend, give priority to vehicles ascending and remember that as your altitude increases, so your engine power decreases. Always give priority to postal coaches travelling in either direction. Their route is usually signposted.

Caravans

Passes suitable for caravans are indicated in the table on the following pages. Those shown to be negotiable by caravans are best used only by experienced drivers in cars with ample power;

the rest are probably best avoided. A correct power-to-load ratio is always essential.

Winter conditions

Mountain passes – key to abbreviations:

Winter conditions are given in italics in the last column of the table on pages 226–235.
UO means 'usually open', although a severe fall of snow may temporarily obstruct the road for 24 to 48 hours, and wheel chains are often necessary; OC means 'occasionally closed'; UC, usually closed, between the dates stated. Dates for opening and closing of passes are approximate only. Warning notices are usually posted at the foot of a pass if it is closed, or if indicating that chains or snow tyres should or must be used.

Wheel chains may be needed early and late in the season, and between short spells (a few hours) of obstruction. At these times, conditions are usually more difficult for caravans on the passes.

In fair weather, wheel chains or snow tyres are necessary only on the higher passes, but in severe weather you will probably need to use them (as a rough guide) at altitudes exceeding 610 metres (2,000ft).

Mountain passes

Pass name, height and country	From and to	Distances from summit and max gradient	Min width of road	Conditions (see page 225 for key to abbreviations)
*Albula 2312 metres (7585ft) Switzerland	Tiefencastel 851 metres (2792ft) La Punt 1687 metres (5535ft)	30km 1 in 10 18.6 miles 9km 1 in 10 5.6 miles	3.5 metres 11ft 6in	UC Nov–early Jun. An inferior alternative to the Julier; tar and gravel, fine scenery. Alternative rail tunnel.
Allos 2250 metres (7382ft) France	Barcelonnette 1132 metres (3714ft) Colmars 1235 metres (4052ft)	20km 1 in 10 12.4 miles 24km 1 in 12 14.9 miles	4 metres 13ft 1n	UC early Nov–early Jun. Very winding, narrow mostly unguarded but not difficult otherwise; passing bays on southern slope, poor surface (maximum width vehicles 1.8 metres, 5ft 11in).
Aprica 1176 metres (3858ft) Italy	Tresenda 375 metres (1230ft) Edolo 699 metres (2293ft)	14km 1 in 11 8.7 miles 15km 1 in 16 9.3 miles	4 metres 13ft 1in	UO Fine scenery, good surface, well graded; suitable for caravans.
Aravis 1498 metres (4915ft) France	La Clusaz 1040 metres (3412ft) Flumet 917 metres (3009ft)	8km 1 in 11 5.0 miles 12km 1 in 11 7.4 miles	4 metres 13ft 1in	OC Dec–Mar. Outstanding scenery, and a fairly easy road.
Arlberg 1802 metres (5912ft) Austria	Bludenz 581 metres (1905ft) Landeck 816 metres (2677ft)	35km 1 in 8 21.7 miles 32km 1 in 7.5 20 miles	6 metres 19ft 8in	OC Dec–Apr. Modern road; short, steep stretch from west easing towards the summit; heavy traffic; parallel toll road tunnel. Suitable for caravans; using tunnel. Pass road closed to vehicles towing trailers.
Aubisque 1710 metres (5610ft) France	Eaux Bonnes 750 metres (2461ft) Argelés-Gazost 463 metres (1519ft)	12km 1 in 10 7 miles 30km 1 in 10 19 miles	3.5 metres 11ft 6in	UC mid Oct–Jun. A very winding road; continuous but easy ascent; the descent incorporates the Col de Soulor (1450 metres, 4757ft); 8km (5 miles) of very narrow, rough unguarded road, with a steep drop.
Ballon d'Alsace 1178 metres (3865ft) France	Giromagny 476 metres (1562ft) St-Maurice-sur-Moselle 549 metres (1801ft)	17km 1 in 9 10.6 miles 9km 1 in 9 5.6 miles	4 metres 13ft 1in	OC Dec–Mar. A fairly straightforward ascent and descent, but numerous bends; negotiable by caravans.
Bayard 1248 metres (4094ft) France	Chauffayer 911 metres (2989ft) Gap 733 metres (2405ft)	18km 1 in 12 11.2 miles 8km 1 in 7 5.0 miles	6 metres 19ft 8in	UO Part of the Route Napoléon. Fairly easy, steepest on the southern side with several hairpin bends; negotiable by caravans from north to south.
*Bernina 2330 metres (7644ft) Switzerland	Pontresina 1805 metres (5922ft) Poschiavo 1019 metres (3343ft)	15.5km 1 in 10 10.5 miles 18.5km 1 in 8 11.5 miles	5 metres 16ft 5in	OC Dec–Mar. A good road on both sides; negotiable by caravans.
Bonaigua 2072 metres (6797ft) Spain	Viella 974 metres (3195ft) Esterri d'Aneu 957 metres (3140ft)	23km 1 in 12 14 miles 23km 1 in 12 14 miles	4.3 metres 14ft 1in	UC Nov–Apr. A sinuous and narrow road with many hairpin bends and some precipitous drops; the alternative route to Lleida (Lérida) through the Viella tunnel is open in winter.
Bracco 613 metres (2011ft) Italy	Riva Trigoso 43 metres (141ft) Borghetto di Vara 104 metres (341ft)	15km 1 in 7 9.3 miles 18km 1 in 7 11.2 miles	5 metres 16ft 5in	UO A two-lane road with continuous bends; passing usually difficult; negotiable by caravans; alternative toll motorway available.

* Permitted maximum width of vehicles 7ft 6in + Permitted maximum width of vehicles 8ft 2.5in ++ Maximum length of vehicle 30ft

Pass name, height and country	From and to	Distances from summit and max gradient	Min width of road	Conditions (see page 225 for key to abbreviations)
Brenner 1374 metres (4508ft) Austria–Italy	Innsbruck 574 metres (1883ft) Vipiteno 948 metres (3110ft)	36km 1 in 12 22miles 15km 1 in 7 9.3 miles	6 metres 19ft 8in	UO Parallel toll motorway open; heavy traffic; suitable for caravans using toll motorway. Pass road closed to vehicles towing trailers.
+Brünig 1007 metres (3304ft) Switzerland	Brienzwiler Station 575 metres (1886ft) Giswil 485 metres (1591ft)	6km 1 in 12 3.7 miles 13km 1 in 12 8.1 miles	6 metres 19ft 8in	UO An easy but winding road, heavy traffic at weekends; suitable for caravans.
Bussang 721 metres (2365ft) France	Thann 340 metres (1115ft) St Maurice-sur-Moselle 549 metres (1801ft)	24km 1 in 14 15 miles 8km 1 in 14 5.0 miles	4 metres 13ft 1in	UO A very easy road over the Vosges; beautiful scenery; suitable for caravans.
Cabre 1180 metres (3871ft) France	Luc-en-Diois 580 metres (1903ft) Aspres sur Buëch 764 metres (2507ft)	24km 1 in 11 15 miles 17km 1 in 14 10.6 miles	5.5 metres 18ft	UO An easy, pleasant road; suitable for caravans.
Campolongo 1875 metres (6152ft) Italy	Corvara in Badia 1568 metres (5144ft) Arabba 1602 metres (5256ft)	6km 1 in 8 3.7 miles 4km 1 in 8 2.5 miles	5 metres 16ft 5in	OC Dec–Mar. A winding but easy ascent; long level stretch on summit followed by easy descent; good surface; suitable for caravans.
Cayolle 2326 metres (7631ft) France	Barcelonnette 1132 metres (3714ft) Guillaumes 819 metres (2687ft)	30km 1 in 10 19 miles 33km 1 in 10 20.5 miles	4 metres 13ft 1in	UC early Nov–early Jun. Narrow and winding road with hairpin bends; poor surface and broken edges; steep drops. Long stretches of single-track road with passing places.
Costalunga (Karer) 1753 metres (5751ft) Italy	Cardano 282 metres (925ft) Pozza 1290 metres (4232ft)	24km 1 in 6 14.9 miles 11km 1 in 8 7 miles	5 metres 16ft 5in	OC Dec–Apr. A good well-engineered road but mostly winding; caravans prohibited.
Croix 1778 metres (5833ft) Switzerland	Villars-sur-Ollon 1253 metres (4111ft) Les Diablerets 1155 metres (3789ft)	8km 1 in 7.5 5.0 miles 9km 1 in 11 5.6 miles	3.5 metres 11ft 6in	UC Nov–May. A narrow and winding route but extremely picturesque.
Croix-Haute 1179 metres (3868ft) France	Monestier-de-Clermont 832 metres (2730ft) Aspres-sur-Buëch 764 metres (2507ft)	34km 1 in 14 21 miles 29km 1 in 14 18 miles	5.5 metres 18ft	UO Well engineered; several hairpin bends on the north side; suitable for caravans.
Envalira 2407 metres (7897ft) Andorra	Pas de la Casa 2091 metres (6860ft) Andorra 1029 metres (3376ft)	5km 1 in 10 3.1 miles 25km 1 in 8 16 miles	6 metres 19ft 8in	OC Nov–Apr. A good road with wide bends on ascent and descent; fine views; negotiable by caravans (maximum height vehicles 3.5 metres/ 11ft 6in on northern approach near L'Hospitalet).
Falzárego 2117 metres (6945ft) Italy	Cortina d'Ampezzo 1224 metres (4016ft) Andraz 1428 metres (4685ft)	17km 1 in 12 10.6 miles 9km 1 in 12 5.6 miles	5 metres 16ft 5in	OC Dec–Apr. Well engineered bitumen surface; many hairpin bends on both sides; negotiable by caravans.

* Permitted maximum width of vehicles 7ft 6in + Permitted maximum width of vehicles 8ft 2.5in ++ Maximum length of vehicle 30ft

Pass name, height and country	From and to	Distances from summit and max gradient	Min width of road	Conditions (see page 225 for key to abbreviations)
Faucille 1323 metres (4341ft) France	Gex 628 metres (2060ft) Morez 702 metres (2303ft)	11km 1 in 10 6.8 miles 27km 1 in 12 17miles	5 metres 16ft 5in	UO Fairly wide, winding road across the Jura mountains; negotiable by caravans, but it is probably better to follow La Cure-St-Cergue-Nyon.
Fern 1209 metres (3967ft) Austria	Nassereith 843 metres (2766ft) Lermoos 995 metres (3264ft)	10km 1 in 10 6 miles 10km 1 in 10 6 miles	6 metres 19ft 8in	UO An easy pass, but slippery when wet; heavy traffic at summer weekends; suitable for caravans.
Flexen 1784 metres (5853ft) Austria	Lech 1447 metres (4747ft) Rauzalpe (near Arlberg Pass) 1628 metres (5341ft)	6.5km 1 in 10 4 miles 3.5km 1 in 10 2.2 miles	5.5 metres 18ft	UO The magnificent 'Flexenstrasse', a well-engineered mountain road with tunnels and galleries. The road from Lech to Warth, north of the pass, is usually closed between November and April due to danger of avalanches.
***Flüela** 2383 metres (7818ft) Switzerland	Davos-Dorf 1563 metres (5128ft) Susch 1438 metres (4718ft)	14km 1 in 10 9 miles 14km 1 in 8 9 miles	5 metres 16ft 5in	OC Nov–May. Easy ascent from Davos; some acute hairpin bends on the eastern side; bitumen surface; negotiable by caravans.
+Forclaz 1527 metres (5010ft) Switzerland France	Martigny 476 metres (1562ft) Argentière 1253 metres (4111ft)	13km 1 in 12 8.1 miles 19km 1 in 12 11.8 miles	5 metres 16ft 5in	UO Forclaz; OC Montets Dec–early Apr. A good road over the pass and to the frontier; in France, narrow and rough over Col des Montets (1461 metres/4793ft); negotiable by caravans.
Foscagno 2291 metres (7516ft) Italy	Bormio 1225 metres (4019ft) Livigno 1816 metres (5958ft)	24km 1 in 8 14.9 miles 14km 1 in 8 8.7 miles	3.3 metres 10ft 10in	OC Nov–May. Narrow and winding through lonely mountains, generally poor surface. Long winding ascent with many blind bends; not always well guarded. The descent includes winding rise and fall over the Passo d'Eira (2200 metres/7218ft).
Fugazze 1159 metres (3802ft) Italy	Rovereto 201 metres (660ft) Valli del Pasubio 350 metres (1148ft)	27km 1 in 7 16.4 miles 12km 1 in 7 7.4 miles	3.5 metres 11ft 6in	UO Very winding with some narrow sections, particularly on northern side. The many blind bends and several hairpin bends call for extra care.
***Furka** 2431 metres (7976ft) Switzerland	Gletsch 1757 metres (5764ft) Realp 1538 metres (5046ft)	10km 1 in 9 6.2 miles 13km 1 in 10 8.1 miles	4 metres 13ft 1in	UC Oct–Jun. A well-graded road, with narrow sections and several sharp hairpin bends on both ascent and descent. Fine views of the Rhône glacier. Alternative rail tunnel available.
Galibier 2645 metres (8678ft) France	Lautaret Pass 2058 metres (6752ft) St-Michel-de-Maurienne 712 metres (2336ft)	7km 1 in 9 4.4 miles 34km 1 in 8 21.1 miles	3 metres 9ft 10in	UC Oct–Jun. Mainly wide, well surfaced but unguarded. Ten hairpin bends on descent then 5km (3.1 miles) narrow and rough. Rise over the Col du Télégraphe (1600 metres/5249ft), then 11 more hairpin bends. (The tunnel under the Galibier summit is closed.)
Gardena (Grödner-Joch) 2121 metres (6959ft) Italy	Val Gardena 1862 metres (6109ft) Corvara in Badia 1568 metres (5144ft)	6km 1 in 8 3.7 miles 10km 1 in 8 6.2 miles	5 metres 16ft 5in	OC Dec–Jun. A well-engineered road, very winding on descent.

* Permitted maximum width of vehicles 7ft 6in + Permitted maximum width of vehicles 8ft 2.5in ++ Maximum length of vehicle 30ft

Pass name, height and country	From and to	Distances from summit and max gradient	Min width of road	Conditions (see page 225 for key to abbreviations)
Gavia 2621 metres (8599ft) Italy	Bormio 1225 metres (4019ft) Ponte di Legno 1258 metres (4127ft)	25km 1 in 5.5 15.5 miles 18km 1 in 5.5 11 miles	3 metres 9ft 10in	UC Oct–Jul. Steep and narrow, but with frequent passing bays; many hairpin bends and a gravel surface; not for the faint-hearted; extra care necessary. (Maximum width for vehicles 1.8 metres/5ft 11in.)
Gerlos 1628 metres (5341ft) Austria	Zell am Ziller 575 metres (1886ft) Wald 885 metres (2904ft)	29km 1 in 12 18 miles 15km 1 in 11 9.3 miles	4 metres 13ft 1in	UO Hairpin ascent out of Zell to modern toll road; the old, steep, narrow, and winding route with passing bays and 1-in-7 gradient is not recommended, but is negotiable with care; caravans prohibited.
+Grand St Bernard 2473 metres (8114ft) Switzerland–Italy	Martigny 476 metres (1562ft) Aosta 583 metres (1913ft)	46km 1 in 9 29 miles 34km 1 in 9 21 miles	4 metres 13ft 1in	UC Oct–Jun. Modern road to entrance of road tunnel (usually open; then narrow over summit to frontier; also good surface in Italy; suitable for caravans using tunnel. Pass road closed to vehicles towing trailers.
*Grimsel 2164 metres (7100ft) Switzerland	Innerkirchen 630 metres (2067ft) Gletsch 1757 metres (5764ft)	26km 1 in 10 16.1 miles 6km 1 in 10 3.7 miles	5 metres 16ft 5in	UC mid-Oct to late Jun. A fairly easy road, but heavy traffic weekends. A long winding ascent, finally hairpin bends; then a terraced descent (six hairpins) into the Rhône valley. Negotiable by caravans.
Grossglockner 2503 metres (8212ft) Austria	Bruck an der Glocknerstrasse 755 metres (2477ft) Heiligenblut 1301 metres (4268ft)	34km 1 in 8 21 miles 15m 1 in 8 9.3 miles	5.5 metres 18ft	UC late Oct–early May. Numerous well-engineered hairpin bends; moderate but very long ascent, toll road; very fine scenery; heavy tourist traffic; negotiable preferably from south to north, by caravans. Road closed 10pm to 5am.
Hochtannberg 1679 metres (5509ft) Austria	Schröcken 1269 metres (4163ft) Warth (near Lech) 1500 metres (4921ft)	5.5km 1 in 7 3.4 miles 4.5km 1 in 11 2.8 miles	4 metres 13ft 1in	OC Jan–Mar. A reconstructed modern road.
Ibañeta (Roncesvalles) 1057 metres (3468ft) France–Spain	St-Jean-Pied-de-Port 163 metres (535ft) Pamplona 415 metres (1362ft)	27km 1 in 10 17 miles 49km 1 in 10 30 miles	4 metres 13ft 1in	UO A slow and winding, scenic route; negotiable by caravans.
Iseran 2770 metres (9088ft) France	Bourg-St-Maurice 840 metres (2756ft) Lanslebourg 1399 metres (4590ft)	47km 1 in 12 29 miles 33km 1 in 9 20.5 miles	4 metres 13ft 1in	UC mid-Oct to late Jun. The second highest pass in the Alps. Well graded with reasonable bends, average surface; several unlit tunnels on northern approach.
Izoard 2360 metres (7743ft) France	Guillestre 1000 metres (3281ft) Briançon 1321 metres (4334ft)	32km 1 in 8 20 miles 22km 1 in 8 14 miles	5 metres 16ft 5in	UC late Oct to mid-Jun. A winding and sometimes narrow road with many hairpin bends. Care is required at several unlit tunnels near Guillestre.

* Permitted maximum width of vehicles 7ft 6in   + Permitted maximum width of vehicles 8ft 2.5in   ++ Maximum length of vehicle 30ft

Mountain passes

Pass name, height and country	From and to	Distances from summit and max gradient	Min width of road	Conditions (see page 225 for key to abbreviations)
*Jaun 1509 metres (4951ft) Switzerland	Broc 718 metres (2356ft) Reidenbach 845 metres (2772ft)	25km 1 in 10 15.5 miles 8km 1 in 10 5 miles	4 metres 13ft 1in	UO A modernised but generally narrow road; some poor sections on ascent, and several hairpin bends on descent; negotiable by caravans.
+Julier 2284 metres (7493ft) Switzerland	Tiefencastel 851 metres (2792ft) Silvaplana 1815 metres (5955ft)	35km 1 in 10 22miles 7km 1 in 7.5 4.4 miles	4 metres 13ft 1in	UO Well-engineered road, approached from Chur by Lenzerheide Pass (1549 metres/5082ft); negotiable by caravans, preferably from north to south.
Katschberg 1641 metres (5384ft) Austria	Spittal 554 metres (1818ft) St Michael 1068 metres (3504ft)	37km 1 in 5 23 miles 6km 1 in 6 3.7 miles	6 metres 19ft 8in	UO Steep though not particularly difficult, parallel toll motorway, including tunnel available; negotiable by light caravans, using tunnel via Tauern Autobahn.
*Klausen 1948 metres (6391ft) Switzerland	Altdorf 458 metres (1503ft) Linthal 662 metres (2172ft)	25km 1 in 10 15.5 miles 23km 1 in 11 14.3 miles	5 metres 16ft 5in	UC Late Oct–early Jun. Narrow and winding in places, but generally easy, in spite of a number of sharp bends; no through route for caravans as they are prohibited from using the road between Unterschächen and Linthal.
Larche (della Maddalena) 1994 metres (6542ft) France–Italy	La Condamine-Châtelard 1308 metres (4291ft) Vinadio 910 metres (2986ft)	19km 1 in 12 11.8 miles 32km 1 in 12 19.8 miles	3.5 metres 11ft 6in	OC Dec–Mar. An easy, well-graded road; narrow ascent, wider on descent; suitable for caravans.
Lautaret 2058 metres (6752ft) France	Le Bourg-d'Oisans 719 metres (2359ft) Briançon 1321 metres (4334ft)	38km 1 in 8 23.6 miles 28km 1 in 10 17.4 miles	4 metres 13ft 1in	OC Dec–Mar. Modern, evenly graded, but winding, and unguarded in places; very fine scenery; suitable for caravans.
Loibl (Ljubelj) 1067 metres (3500ft) Austria–Slovenia	Unterloibl 518 metres (1699ft) Kranj 385 metres (1263ft)	10km 1 in 5.5 6.2 miles 26km 1 in 8 16 miles	6 metres 19ft 8in	UO Steep rise and fall over Little Loibl pass to tunnel (1.6km/1 mile long) under summit. The old road over the summit is closed to through traffic.
*Lukmanier (Lucomagno) 1916 metres (6286ft) Switzerland	Olivone 893 metres (2930ft) Disentis 1133 metres (3717ft)	20km 1 in 11 12 miles 20km 1 in 11 12 miles	5 metres 16ft 5in	UC early Nov–late May. Rebuilt, modern road; suitable for caravans.
+Maloja 1815 metres (5955ft) Switzerland	Silvaplana 1815 metres (5955ft) Chiavenna 333 metres (1093ft)	11km level 6.8 miles 32km 1 in 11 19.8 miles	4 metres 13ft 1in	UO Escarpment facing south; fairly easy, but many hairpin bends on descent; negotiable by caravans, possibly difficult on ascent.
Mauria 1298 metres (4258ft) Italy	Lozzo Cadore 753 metres (2470ft) Ampezzo 560 metres (1837ft)	13km 1 in 14 8 miles 31km 1 in 14 19.2 miles	5 metres 16ft 5in	UO A well-designed road with easy, winding ascent and descent; suitable for caravans.

* Permitted maximum width of vehicles 7ft 6in + Permitted maximum width of vehicles 8ft 2.5in ++ Maximum length of vehicle 30ft

Pass name, height and country	From and to	Distances from summit and max gradient	Min width of road	Conditions (see page 225 for key to abbreviations)
Mendola 1363 metres (4472ft) Italy	Appiano (Eppan) 411 metres (1348ft) Sarnonico 978 metres (3208ft)	15km 1 in 8 9.3 miles 9km 1 in 10 6 miles	5 metres 16ft 5in	UO A fairly straightforward but winding road, well guarded; suitable for caravans.
Mont Cenis 2083 metres (6834ft) France–Italy	Lanslebourg 1399 metres (4590ft) Susa 503 metres (1650ft)	11km 1 in 10 6.8 miles 28km 1 in 8 17.4 miles	5 metres 16ft 5in	UC Nov–May. Approach by industrial valley. An easy highway, with mostly very good surface; spectacular scenery; suitable for caravans. Alternative Fréjus road tunnel.
Monte Croce di Comélico (Kreuzberg) 1636 metres (5368ft) Italy	San Candido 1174 metres (3852ft) Santo Stefano di Cadore 908 metres (2979ft)	15km 1 in 12 9.3 miles 21km 1 in 12 13 miles	5 metres 16ft 5in	UO A winding road with moderate gradients, beautiful scenery; suitable for caravans.
Montgenèvre 1850m (6070ft) France–Italy	Briançon 1321 metres (4334ft) Cesana Torinese 1344 metres (4409ft)	12km 1 in 14 7.4 miles 8km 1 in 11 5 miles	5 metres 16ft 5in	UO An easy, modern road; suitable for caravans.
Monte Giovo (Jaufen) 2094 metres (6870ft) Italy	Merano 324 metres (1063ft) Vipiteno 948 metres (3110ft)	40km 1 in 8 24.8 miles 19km 1 in 11 11.8 miles	4 metres 13ft 1in	UC Nov–May. Many well engineered hairpin bends; caravans prohibited.
Montets (see Forclaz)				
Morgins 1369 metres (4491ft) France–Switzerland	Abondance 930 metres (3051ft) Monthey 424 metres (1391ft)	14km 1 in 11 8.7 miles 15km 1 in 7 9.3 miles	4 metres 13ft 1in	UO A lesser used route through pleasant, forested countryside crossing the French-Swiss border.
*Mosses 1445m (4740ft) Switzerland	Aigle 417 metres (1368ft) Château d'Oex 958 metres (3143ft)	16km 1 in 12 10 miles 15km 1 in 12 9.3 miles	4 metres 13ft 1in	UO A modern road; suitable for caravans.
Nassfeld (Pramollo) 1530m (5020ft) Austria–Italy	Tröpolach 601 metres (1972ft) Pontebba 568 metres (1864ft)	10km 1 in 5 6.2 miles 10km 1 in 10 6.2 miles	4 metres 13ft 1in	OC late Nov–Mar. The winding descent in Italy has been improved.
*Nufenen (Novena) 2478 metres (8130ft) Switzerland	Ulrichen 1346 metres (4416ft) Airolo 1142 metres (3747ft)	13km 1 in 10 8.1 miles 24km 1 in 10 14.9 miles	4.0 metres 13ft 1in	UC mid-Oct to mid-Jun. The approach roads are narrow, with tight bends, but the road over the pass is good; negotiable by caravans.
*Oberalp 2044 metres (6706ft) Switzerland	Andermatt 1447 metres (4747ft) Disentis 1133 metres (3717ft)	10km 1 in 10 6.2 miles 21km 1 in 10 13 miles	5 metres 16ft 5in	UC Nov–late May. A widened road with a modern surface; many hairpin bends, but long level stretch on summit; negotiable by caravans. Alternative rail tunnel for winter.

* Permitted maximum width of vehicles 7ft 6in + Permitted maximum width of vehicles 8ft 2.5in ++ Maximum length of vehicle 30ft

Mountain passes

Pass name, height and country	From and to	Distances from summit and max gradient	Min width of road	Conditions (see page 225 for key to abbreviations)
*Ofen (Fuorn) 2149 metres (7051ft) Switzerland	Zernez 1474 metres (4836ft) Santa Maria im Münstertal 1375 metres (4511ft)	22km 1 in 10 13.6 miles 14km 1 in 8 8.7 miles	4 metres 13ft 1in	UO Good, fairly easy road through the Swiss National Park; negotiable by caravans.
Petit St Bernard 2188 metres (7178ft) France–Italy	Bourg-St-Maurice 840 metres (2756ft) Pré St-Didier 1000 metres (3281ft)	30km 1 in 16 19 miles 23km 1 in 12 14.3 miles	5 metres 16ft 5in	UC mid Oct–Jun. Outstanding scenery; a fairly easy approach, but poor surface and unguarded broken edges near the summit; good on the descent in Italy; negotiable by light caravans.
Peyresourde 1563 metres (5128ft) France	Arreau 704 metres (2310ft) Luchon 630 metres (2067ft)	18km 1 in 10 11.2 miles 14km 1 in 10 8.7 miles	4 metres 13ft 1in	UO Somewhat narrow with several hairpin bends, though not difficult.
*Pillon 1546 metres (5072ft) Switzerland	Le Sépey 974 metres (3196ft) Gsteig 1184 metres (3885ft)	15km 1 in 11 9 miles 7km 1 in 11 4.4 miles	4 metres 13ft 1in	OC Jan–Feb. A comparatively easy modern road; suitable for caravans.
Plöcken (Monte Croce-Carnico) 1362 metres (4468ft) Austria–Italy	Kötschach 706 metres (2316ft) Paluzza 600 metres (1968ft)	16km 1 in 7 10 miles 16km 1 in 14 10 miles	5 metres 16ft 5in	OC Dec–Apr. A modern road with long, reconstructed sections; heavy traffic at summer weekends; delay likely at the frontier; negotiable by caravans, best used only by experienced drivers in cars with ample power.
Pordoi 2239 metres (7346ft) Italy	Arabba 1602 metres (5256ft) Canazei 1465 metres (4806ft)	9km 1 in 10 5.6 miles 12km 1 in 10 7.4 miles	5 metres 16ft 5in	OC Dec–Apr. An excellent modern road with numerous hairpin bends; negotiable by caravans.
Port 1249 metres (4098ft) France	Tarascon 474 metres (1555ft) Massat 650 metres (2133ft)	18km 1 in 10 11.2 miles 12km 1 in 10 7.4 miles	4 metres 13ft 1in	OC Nov–Mar. A fairly easy road, but narrow on some bends; negotiable by caravans.
Portet-d'Aspet 1069 metres (3507ft) France	Audressein 508 metres (1667ft) Fronsac 472 metres (1548ft)	18km 1 in 7 11.2 miles 29km 1 in 7 18 miles	3.5 metres 11ft 6in	UO Approached from the west by the easy Col des Ares (797 metres/2615ft) and Col de Buret (599 metres/1965ft); well-engineered road, but calls for particular care on hairpin bends; rather narrow.
Pötschen 982 metres (3222ft) Austria	Bad Ischl 469 metres (1539ft) Bad Aussee 659 metres (2162ft)	19km 1 in 11 11.8 miles 9km 1 in 11 5.6 miles	7 metres 23ft	UO A modern road; suitable for caravans.
Pourtalet 1792 metres (5879ft) France–Spain	Eaux-Chaudes 656 metres (2152ft) Biescas 860 metres (2822ft)	23km 1 in 10 14.3 miles 32km 1 in 10 20 miles	3.5 metres 11ft 6in	UC late Oct–early Jun. A fairly easy, unguarded road, but narrow in places.
Puymorens 1915 metres (6283ft) France	Ax-les-Thermes 720 metres (2362ft) Bourg-Madame 1130 metres (3707ft)	28km 1 in 10 17.4 miles 27km 1 in 10 16.8 miles	5.5 metres 18ft	OC Nov–Apr. A generally easy, modern tarmac road, but narrow, winding and with a poor surface in places; not suitable for night driving; not suitable for caravans (max height vehicles 3.5 metres/11ft 6in). Parallel toll road tunnel available.

* Permitted maximum width of vehicles 7ft 6in + Permitted maximum width of vehicles 8ft 2.5in ++ Maximum length of vehicle 30ft

Pass name, height and country	From and to	Distances from summit and max gradient	Min width of road	Conditions (see page 225 for key to abbreviations)
Quillane 1714 metres (5623ft) France	Quillan 291 metres (955ft) Mont-Louis 1600 metres (5249ft)	63km 1 in 12 39.1 miles 6 km 1 in 12 3.5 miles	5 metres 16ft 5in	OC Nov–Mar. An easy, straightforward ascent and descent; suitable for caravans.
Radstädter-Tauern 1738 metres (5702ft) Austria	Radstadt 862 metres (2828ft) Mauterndorf 1122 metres (3681ft)	21km 1 in 6 13.0 miles 17km 1 in 7 10.6 miles	5 metres 16ft 5in	OC Jan–Mar. Northern ascent steep, but not difficult otherwise; parallel toll motorway including tunnel; negotiable by light caravans, using tunnel.
Résia (Reschen) 1504 metres (4934ft) Italy–Austria	Spondigna 885 metres (2903ft) Pfunds 970 metres (3182ft)	29km 1 in 10 18 miles 21km 1 in 10 13 miles	6 metres 19ft 8in	UO A good, straightforward alternative to the Brenner Pass; suitable for caravans.
Restefond (La Bonette) 2802 metres (9193ft) France	Jausiers (near Barcelonnette) 1220 metres (4003ft) St-Etienne-de-Tinée 1144 metres (3753ft)	23km 1 in 8 14.3 miles 27km 1 in 6 16.8 miles	3 metres 9ft 10in	UC Oct–Jun. The highest pass in the Alps, completed in 1962. Narrow, rough, unguarded ascent with many blind bends, and nine hairpins. Descent easier, winding with 12 hairpin bends. Not for the faint-hearted; extra care required.
Rolle 1970 metres (6463ft) Italy	Predazzo 1018 metres (3340ft) Mezzano 637 metres (2090ft)	21km 1 in 11 13.0 miles 27km 1 in 14 17 miles	5 metres 16ft 5in	OC Dec–Mar. A well-engineered road with many hairpin bends on both sides; very beautiful scenery; good surface; negotiable by caravans.
Rombo (see Timmelsjoch)				
Routes des Crêtes 1283 metres (4210ft) France	St-Dié 343 metres (1125ft) Cernay 296 metres (971ft)	1 in 8 1 in 8	4 metres 13ft 1in	UC Nov–Apr. A renowned scenic route crossing seven ridges, with the highest point at 'Hôtel du Grand Ballon'.
+St Gotthard (San Gottardo) 2108 metres (6916ft) Switzerland	Göschenen 1106 metres (3629ft) Airolo 1142 metres (3747ft)	18km 1 in 10 11 miles 15km 1 in 10 9.3 miles	6 metres 19ft 8in	UC mid-Oct to early Jun. Modern, fairly easy two- to three-lane road. Heavy traffic; negotiable by caravans. Alternative road tunnel.
*San Bernardino 2066 metres (6778ft) Switzerland	Mesocco 790 metres (2592ft) Hinterrhein 1620 metres (5315ft)	21km 1 in 10 13 miles 9.5km 1 in 10 5.9 miles	4 metres 13ft 1in	UC Oct–late Jun. Easy, modern roads on northern and southern approaches to tunnel. Narrow and winding over summit, via tunnel suitable for caravans.
Schlucht 1139 metres (3737ft) France	Gérardmer 665 metres (2182ft) Munster 381 metres (1250ft)	15km 1 in 14 9.3 miles 18km 1 in 14 11 miles	5 metres 16ft 5in	UO An extremely picturesque route crossing the Vosges mountains, with easy, wide bends on the descent; suitable for caravans.
Seeberg (Jezersko) 1218 metres (3996ft) Austria–Slovenia	Eisenkappel 555 metres (1821ft) Kranj 385 metres (1263ft)	14km 1 in 8 8.7 miles 33km 1 in 10 20.5 miles	5 metres 16ft 5in	UO An alternative to the steeper Loibl and Wurzen passes; moderate climb with winding, hairpin ascent and descent.

* Permitted maximum width of vehicles 7ft 6in + Permitted maximum width of vehicles 8ft 2.5in ++ Maximum length of vehicle 30ft

Mountain passes

Pass name, height and country	From and to	Distances from summit and max gradient	Min width of road	Conditions (see page 225 for key to abbreviations)
Sella 2240 metres (7349ft) Italy	Plan 1606 metres (5269ft) Canazei 1465 metres (4806ft)	9km 1 in 9 5.6 miles 12km 1 in 9 7 miles	5 metres 16ft 5in	OC Dec–Jun. A finely engineered, winding road; exceptional views of the Dolomites.
Semmering 985 metres (3232ft) Austria	Mürzzuschlag im Mürztal 672 metres (2205ft) Gloggnitz 457 metres (1499ft)	14km 1 in 16 8.7 miles 17km 1 in 16 10.6 miles	6 metres 19ft 8in	UO A fine, well-engineered highway; suitable for caravans.
Sestriere 2033 metres (6670ft) Italy	Cesana Torinese 1344 metres (4409ft) Pinerolo 376 metres (1234ft)	12km 1 in 10 7.4 miles 55km 1 in 10 34.2 miles	6 metres 19ft 8in	UO Mostly bitumen surface; negotiable by caravans.
Silvretta (Bielerhöhe) 2032 metres (6666ft) Austria	Partenen 1051 metres (3448ft) Galtür 1584 metres (5197ft)	16km 1 in 9 9.9 miles 10km 1 in 9 6.2 miles	5 metres 16ft 5in	UC late Oct–early Jun. For the most part reconstructed; 32 easy hairpin bends on western ascent; eastern side more straightforward. Toll road; caravans prohibited.
+Simplon 2005 metres (6578ft) Switzerland–Italy	Brig 681 metres (2234ft) Domodóssola 280 metres (919ft)	22km 1 in 9 13.6 miles 41km 1 in 11 25.5 miles	7 metres 23ft	OC Nov–Apr. An easy, reconstructed modern road, but 20.8km/13 miles long, continuous ascent to summit; suitable for caravans.
Somport 1632 metres (5354ft) France–Spain	Bedous 416 metres (1365ft) Jaca 820 metres (2690ft)	31km 1 in 10 19.2 miles 32km 1 in 10 20 miles	3.5 metres 11ft 6in	UO A favoured, old-established route; generally easy, but in parts narrow and unguarded; fairly well-surfaced road; suitable for caravans.
*Splügen 2113 metres (6932ft) Switzerland–Italy	Splügen 1457 metres (4780ft) Chiavenna 330 metres (1083ft)	9km 1 in 9 5.6 miles 30km 1 in 7.5 18.6 miles	3.5 metres 11ft 6in	UC Nov–Jun. Mostly narrow and winding, with many hairpin bends, and not well guarded; care is also required at many tunnels and galleries (max height vehicles 9ft 2in).
++Stelvio 2757 metres (9045ft) Italy	Bormio 1225 metres (4019ft) Spondigna 885 metres (2903ft)	22km 1 in 8 13.6 miles 28km 1 in 8 12.9 miles	4 metres 13ft 1in	UC Oct–late Jun. The third highest pass in the Alps; the number of acute hairpin bends, all well engineered, is exceptional – from 40 to 50 on either side; the surface is good, the traffic heavy. Hairpin bends are too acute for long vehicles.
+Susten 2224 metres (7297ft) Switzerland	Innertkirchen 630 metres (2067ft) Wassen 916 metres (3005ft)	28km 1 in 11 12.9 miles 19km 1 in 11 11.8 miles	6 metres 19ft 8in	UC Nov–Jun. A very scenic and well-guarded mountain road; easy gradients and turns; heavy traffic at weekends; negotiable by caravans – extra care required. Not for the faint-hearted.
Tenda (Tende) 1321 metres (4334ft) Italy–France	Borgo S Dalmazzo 641 metres (2103ft) La Giandola 308 metres (1010ft)	24km 1 in 11 14.9 miles 29km 1 in 11 18 miles	6 metres 19ft 8in	UO Well-guarded, modern road with several hairpin bends; road tunnel at summit; suitable for caravans, but prohibited during the winter.
+Thurn 1274 metres (4180ft) Austria	Kitzbühel 762 metres (2500ft) Mittersill 789 metres (2588ft)	19km 1 in 12 11.8 miles 10km 1 in 16 6.2 miles	5 metres 16ft 5in	UO A good road with narrow stretches; northern approach rebuilt; suitable for caravans.

* Permitted maximum width of vehicles 7ft 6in   + Permitted maximum width of vehicles 8ft 2.5in   ++ Maximum length of vehicle 30ft

Pass name, height and country	From and to	Distances from summit and max gradient	Min width of road	Conditions (see page 225 for key to abbreviations)
Timmelsjoch (Rombo) 2509 metres (8232ft) Austria–Italy	Obergurgl 1910 metres (6266ft) Moso 1007 metres (3304ft)	14km 1 in 7 8.7 miles 23km 1 in 8 14 miles	3.5 metres 11ft 6in	UC mid-Oct to late Jun. Pass open to private cars (without trailers) only as some tunnels on the Italian side are too narrow for larger vehicles; toll road. Border closed 8pm to 7am.
Tonale 1883 metres (6178ft) Italy	Edolo 699 metres (2293ft) Dimaro 766 metres (2513ft)	30km 1 in 12 18.6 miles 27km 1 in 10 16.7 miles	5 metres 16ft 5in	UO A relatively easy road; suitable for caravans.
Toses (Tosas) 1800 metres (5906ft) Spain	Puigcerdá 1152 metres (3780ft) Ribes de Freser 920 metres (3018ft)	26km 1 in 10 16 miles 25km 1 in 10 15.5 miles	5 metres 16ft 5in	UO Now a fairly straightforward, but continuously winding, two-lane road with many sharp bends; negotiable by caravans.
Tourmalet 2114 metres (6936ft) France	Luz 711 metres (2333ft) Ste-Marie-de-Campan 857 metres (2812ft)	18km 1 in 8 11 miles 17km 1 in 8 10.6 miles	4 metres 13ft 1in	UC Oct to mid-Jun. The highest of the French Pyrenean routes; the approaches are good, though winding and exacting over summit; sufficiently guarded.
Tre Croci 1809 metres (5935ft) Italy	Cortina d'Ampezzo 1224 metres (4016ft) Auronzo di Cadore 864 metres (2835ft).	7km 1 in 9 4.4 miles 26 km 1 in 9 16 miles	6 metres 19ft 8in	OC Dec–Mar. An easy pass; very fine scenery; suitable for caravans.
Turracher Höhe 1763 metres (5784ft) Austria	Predlitz 922 metres (3024ft) Ebene-Reichenau 1062 metres (3484ft)	20km 1 in 5.5 12.4 miles 8km 1 in 4.5 5 miles	4 metres 13ft 1in	UO Formerly one of the steepest mountain roads in Austria; now much improved. A steep, fairly straightforward ascent is followed by a very steep descent; good surface and mainly two-lane width; fine scenery.
*Umbrail 2501 metres (8205ft) Switzerland–Italy	Santa Maria im Münstertal 1375 metres (4511ft) Bormio 1225 metres (4019ft)	14km 1 in 11 9 miles 19km 1 in 11 11.8 miles	4.3 metres 14ft 1in	UC early Nov–early Jun. Highest of the Swiss passes; narrow; mostly gravel surfaced with 34 hairpin bends, but not too difficult.
Vars 2109 metres (6919ft) France	St-Paul-sur-Ubaye 1470 metres (4823ft) Guillestre 1000 metres (3281ft)	8km 1 in 10 5 miles 20km 1 in 10 12.4 miles	5 metres 16ft 5in	OC Dec–Mar. Easy winding ascent with seven hairpin bends; gradual winding descent with another seven hairpin bends; good surface; negotiable by caravans.
Wurzen (Koren) 1073 metres (3520ft) Austria–Slovenia	Riegersdorf 541 metres (1775ft) Kranjska Gora 810 metres (2657ft)	7km 1 in 5.5 4.5 miles 6km 1 in 5.5 3.5 miles	4 metres 13ft 1in	UO A steep two-lane road, which otherwise is not particularly difficult; heavy traffic at summer weekends; delay likely at the frontier; caravans prohibited.
Zirler Berg 1009 metres (3310ft) Austria	Seefeld 1180 metres (3871ft) Zirl 622 metres (2041ft)	6km 1 in 7 3.5 miles 5km 1 in 6 3.1 miles	7 metres 23ft	UO An escarpment facing south, part of the route from Garmisch to Innsbruck; a good, modern road, but heavy tourist traffic and a long steep descent, with one hairpin bend, into the Inn Valley. Steepest section from the hairpin bend down to Zirl; caravans prohibited northbound.

* Permitted maximum width of vehicles 7ft 6in + Permitted maximum width of vehicles 8ft 2.5in ++ Maximum length of vehicle 30ft

Port plans

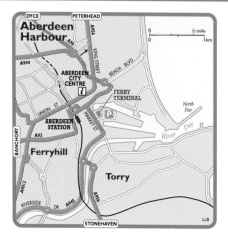

Aberdeen Harbour

DYCE · PETERHEAD · A956 · A92 · KING STREET · A944 · ABERDEEN CITY CENTRE · BEACH BLVD · FERRY TERMINAL · North Pier · UNION ST · MARKET ST · ABERDEEN STATION · BANCHORY · A93 · Ferryhill · River Dee · Torry · A9013 · RIVERSIDE DR · A956 · A956 · A90 · STONEHAVEN · LLB

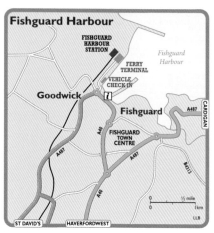

Fishguard Harbour

FISHGUARD HARBOUR STATION · Fishguard Harbour · FERRY TERMINAL · VEHICLE CHECK IN · Goodwick · Fishguard · A487 · CARDIGAN · A40 · FISHGUARD TOWN CENTRE · A487 · A487 · B4313 · A40 · ST DAVID'S · HAVERFORDWEST · LLB

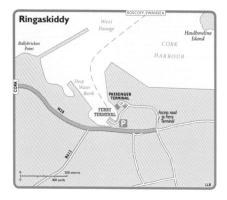

Ringaskiddy

ROSCOFF, SWANSEA · West Passage · Haulbowline Island · Ballybricken Point · CORK HARBOUR · CORK · Deep Water Berth · PASSENGER TERMINAL · N28 · FERRY TERMINAL · Access road to Ferry Terminal · R613 · 500 metres · 400 yards · LLB

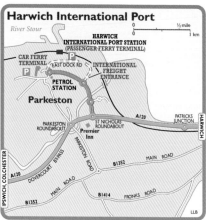

Harwich International Port

River Stour · HARWICH INTERNATIONAL PORT STATION (PASSENGER FERRY TERMINAL) · CAR FERRY TERMINAL · EAST DOCK RD · INTERNATIONAL FREIGHT ENTRANCE · PETROL STATION · Parkeston · A120 · PATRICKS JUNCTION · HARWICH · PARKESTON ROUNDABOUT · ST NICHOLAS ROUNDABOUT · Premier Inn · PARKESTON ROAD · IPSWICH, COLCHESTER · A120 · DOVERCOURT BYPASS · MAIN ROAD · B1352 · MAIN ROAD · B1352 · MAIN ROAD · B1414 · FRONKS ROAD · LLB

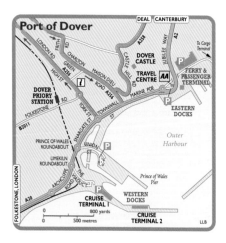

Port of Dover

DEAL · CANTERBURY · A258 · JUBILEE WAY · A2 · LONDON RD · FRITH RD · CHARLTON · GREEN · MAISON DIEU ROAD · A256 · DOVER CASTLE · CASTLE HILL RD · TRAVEL CENTRE · AA · To Cargo Terminal · FERRY & PASSENGER TERMINAL · DOVER PRIORY STATION · HIGH ST · YORK ST · MARINE PDE · EASTERN DOCKS · FOLKESTONE RD · B2011 · TOWNWALL ST · SNARGATE ST · PRINCE OF WALES ROUNDABOUT · UNION ST · Outer Harbour · LIMEKILN ROUNDABOUT · ARCHCLIFFE · THE · Prince of Wales Pier · FOLKESTONE, LONDON · A20 · ROAD VIADUCT · CRUISE TERMINAL 1 · WESTERN DOCKS · CRUISE TERMINAL 2 · 800 yards · 500 metres · LLB

Heysham Harbour

MORECAMBE · Lower Heysham · A589 · Half Moon Bay · FREIGHT FERRY TERMINAL · PORT WAY · Higher Heysham · HEYSHAM PORT STATION · A589 · South Jetty · CAR FERRY TERMINAL · A683 · LANCASTER · MONEY CLOSE LANE · NUCLEAR POWER STATIONS · 800 yards · 500 metres · LLB

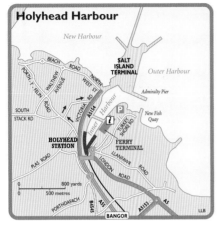

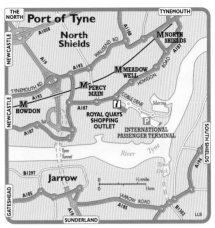

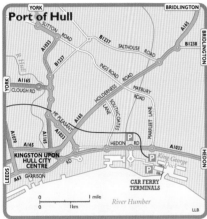

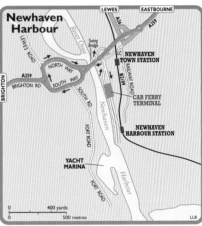

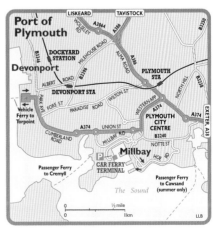

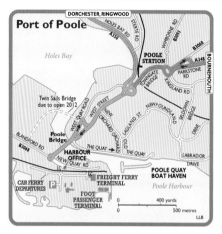

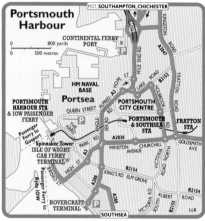

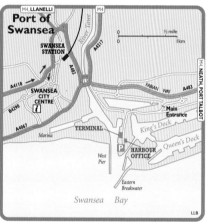

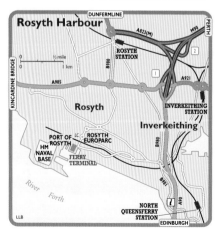

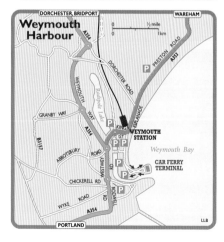

Index